Rich Country, Poor Country

The Multinational as Change Agent

BENJAMIN F. BOBO

PRAEGER

Westport, Connecticut
London

Library of Congress Cataloging-in-Publication Data

Bobo, Benjamin F.
    Rich country, poor country : the multinational as change agent / Benjamin F. Bobo.
        p. cm.
    Includes bibliographical references and index.
    ISBN 0-275-97928-8 (alk. paper)
    1. International business enterprises—Social aspects—Developing countries. 2. Social responsibility of business. 3. Economic assistance—Developing countries. 4. Poor—Developing countries. 5. Economic development. 6. International economic relations. I. Title.
    HD2755.5.B596 2005
    338.8'881724—dc22   2004028189

British Library Cataloguing in Publication Data is available.

Library of Congress Catalog Card Number: 2004028189
ISBN: 0-275-97928-8

First published in 2005

Praeger Publishers, 88 Post Road West, Westport, CT 06881
An imprint of Greenwood Publishing Group, Inc.
www.praeger.com

Printed in the United States of America

The paper used in this book complies with the Permanent Paper Standard issued by the National Information Standards Organization (Z39.48-1984).

10   9   8   7   6   5   4   3   2   1

Every reasonable effort has been made to trace the owners of copyright materials in this book, but in some instances this has proven impossible. The author and publisher will be glad to receive information leading to more complete acknowledgments in subsequent printings of the book and in the meantime extend their apologies for any omissions.

Some writers pursue an interest
Others pursue a cause
Some pursue success
Others pursue significance

To Patricia, Benjelani, and Yohancé

Contents

Exhibits		*ix*
Preface		*xiii*
Acknowledgments		*xvii*
Perspective		*xix*
1.	Introduction	1
2.	The Historical Context in Brief	7
3.	Multinational Corporations in the Economic Development of Black Africa: Some Problems that Affect an Equitable Relationship	25
4.	Issues in North–South Relations and the New World Order	43
5.	MNC–Third World Relations: A Comparative Study of Policymakers' Attitudes and Perceptions	63
6.	Multinationals in the Third World: Reciprocity, Conflict Resolution and Economic Policy Formulation	75
7.	Multinationals, the North and the New World Order: Objectives and Opportunities	95
8.	Internationalization Decision Making and the Global Interdependency Sensitivity Thesis	111
9.	Multinationals and the Caribbean: A Post-Colonial Perspective	129
10.	Third World Investment Strategy: The African Predicament	139

11. Whose Wealth to Maximize: The Third World
     as Stakeholder   153

12. GIST and Profit Satisficing: Toward More
     User-Friendly Shareholder Wealth Maximization   169

13. User-Friendly Shareholder Wealth Maximization
     and B-School Pedagogy   197

14. Epilogue   209

Bibliography   217

Index   229

Exhibits

2.1 Sales and Assets of Global Corporations 2000 ($ billions) — 9

2.2 Gross National Product, Selected Countries 1990 and 2000 ($ billions) — 11

2.3 Poor Countries and Per Capita Income: A Model of the Debate — 13

2.4 Gross National Product Per Capita, Selected Countries 1990 and 2000 ($) — 16

2.5 Direct Foreign Investment by Region ($ million) — 17

2.6 Direct Foreign Investment in Third World Economies, Selected Countries ($ million) — 18

2.7 Gross National Product Per Capita, Selected Countries, Relative Position in 1990 by Comparison to 2000 ($) — 21

3.1 Africa's Share of World Mineral Resources — 27

4.1 Issues in North-South Relations and the New World Order, Third World Population and GNP Per Capita, 1991 — 45

4.2 Approaches to the Analysis of Inequality Between and Within Nations — 51

4.3 U.S. Direct Foreign Investment in All Industries in Developing Countries: 1980–1991 ($ billions) — 53

4.4 U.S. Direct Investment Position Abroad, 1991 — 53

4.5 External Public Debt of Developing Countries — 54

4.6   Natural Resource Reserves of Third World Countries   55

4.7   Mean Exports and Imports for Third World Countries,
      1991 ($ millions)   57

4.8   Additional Developing Country Exports
      Resulting from the Elimination of Trade
      Barriers 1991 ($ billions)   58

5.1   Comparative Attitude Profile, Impact of Joint
      Ventures on MNC-LDC Relations, Weighted
      Average Rating and Ranking   67

5.2   Comparative Attitude Profile, Method of
      Ownership and Resentment Towards MNCs
      by LDCs, Weighted Average Rating and Ranking   69

5.3   Comparative Attitude Profile, Government Codes
      and Business Practices, Weighted Average
      Rating and Ranking   71

5.4   Comparative Attitude Profile, Labor Relations
      and Personnel Training, Weighted Average
      Rating and Ranking   73

6.1   Attitude Profile, Impact of Joint Ventures on
      MNC-LDC Relations, Weighted Average Rating   79

6.2   Attitude Profile, Method of Ownership and
      Resentment Towards MNCs by LDCs, Weighted
      Average Rating   81

6.3   Attitude Profile, Contributions, Expectations
      and Sources of Conflict, Weighted Average Rating   83

6.4   Attitude Profile, Government Codes and Business
      Practices, Weighted Average Rating   85

6.5   Attitude Profile, Labor Relations and Personnel
      Training, Weighted Average Rating   86

6.6   Attitude Profile, Technology Transfer, Industrial
      Infrastructure and Import Substitution, Weighted
      Average Rating   87

6.7   Attitude Profile, Cultural Factors and MNC-LDC
      Relationships, Weighted Average Rating   88

6.8   Attitude Profile, Political Influence and Domestic
      Policy Formulation, Weighted Average Rating   89

6.9   Attitude Profile, NIEO and the Present, Weighted
      Average Rating   90

7.1   U.S. Direct Investment Position Abroad, 1991   98

7.2   Natural Resource Reserves of Third World Countries   101

7.3   Attitude Profile, Importance of Selected Factors in
      Improving MNC-LDC Relations, Weighted
      Average Ratings   103

9.1   Ladder of Comparative Advantage   134

11.1 Output of the Firm Under Profit Maximizing
      and Profit Satisficing   157

12.1 Shareholder Wealth Maximization   174

12.2 Shareholder Wealth Maximization, The MNC
      Decision-Making Structure   176

12.3 Shareholder Wealth Maximization
      with Stakeholder Emphasis   178

12.4 Shareholder Wealth Maximization with
      Inclusive Stakeholder Emphasis   181

12.5 Shareholder Wealth Maximization–Stakeholder Wealth
      Enhancement: Corporate Social Responsibility   183

12.6 Shareholder-Stakeholder Partnership:
      The Multinational, GIST, and Profit Satisficing   185

12.7 Stakeholder Givebacks   187

12.8 Shareholder-Stakeholder/Rich Country–Poor
      Country: Ethics and "Ready, Willing, and Able"   190

12.9 Rich Country–Poor Country, A Win-Win Scenario   194

13.1 Human Development Paradigm   201

13.2 The Rich Country–Poor Country Makeup   202

13.3 Shareholder Wealth Maximization, A Query
      and Deliberation Framework   204

13.4 Thinking Outside the Box   206

Preface

Thinking about this initiative, I was drawn to my work on multinational corporations (MNCs) and Third World relations. This topic is the other facet of my research agenda, which has a dual purpose. *Locked In and Locked Out: The Impact of Urban Land Use Policy and Market Forces on African Americans* expresses my concern about the life-choice constraints of the economically disadvantaged, in this case, African Americans. Because I am also concerned about the plight of Third World people and their life-choice constraints, in this book I have focused on the vexing problem of Third World development. The common thread connecting the dual purpose is income inequality, which is clearly driven by a host of factors including race and class struggle, systemic rigors, intergenerational poverty, imbalanced economic capacity, and so on. Cause notwithstanding, I am concerned about the plight of the poor despite where they live. This dual focus has been my driving force in pursuing certain scholarly initiatives over the years.

Because I feel strongly that income inequality between rich and poor nations and the deep poverty engulfing people in the Third World can be effectively addressed by the multinational corporation, I decided to prepare an extensive exposition on the matter. This is not to suggest that government involvement—for example, foreign aid and tariff policy—can be supplanted, but the multinational corporation can offer decidedly poignant redress.

I have published a number of articles designed to facilitate better understanding of the Third World condition, to articulate premises and prescriptions that encourage and assist problem solving, and to further enrich the body of knowledge on the topic. The articles, quite interestingly

I believe, exhibit a rather sequential and evolutionary pattern of my thinking over time; hence, I thought it prudent to arrange and highlight a collection of these publications in a single volume, augmented by new material reflecting my more recent thinking.

The central theme over the course of the writings has been my concern about the constrained life-choice options available to Third World people and how multinational corporations can play the very significant role of change agent through the process of direct foreign investment (often referred to as foreign direct investment in the literature, and used interchangeably in this discourse). I have labored for many years to articulate a framework for establishing a more user-friendly investment relationship between multinational firms and Third World nations. The reader will find a progression of thinking on the Third World poverty and economic development problem with an ongoing view toward conception of seriously effective aids to its resolution. Several concepts and approaches to assessing and redressing the Third World condition are introduced including *profit satisficing*, the global interdependency sensitivity thesis (GIST), stakeholder givebacks, and a new business school pedagogy framework, among others that punctuate the discussion in the book. The business community, particularly multinational firms, in all likelihood will find the global interdependency sensitivity thesis as well as the *profit satisficing* concepts very formidable challenges to accepted business practices. And the notion that *profit satisficing* may warrant inclusion in business school pedagogy with much the same treatment as *profit maximization*, as I propose, could engender much debate on the topic in the business school community.

AN OVERVIEW OF THE BOOK

The presented published works on referenced topics and issues are arranged chronologically. The preface is followed by a general introduction. Each succeeding chapter opens with an interfacing mini-introduction to assist the reader in following the progression and evolution of thought as the articles were developed over time. To provide further breadth and scope, new and more current work is incorporated. These materials further articulate the nature of the problem and the importance of the prescribed approaches.

Chapter 1 introduces pertinent issues related to the conditioning of rich and poor countries. The debate surrounding the rich country–poor country makeup of the world is reviewed. Capital diffusion as a means of facilitating economic development, the principle of comparative advantage, and the stage theory of economic growth are highlighted. The discussion concludes with analytical, prescriptive, and moral perspectives advanced to give guidance and direction to the succeeding dialogue.

Chapter 2 presents brief historical facts concerning the emergence of the multinational corporation, including salient details on the nature of the Third World. Past and present forms of the multinational organization are outlined with a focus on early investment practices, factors leading to the multinational's phenomenal growth, and the wealth of multinationals by comparison to selected countries. A clear indication of the enormity and power of the multinational is conveyed. Matters of economic significance concerning Third World development are discussed, centering on the regional makeup of the Third World and drawing on pertinent experiences of Africa, Asia, and Latin America.

Chapter 3 is the initial published product of the many years of research and writing that make this undertaking possible. "Multinational Corporations in the Economic Development of Black Africa" offers a good entry way, particularly in the context of this book, to the study and analysis of the relationship of multinational corporations and Third World nations. Africa has a history of poor economic performance relative to other Third World regions and therefore offers a ready environment in which to explore important problems and issues impacting the MNC–host country relationship. Technology transfer, transfer pricing, taxation, and corporate ethics are the focus of the discussion.

In Chapter 4, matters concerning corporate and host country independence are explored; the concept of the North-South arrangement of countries is reviewed; the inequality issue is assessed; and demands of the call for a new world order are examined, particularly in light of the proposed wealth redistribution doctrine.

In the course of conducting research and writing on the general theme of multinational corporations and Third World relations, Chapters 5 and 6 are most closely related in that they report the results of international surveys conducted in 1980 and 1994. The dialogue in Chapter 5 is essentially the same as that in the first half of Chapter 6, except that it discusses both surveys and Chapter 6 addresses only the 1994 results. The latter part of Chapter 6 utilizes the 1994 survey results in a broader and more extensive fashion, allowing address of a wider range of issues.

Using the wealth redistribution doctrine in the call for a new world order as a backdrop, Chapter 7 discusses important objectives necessary to accomplishing redistribution, and examines opportunities available to the multinational corporation to facilitate such efforts. Results from the 1994 international survey provide empirical substance and support.

Because of the issues and problems facing multinationals and Third World nations as they engage each other in the pursuit of corporate and host country objectives, conflict invariably arises. Chapter 8 reviews sources of conflict and conflict resolution models, and proposes a bargaining framework that adds a new dimension to the multinational–host country relationship.

Ideally, corporate and host country objectives can merge into a uniform business rationale that accomplishes the desires of both parties. Chapter 9 examines the Caribbean model of development and proposes an integration strategy that combines corporate and host objectives in moving the island nations of the Caribbean toward sustained economic development.

Economic development problems in Africa are among the most difficult in the world to reconcile. Chapter 10 examines the African predicament with a view toward clarifying the nature of the difficulties confronting development efforts and assessing the economic impact of both internal and external forces.

Fully and inexorably essential to correcting the problems of development is increasing the wealth of Third World countries. Recognizing the multinational corporation as the change agent having the capacity to significantly facilitate development, hence wealth expansion, Chapter 11 assesses the primary goal of the corporation—shareholder wealth maximization—in an effort to broaden the concept of wealth maximization to include the Third World stakeholder. And, a new model of shareholder wealth maximization is proposed to facilitate Third World development.

Preparing the corporation to adopt this new model of shareholder wealth maximization requires an implementation strategy and procedure. Chapter 12 outlines an approach to implementing the model, and presents pertinent details along with schematic illustrations of the model and the decision-making process.

Such implementation may require a new pedagogy to assist with mainstreaming the model, a necessary condition for legitimacy as well as longevity. Chapter 13 discusses the issue of a new pedagogy and identifies the business school as its focal point.

Finally, through presentation of issues and problems associated with multinational corporations and Third World relations, this book endeavors to draw direct focus to the relationship and how its structure can affect the realization of objectives by both parties. Moreover, in articulating a new model of wealth maximization and an approach to implementation, a clear prescription for redressing the rich country–poor country dilemma is engaged. With this in mind, however, Chapter 14 identifies forces at play that may challenge the capacity of the model to realize its intent, and indeed may even render it ineffective.

Acknowledgments

Such an undertaking cannot materialize without the benefit of many contributions. I owe deep appreciation to Loyola Marymount University for extensive research assistance that supported completion of this work.

I am especially indebted to Dean John Wholihan of the Loyola Marymount University College of Business Administration for encouraging me to develop the course Multinationals and the Third World that in many ways inspired this work. I extend further gratitude to Dean Wholihan for continuous encouragement as this work progressed, and for the generous research support, without which completion may not have resulted.

Profound thanks to Dr. Lawrence Tai for his collaboration on the reprinted articles that provide a foundation for the discourse and add richness to the deliberation.

I thank the journals in which the reprinted articles appear for granting permission to use the material as requested, as well as the numerous other sources cited for permission to use various materials.

Special gratitude to the many students at Loyola Marymount University who have attended my lectures on multinationals and the Third World, and for their reactions to the many topics and issues explored therein.

I acknowledge the dedicated effort of my graduate research assistant, Einat Metzl, for invaluable attention to detail and for data collection assistance. Thanks also to my graduate research assistant, Yesim Merter, for very helpful assistance gathering data. Gratitude is also extended to my undergraduate research assistant, Taibatu Obasi.

Special thanks to Kathe Segall, who held steadfastly as the monumental task of orchestrating and preparing the final presentation was cast upon her. Many, many thanks, Kathe, for delivering the goods.

And I thank family and friends for intellectual, moral, and spiritual support as I labored with the effort of bringing this undertaking to fruition.

Perspective

There are poor countries around the globe in need of a hand up.
Multinationals can provide the hand.

Some three-quarters of the countries in the world fall into the Third World
classification. These countries are comparatively poor and, in some cases,
acutely so when the United States, Canada, Great Britain, Japan, Italy,
Germany, and France are used as measures of economic success. Today
some four-fifths of the world's peoples live in Third World countries; Like
their countries, they are largely poor, many desperately so, and there
appears to be little or no opportunity to significantly improve their economic state. Seemingly they are playing a game of "haves and have-nots,"
the latter being their inherited role. The economic condition of the fore-
parent is cast upon the offspring, forging an intergenerational blueprint—
a predestination, perhaps. But if predestination is simply a state of mind,
repudiation of the game of "haves and have-nots" is a rational choice.
Should they choose to do so fully and unequivocally, how will they
behave? Perhaps we don't want to know. If you were desperately poor
and felt no chance of pulling yourself up by your bootstraps, what would
you do? Perhaps you don't want to know.

Look around us. Everywhere, we see people living in poverty, even
abjectly so. We also see people living in decadence, even strikingly so. So
few have so much and so many have so little. Today's technology places
the eyes of the world upon one and all. Satellite vision brings everyone's
lifestyle directly into the living room; everybody sees how everybody

lives. The lifestyles of the rich and famous are flaunted, the well-off demand high respect from the poor, and poor people are relegated to society's backseat. I often wonder how poor people wake every day to toil in what seems to be an endless existence of degradation and yet manage to mask their condition with moments of humor. Changing suffrage into moods of laughter is no less than astounding. This indeed is toleration at its finest.

I am reminded of the words of Martin Luther King, Jr.: "I can never be what I ought to be until you are what you ought to be. . . ."[1] Little do we realize that every day poverty exists means another day of loss to the world economy. Every day a laborer produces less than his or her most efficient output, the world economy loses another day of maximized expansion. In the larger scheme of things, everybody loses. So how can anyone be what he or she ought to be until everyone is what he or she ought to be? Is this mere naiveté? Perhaps, perhaps not.

Many of us seemingly rationalize poverty as if it is conceived in the womb. On the contrary, poverty is not a personality trait, but is rather much like racism. It has its roots in one's inability to truly care about others; to truly feel another's pain; to truly feel another's suffrage; in short, to truly internalize the wretchedness of being. Even in one's moments of good wishes and laudable deeds, one often does not truly connect words and actions to meanings and outcomes. What do words spoken really mean and what do actions taken really produce? This is most apparent in the world at large, particularly in poor countries. Much is talked about and much is acted on, but there is little change, to be sure, little sustainable change.

The inability to induce sustainable change may be due more to application of an ineffective change model than lack of effort. In the same way we tackled smallpox, for example, we can conduct a winning assault on poverty. This doesn't mean that a cure can be developed in a laboratory test tube and injected into all exposed. Rather, it recognizes that smallpox threatened the very existence of mankind. Sufficient know-how and resources were deployed to eradication of the problem; hence, its demise became a reality. Poverty is no less threatening to mankind. It simply has a different gene structure, you might say, so that different know-how and resources may be called for to achieve a solution. The poverty problem is immense; the solution must be even more so. We must be willing to tread where we have yet to explore, to pursue what we have yet to imagine, to try the untried. We must sound a call to arms, and in so doing deploy resources so massive in content, so imposing in stature, and so profound in context as to provide a clear gateway to poverty abatement.

Poverty in many ways behaves like a contagious disease, like smallpox if you will, engulfing all that come too close. And like a contagious disease, poverty is curable. The right serum, antidote, or solution will do the trick.

In the case of poverty, the multinational corporation can be a potent serum. To be sure, many criticize the notion that the multinational can or will do such good, citing many examples of impropriety. What is overlooked in the critique are the many examples of good deeds, not the least of which is the promotion of improved standard of living. Some of the critics are employed by multinationals and rely on them for their livelihood. Others stand in the path of their good deeds and are swept up in their prosperity. Without doubt, multinationals are given to misdeeds and deserve criticism, but critics should be mindful that when the Fortune 500 companies—a vanguard of multinational enterprise—get a cough, the labor market gets a sore throat. When the Fortune 500 gets a sore throat, workers come down with a cold. When the Fortune 500 gets a cold, pneumonia is contracted throughout the labor force. What power the big corporation!

Critics' fears, however, should not be taken lightly. There is much evidence of corporate misdeeds—some intentional, others not. One perpetrator of misdeeds is the profit motive. The pursuit of profit often means charging whatever the market will bear, or selecting only those investments or business ventures that produce the highest return or highest net present value to the firm. This practice, while financially sound, may not show warranted regard for the broader stakeholder community. The interest of poor people and poor countries, clear stakeholders in the larger scheme of business enterprise, may not be best served under profit maximization objectives. An alternative objective, *profit satisficing*, may better serve this stakeholder community. Poverty abatement requires a special apparatus and a unique approach; the multinational corporation may be that apparatus, and *profit satisficing* may be that approach. Thus, rather than rejecting the multinational's power, however valid the criticism, why not harness it? Why not use its great capacity to perform a wonder cure? Wonders do happen.

NOTES

1. Martin Luther King, Jr., *Why We Can't Wait* (New York: Harper & Row Publishers, 1963), 150–152. See also Martin Luther King, Jr., "Remaining Awake Through a Great Revolution," Commencement Address for Oberlin College, Oberlin, OH, 1965; Martin Luther King, Jr., "Remaining Awake Through a Great Revolution," *Congressional Record*, Washington, DC, 1968; Gerene L. Freeman, *What About My 40 Acres & a Mule?* (New Haven, CT: Yale-New Haven Teachers Institute, 1994); and Benjamin F. Bobo, *Locked In and Locked Out: The Impact of Urban Land Use Policy and Market Forces on African Americans* (Westport, CT: Praeger Publishers, 2001).

CHAPTER 1

Introduction

Do it today.
Give tomorrow a chance.

In Robert Gilpin's book, *U.S. Power and the Multinational Corporation*, written more than 25 years ago, he questioned whether America was repeating the error committed by other economic powers—such as the Netherlands in the seventeenth century and Great Britain in the nineteenth—of overinvesting abroad to the detriment of the home economy.[1] The concern appeared to be that the multinational corporation, the purveyor of direct foreign investment, would aid and abet the emergence of new centers of economic power and that such benevolence would not serve well America's national interest. This argument is validated by the emergence of the G8 (Group of 8) pact of countries, some observers argue. Another take on American capitalism, although not limited to U.S. foreign investment, is as noteworthy. In his exposition "The Development of Underdevelopment," Andre Gunder Frank argues that capital diffusion from the developed world (the core or metropolis) to particularly developing nations (the periphery or satellite) has directly resulted in their underdevelopment.[2] According to some observers, the emergence of the "Third World" validates the point.

Does today's world marketplace exemplify the Gilpin economic structure or does the Frank proposition appear more relevant? If Gilpin's concern were limited to the resulting emergence of new centers of economic power now held by G8 countries, clearly multinational enterprise produced a more diverse power structure. If Frank's argument accurately reflects the result of intimate economic relations between Third World countries and the capitalist system, multinational enterprise produced a very exclusive power structure. It is evident that both bear validity. But precisely how did the world order of countries arrive at the rich country–poor country makeup?

In contemporary expositions on international economic relations, much debate surrounds the notion that wealth and power tend to concentrate, and that distribution effects tend to be limited to certain locales within the world system. One view is that extremes of wealth and poverty have been created by the strong through exploitation and underdevelopment of the weak. This has led to a world order of disadvantaged and advantaged nations in which a transfer of wealth and power has occurred from the disadvantaged to the industrial core resulting in the marginalization of a sector of mankind to support economic activity for the rich. The power of the rich enables creation of an international division of labor, which favors ongoing accumulation of wealth at the core and fosters extensive under-development elsewhere.[3]

The other major view is that wealth and power tend to concentrate at the core with limited diffusion outward to the periphery. This is due to the higher rate of profit at the core where economic growth primarily occurs, and further due to operation of unfettered market and price mechanisms. A range of circumstances may be responsible for the higher rate of profit, including good governance, resource availability (skilled labor, raw mate-rials, etc.), superior technology, comparative advantage, efficient infra-structure, external economies, high savings rate, and economies of scale. The higher rate of profit, it is argued, attracts and absorbs labor, capital, and resources to the detriment of the periphery. These features of the core give it technical and organizational superiority, hence, market power and competitive advantage. The core is therefore in a position to command "monopoly" or "technological" rents from the periphery. As such, the core realizes a high rate of profit or return relative to the marginal incre-ment of investment or input required.[4] Exploitation or market efficiency, as explained, leads in many respects to sustained economic superiority at the core, as well as sustained underdevelopment at the periphery. A coun-tervailing argument is that market efficiency or sustained economic growth at the core spreads throughout the world system through positive exploitation of natural resources and even cheap labor, thereby enabling the periphery and creating a more enterprising world order. Factors of production—labor, capital, technology, and even land itself as related to food stuffs and raw material—have become more mobile with industrial-ism and rising global economic interdependency. Industry spreads to the periphery through foreign investment, trade expansion, and technology transfer from the core. While the diffusion of the growth process does not occur evenly throughout the world system, peripheral locations eventu-ally become new concentrations of economic power.[5]

The notion of economic diffusion meets heavy rejection in some circles. Frank argues that it is largely erroneous to presume that the diffusion of capital, institutions, values, and the like to the periphery foster economic development there. He contends that such relations with the core do little more than promote the structure and development of the capitalist system, and intensify and perpetuate the very conditions they are supposedly designed to remedy. Further, as Frank sums up, past experiences of under-developed countries suggest that economic development there can take place only largely independently of diffusion from developed countries.[6]

No doubt the prevailing debate over the conditioning of rich and poor countries will persist. It is clear that doing it alone, as Frank suggests, would require that rich countries, principally the G8, give poor countries complete autonomy in the world marketplace. Even if this were possible, is it practical? It would mean that poor countries quite literally would have to pull themselves up by their bootstraps. To be sure, the diffusion of cap-ital to poor countries either has little occurred or has hardly succeeded, depending on the side of the debate taken. But this may well suggest a fail-ure of the approach to capital diffusion, not the concept itself. In the absence of countervailing forces, particularly rich country preferences or poor country economic planning, the market mechanism should effect a reasonably efficient redistribution of wealth and power to poor countries via capital diffusion. It is clear that industrial centers frequently endeavor to prevent or control the spread of industrialism to protect competitive as well as comparative advantage. And, poor countries engage in economic planning that often inhibits capital diffusion from the outside in efforts to pick and choose the direction of economic growth, and to protect them-selves from unwanted intrusion in national economic processes.[7]

It is useful to recognize that capital diffusion is far more complex than it may appear on the surface. Concerns regarding exploitation, market efficiency, and distribution effects mask the industrial development process, which requires the full range of growth support attributes. These include good governance—political, social, and institutional framework—and reasonably plentiful factors of production—raw materials, skilled labor (cheap labor may be a substitute as a starter), capital, entrepreneur-ship, and foreign exchange. Even with these reasonably available and even with the multinational corporation engaged in capital diffusion, that is, providing a hand up as change agent, Third World countries (indeed, every country) may be confined to walking the ladder of com-parative advantage.[8] The principle of comparative advantage, advanced by the English economist David Ricardo in 1817, holds that a country has a comparative advantage in a product or service when it can produce that product or service at a lower cost than it can be produced by another country. In this vein, a commonly accepted argument is that trade between and among countries makes everyone better off because countries specialize in producing those products and services in which they have comparative advantage. Specialization results in an efficient international division of labor, giving each country a higher real national income than it would have with no trade, thus enabling it to more aggressively climb the ladder.[9]

Each rung on the ladder represents a stage in the development process. Countries typically begin the process through accessing export markets and world trade via a supply of resource-intensive products (oil, timber, sugar, etc.). The next rung involves products that are unskilled labor-intensive, such as textiles and foodstuffs. Further advancement requires semiskilled and skilled labor-intensive production, notably electronics and small appliances. The next destination on the ladder is perhaps the most defining indicator of industrialization—capital-intensive machinery production. Achieving comparative advantage at this level thrusts the nation squarely into the high-stakes game of big-ticket exports. Competing head-on with G8 nations is a must and establishing clear cost advantage is paramount. Machinery production and export is the coming-of-age in economic development. The know-how and initiative required for project design, development, and implementation at this level sets the stage for movement to the most advanced step on the ladder—knowledge-intensive research and development (R&D). R&D is the ultimate target in the economic development process, involving high-tech data communications infrastructure, and highly educated and skilled labor that is required for production of computers, computer information systems, pharmaceuticals, and other knowledge-intensive products.[10] Each step up the ladder is virtually a monumental task, consuming many years and much effort.

The ladder of comparative advantage process can be likened to Rostow's stages of economic growth. In his treatise, emphasis is placed on the composition of investment and the growth of certain leading sectors thought to be instrumental in propelling the economy.[11]

Kuznets summarized the stage process as a theory that implies: (1) distinct time segments, characterized by different sources and patterns of economic changes; (2) a specific succession of these segments, so that b cannot occur before a, or c before b; and (3) a common matrix, in that the successive segments are stages in one broad process—usually one of development and growth rather than of devolution and shrinkage. Stage theory is most closely associated with a uni-directional rather then cyclic view of history. In the cyclic view the stages are recurrent; in a uni-directional view, a stage materializes, runs its course, and never recurs. Even in the process of devolution and decline, the return to a level experienced previously is not viewed as a recurrence of the earlier stage.[12]

As previously suggested, Third World economic development may be confined to the stage path to growth. Opponents of such notion argue that stage development is misleading, particularly the implication that all economies tend to pass through the same series of stages. While there may be similarity and likeness in the sequence of development for some countries, historical evidence does not support a single sequence representing the history of all countries. Opposing argument further asserts that an economy may achieve a later stage of development without first having passed through an earlier stage,[13] and may presumably start on a higher rung on the ladder of comparative advantage. Stages and rungs are not necessarily mutually exclusive and features of earlier activities may be associated with or overlap features of later activities.

Despite the arguments surrounding the economic development process, the rise and persistence of a rich country–poor country world order is clear and indisputable. The various essentially conceptual frameworks—efficient markets, exploitation, capital diffusion, ladder of comparative advantage, and stage theory of economic growth—assist the focus on strategic factors that promote or restrict development. But the intelligence of the frameworks has yet to lead us to resolution of the poor country status of a preponderance of nations. In an attempt to enhance the dialogue on the topic what follows is a different approach to assessing the situation of poor countries and to prescribing aids for redressing their condition.

The analytical perspective rests upon the relationship of multinational enterprise and Third World development as an operating system that drives the economic development process. The prescriptive perspective engages the multinational corporation as the agent of change with the capacity to energize the economic development process in the Third World. The moral perspective lies in the goodness of the human spirit, the intellectual capacity to adjust traditional thought to accommodate new conceptual approaches, and the ethical imperative to fix what's wrong with the world.

NOTES

1. Robert Gilpin, *U.S. Power and the Multinational Corporation* (New York: Basic Books, Inc., 1975), 8.

2. Andre Gunder Frank, "The Development of Underdevelopment," in David N. Balaam and Michael Veseth, *Readings in International Political Economy* (Upper Saddle River, NJ: Prentice Hall, Inc., 1996), 64–73. See also Gilpin, ibid., 47–48. Capitalist and Marxist theorists differ on the definition of core and periphery. The capitalist sees the world generally as having several cores and peripheries scattered throughout, while the Marxist tends to regard the core as being distinctly comprised of all the capitalist economies and the periphery as distinctly Third World countries.

3. Gilpin, ibid., 50.

4. Ibid., 50–51.

5. Ibid., 51–52.

6. Balaam and Veseth, ibid., 65.

7. Gilpin, ibid., 51–52.

8. Gerald M. Meier, *Leading Issues in Economic Development* (New York: Oxford University Press, 1995), 458.

9. Ibid., 455.

10. Ibid., 456–457.

11. Ibid., 69. See also W.W. Rostow, "The Stages of Economic Growth," *Economic History Review* (August 1959); W.W. Rostow, *The Stages of Economic Growth* (New York: Cambridge University Press, 1990); and W.W. Rostow et al., *The Economics of Take-Off into Sustained Growth* (New York: St. Martin's Press, 1963).

12. Meier, ibid., 69. See also Simon Kuznets, "Notes on Stage of Economic Growth as a System Determinant," in Alexander Eckstein, ed., *Comparison of Economic Systems* (Berkeley: University of California Press, 1971), 243.

13. Meier, ibid., 71.

CHAPTER 2

The Historical Context in Brief

All that follows emerges from a concern about life-choice constraints of the economically disadvantaged and a belief that disadvantagement can be remedied. The multinational corporation stands steadfastly as a beacon of hope and an instrument of change, certainly to this researcher, with the capacity to orchestrate resolve to the desperate conditions of Third World nations. Some history of the multinational corporation offers insight into the unique character of this organizational form and its potential as an agent of change in the Third World environment. In addition, some history of the Third World, especially of economic significance, helps to draw attention more directly to the conditions at hand and the need for a special change agent to lead necessary economic transformation. This chapter sets forth historical facts that underscore the need for a more formal relationship between multinational corporations and Third World countries.

The post–World War II era has witnessed the emergence of a powerful agent of world social and economic change—the multinational corporation. Owning and managing business facilities in foreign countries, it is often wealthier in assets than many of the nations, particularly Third World nation-states, in which it conducts business. Though the multinational corporation exists under the jurisdiction of the host countries' laws and pays them taxes, it has its own goals and objectives and responds to a supreme management authority located in its home country.

Predecessors of multinational corporations were the companies of merchant traders of medieval Venice, including English, Dutch, and French trading companies of the seventeenth and eighteenth centuries. Unlike today's multinational corporations, they were trading rather than manufacturing organizations, with little fixed investment and rarely operating under the jurisdiction of foreign sovereign states. Comparatively, multinational corporations so visible in the global marketplace today have enormous fixed investment and engage in a host of activities under foreign jurisdiction, including establishing sales and service organizations, licensing foreign firms to produce and sell their products, conducting research and development, establishing and operating manufacturing facilities, and multinationalizing management and corporate stock ownership.

Apart from the operating of trading companies in the seventeenth and eighteenth centuries, the stage was further set for development of the multinational corporation by foreign investment activities conducted by Western Europe during the nineteenth century. While little direct capital flow took place outside colonial territories or spheres of influence in the early years, investment was extensive within what was perhaps considered safe domains. British firms made large investments in India, Canada, Australia, and South Africa. Dutch firms deployed capital in the East Indies, and French companies concentrated their investments in Indochina, Algeria, and other French colonies. The United States was also a recipient of European investments, but this was done through the purchase of corporate and American government securities rather than direct foreign investment. Direct commitments in brick and mortar in alien territory was not yet the modus operandi. By the turn of the twentieth century, however, American firms were engaged in foreign investment activity and were well on their way to making the practice of direct foreign investment commonplace. This was particularly evident in Britain, where American firms were producing farm equipment, printing presses, and other products.[1]

During the early twentieth century, the first substantial multinational corporate investments were made; in fact, the multinational corporation is considered to have had its inception during this period. The mining and petroleum industries were the initial targets of early direct investment. Large oil companies like British Petroleum and Standard Oil emerged, along with hard mineral corporations such as Anaconda Copper, Kennecott Copper, and International Nickel, and manufacturing and merchandising multinationals such as Singer, Woolworth, and Coca-Cola. Manufacturers of automobiles, tires, and auto spare parts and accessories joined the list of multinationals, which originate primarily from the United States, Britain, Canada, the Netherlands, Switzerland, France, Germany, Italy, Sweden, and Japan.[2]

The twentieth century also witnessed the emergence of a new category of international enterprise in the Third World multinational. While Third World corporate multinationalism is in the embryonic stage, a few examples of the time are noteworthy. Saudi Arabian businessman Ghaith

R. Pharaon purchased majority interest in the Mainbank of Houston and the National Bank of Georgia. Multinational firms headquartered in South Korea, Taiwan, and the Philippines spearheaded construction in foreign countries. Taiwanese companies built steel mills in Nigeria; Koreans paved roads in Ecuador; and Filipinos developed deep-water port facilities in the Persian Gulf. The watchmaker Stelux Manufacturing Company of Hong Kong purchased a large equity interest in Bulova Watch Company. India's Hindustan Machine and Tools Company helped Algeria launch a machine tools industry; and other Indian multinationals assisted with the construction of Libyan steel mills and Yugoslavian electronics plants.[3]

From its advent, the multinational corporation grew at a phenomenal pace. By the early 1970s, the annual sales of some multinationals were larger than the gross national product (GNP) of many countries, particularly Third World.[4] For example, General Motors (GM) was bigger than Pakistan and South Africa; Royal Dutch Shell was bigger than Iran and Turkey; and Goodyear Tire was bigger than Saudi Arabia.[5] Over time, as gross national product has grown, so have sales. By 2000, as may be gleaned from Exhibits 2.1 and 2.2, the number of multinationals that were larger than Third World countries comprised an extensive list. And, at the 2000 mark, the sales of multinationals were not just larger than the GNP of Third World countries, as may be expected, but developed countries as well. For example, Exxon Mobil rivaled Sweden; Royal Dutch Shell and

Exhibit 2.1
Sales and Assets of Global Corporations 2000 ($ billions)

Corporation	Sales	Assets
Altria Group	80.4	79.1
AT&T	66.0	208.1
Boeing Company	51.3	43.5
BP	148.1	144.9
Cardinal Health	25.2	10.3
Chevron	50.6	41.3
ConocoPhillips	22.2	20.5
DaimlerChrysler	152.5	187.1
Delphi	29.1	18.5
Dow	23.0	27.7
DuPont	28.3	39.4
Electronic Data Systems	19.2	12.7
Exxon Mobil	231.8	149.0
Ford Motor	170.1	284.4
General Electric	129.9	437.0
Georgia-Pacific	22.2	30.9
GM	184.6	303.1
Hewlett-Packard	48.8	34.0

Exhibit 2.1 *(continued)*

Home Depot	45.7	21.4
Honda Motor	57.5	46.2
Honeywell International	25.0	25.2
IBM	88.4	88.4
Johnson & Johnson	29.1	31.3
Matsushita	68.9	72.5
McKesson	36.7	10.4
Merck & Co.	40.4	39.9
Microsoft	23.0	52.1
Mitsubishi	127.3	78.6
Mitsui	128.2	62.1
Nippon Steel	25.3	39.3
Nippon Telegraph & Telephone	98.0	180.2
Nissan Motor	49.1	52.0
Nokia	27.9	18.3
Procter & Gamble	40.0	34.2
RoyalDutch/Shell Group	191.5	122.5
RWE	14.5	72.2
Samsung	32.3	5.8
SBC Communications	51.5	98.7
Sears	40.9	36.9
Siemens	72.1	73.0
Sony	63.1	64.2
Suez	31.8	78.7
Texaco	51.1	30.9
Total	105.8	80.7
Toyota Motor	121.3	155.2
Tyco International	28.9	40.4
Unilever	43.8	27.0
United Technologies	26.6	25.4
Verizon Communications	64.7	164.7
Wal-Mart	165.0	70.3

Source: Data compiled from the annual reports of the respective corporations for the year 2000.

GM were larger than Denmark; Ford Motor and Wal-Mart were larger than Norway; DaimlerChrysler and BP were larger than Finland; and General Electric was larger than Greece. Collectively, the sales of the top 12 multinationals represented in Exhibit 2.1—about $1.8 trillion—exceeded gross national product of several G8 (Group of Eight) countries, including the United Kingdom, France, Italy, Canada, and Russia.

Size translates to power and influence. Multinationals are making daily decisions that have more impact on the lives of people than those of many sovereign governments. As multinationalism shapes the globalization of

Exhibit 2.2
Gross National Product, Selected Countries 1990 and 2000 ($ billions)

Country	Gross National Product		Country	Gross National Product	
	1990	*2000*		*1990*	*2000*
United States	5,846	9,602	Ireland	42	86
Japan	3,348	4,519	Colombia	41	85
Germany	1,612	2,064	Malaysia	43	79
United Kingdom	934	1,459	Philippines	45	79
France	1,142	1,438	Chile	29	70
Italy	988	1,163	Pakistan	43	61
China	368	1,063	Czech Republic	(NA)	54
Canada	550	650	Peru	17	53
Brazil	411	610	New Zealand	43	50
Spain	458	595	Algeria	61	48
Mexico	236	497	Bangladesh	31	48
India	332	455	Hungary	30	47
South Korea	246	421	United Arab Emirates	37	(NA)
Netherlands	285	398	Romania	40	37
Australia	300	388	Ukraine	83	35
Argentina	104	276	Morocco	25	34
Switzerland	225	274	Nigeria	26	33
Belgium	183	252	Vietnam	(NA)	30
Russia	(NA)	241	Belarus	35	29
Sweden	214	241	Croatia	(NA)	20
Turkey	128	202	Slovakia	18	20
Hong Kong	72	176	Slovenia	(NA)	20
Denmark	120	172	Uruguay	9	20
Poland	(NA)	162	Guatemala	8	19
Norway	108	155	Kazakhstan	(NA)	19
Saudi Arabia	105	150	Luxembourg	12	18
Finland	124	130	Lebanon	(NA)	17
South Africa	102	129	Sri Lanka	8	16
Greece	79	126	Costa Rica	5	15
Thailand	84	122	Ecuador	10	15
Indonesia	111	120	Syria	11	15
Portugal	64	111	El Salvador	5	13
Iran	141	107	Bulgaria	20	12
Israel	51	104	Cote d'Ivoire	9	10
Venezuela	52	104	Uzbekistan	(NA)	9
Singapore	36	99	Congo (Kinshasa)	8	(NA)
Egypt	42	95	Ethiopia	8	7

Source: Statistical Abstract of the United States, U.S. Census Bureau, 2002; and World Development Indicators (Washington, DC: The World Bank, 1991).

production, decisions about the allocation and utilization of world resources become more and more concentrated in the hands of fewer and fewer decision makers. In the early 1970s, it was expected that by 1985, 200 to 300 global corporations would control 80 percent of all productive assets of the noncommunist world, and by the turn of the century a few hundred global companies would own productive assets in excess of $4 trillion, or more than 50 percent of everything worth owning for the creation of wealth.[6] While it is unclear whether the full measure of these expectations has actually materialized or for that matter is even ascertainable, current data as shown in Exhibit 2.1 reveal several interesting facts in the context of earlier expectations. By the turn of the century, some 50 global corporations alone owned productive assets in excess of $4 trillion. Clearly, the growth of global corporations has far exceeded expectations; more importantly, their influence on the allocation and utilization of world resources presumably has intensified quite significantly, perhaps even more so than earlier expected.

Over time multinationalism has become truly global, touching not only the full scope of developed countries, but reaching into Third World countries as well. Historically, the term "Third World" has been used in reference to African, Asian, and Latin American countries (including the Middle East and the Pacific islands) as a means of identifying these areas of the world as generally economically poor. There is some concern that the term may be no longer relevant as a collective description of countries facing common issues and problems of development.[7] This notwithstanding, there are groupings of countries that are economically poor by comparison to a select grouping of other countries—Sub-Saharan African countries relative to the G8 for example—particularly in terms of gross national product. Such imbalanced international economics gives rise to a rich country–poor country world order. Exhibit 2.2 offers a poignant expose of the relative wealth or well-being of countries as suggested by gross national product. Gross national product is viewed as the most comprehensive individual indicator of the general economic well-being of a nation. Historically, wealth has been concentrated within and among the higher GNP countries; data from 1990 and 2000 support this observation in that generally the same countries are located in the top tier of GNP. On the other hand, there is a grouping of countries (as depicted in Exhibit 2.2) falling noticeably at the lower end of GNP, which have been unable to achieve substantial economic development. Countries in this predicament—typically those in Africa, Asia, and Latin America—have a history of general poverty and appear to have no means of generating significant wealth, certainly not independently.

Further, there has been much debate surrounding the historical experience and indeed the misfortunes of poor countries. What has led to the paucity in gross national product so evident among an array of countries in the world? Exhibit 2.3 may be helpful in this regard. There is a generally accepted argument that Third World development can be best orchestrated

Exhibit 2.3
Poor Countries and Per Capita Income: A Model of the Debate

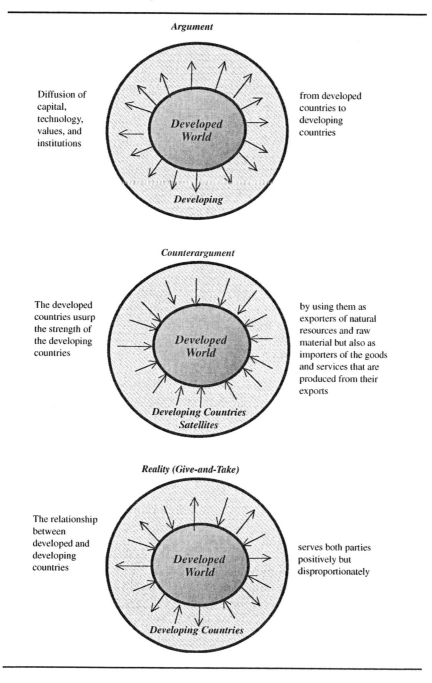

Argument

Diffusion of capital, technology, values, and institutions

Developed World

Developing

from developed countries to developing countries

Counterargument

The developed countries usurp the strength of the developing countries

Developed World

Developing Countries Satellites

by using them as exporters of natural resources and raw material but also as importers of the goods and services that are produced from their exports

Reality (Give-and-Take)

The relationship between developed and developing countries

Developed World

Developing Countries

serves both parties positively but disproportionately

through relations with the developed countries. Essentially, the idea is that through a diffusion of the developed world's capital, technology, values, and institutions to developing countries, a spawning of economic development will result. Modernization, where evident in developing countries, is viewed as the outcome of this relationship. This is countered with the argument that the developed world's relationship with developing countries merely serves to intensify the underdeveloped conditions it purports to remedy. The substance of this viewpoint is that the developed countries usurp the strength of the developing countries by using them purely as exporters of the natural resources that are so important to fueling the engines of growth in developed countries. At the same time, as the counterargument contends, developing countries are little more than importers of goods and services from developed countries with price tags that far exceed their share of value added to the natural resource exports used in producing the imported goods and services. The implication here is perhaps obvious—developing countries are not receiving a fair share of value added to resources that they supply.[8]

Though the argument and counterargument present interesting positions on the subject at hand, in reality an interfacing of the two viewpoints may reflect a more representative depiction of the relationship between developed and developing countries. Pragmatically, there is give-and-take between the parties with a sharing of the gain realized from exploitation of Third World natural resources. However, there is such a disproportionate sharing of the gain that the allocation of wealth between the parties has become heavily skewed toward the developed world over time, hence the rich country–poor country makeup.

Historically, the process of give-and-take has been engineered by the multinational corporation. From Africa to Asia to Latin America, rich countries, through the exploits of multinational corporations, have pursued the acquisition of raw materials, and also the consumer market. The sheer enormity of the developing world in natural resources and population has provided a marketplace of business opportunities and will continue to do so as time passes. Each developing region has special characteristics and circumstances.

Africa, comprising some 55 independent nations and other territories (including offshore islands), is the second largest continent. It is more than three times the size of the United States. Its population has risen from 350 million in the late 1970s to more than 830 million today. The continent's mineral reserves place it among the most heavily endowed regions of the world, ranking first or second in quantity of world reserves of bauxite, chromite, cobalt, diamond, gold, manganese, phosphate rock, platinum, titanium, vanadium, vermiculite, and zirconium.[9]

Africa has been largely regarded as a source of raw materials and a market for exports. In recent decades, however, limited industrial development has emerged on the continent, owing primarily to increased demand, the introduction of locally produced goods as substitution for imports, and the encouragement of manufacturing by individual African administrations. Even so, African economies experienced general stagnation or decline until the early 1990s. In fact, real gross domestic product (GDP) for the continent (Sub-Saharan Africa) had approached a virtual no-growth stage by the beginning of the 1990s,[10] when general growth resumed. From 1990 to 1994, Africa's GDP averaged about 2.2 percent a year, with 1992 being the weak link at 1.4 percent. The latter half of the 1990s recorded rather impressive gains. Beginning in 1995, GDP climbed to 4.0 percent and averaged about 4.5 percent through 2000, with 1996 and 1997 reaching 5.2 percent annually.[11] Economic growth in Africa has relied in large part on economic reform programs. While the outcome of such efforts is generally reflected in higher GDP, the growth has been unevenly experienced across the continent. Moreover, Africans on average have not experienced much improvement in well-being, as reflected in increases in per capita income over time.[12] Exhibit 2.4 provides some testimony in this regard. Ethiopia, Nigeria, and Cote d'Ivoire actually lost ground from 1990 to 2000. Comparatively, developed countries posted sizeable advances during the period, resulting in a widening of the income gap between rich and poor nations. The decline of per capita income in African countries suggests a general deterioration in the well-being of their inhabitants.

African economic growth has depended also on direct foreign investment and foreign aid, but there has not been much in the way of such capital flows from the developed countries, their primary source. This in part may reflect a decline in external political interest in Africa following the end of the cold war, as well as economic problems in developed countries. Though capital flows to the Third World increased rather dramatically during the 1990s, African countries were generally not the beneficiaries.[13] In fact, "many African countries are not even listed for consideration by transnational corporations—let alone make it onto the 'short list'—when it comes to locational decisions for FDI [Foreign Direct Investment], despite offering a number of attractions to foreign investors."[14]

Exhibit 2.5 provides an indication of foreign capital flows to the African continent over time. With the exception of the Middle East, the region on the whole has seen acceleration in investment capital in recent decades, but its success in attracting direct foreign investment pales by comparison to Asia and Latin America. Flows to individual African countries as depicted in Exhibit 2.6, while not dramatic in general, have remained rather paltry, stagnant, or declined in selected cases. Those particularly represented here include Cote d'Ivoire, Ethiopia, Malawi, Cameroon, Togo, Benin, Botswana, Chad, Rwanda, Congo, Burundi, Burkina Faso, Morocco, Algeria, Central African Republic, Mauritania, and Sierra Leone. These are but a portion of the countries on the continent that show

Exhibit 2.4
Gross National Product Per Capita, Selected Countries 1990 and 2000 ($)

Country	Gross National Product Per Capita		Country	Gross National Product Per Capita	
	1990	*2000*		*1990*	*2000*
Luxembourg	31,350	42,060	Lebanon	(NA)	4,010
Switzerland	33,510	38,140	Costa Rica	1,790	3,810
Japan	27,100	35,620	Slovakia	3,340	3,700
Norway	25,490	34,530	Brazil	2,780	3,580
United States	23,440	34,100	Malaysia	2,380	3,380
Denmark	23,430	32,280	Turkey	2,280	3,100
Sweden	25,050	27,140	South Africa	2,890	3,020
Hong Kong	12,680	25,920	Belarus	3,460	2,870
Finland	24,890	25,130	Peru	780	2,080
Germany	20,290	25,120	Colombia	1,180	2,020
Netherlands	19,070	24,970	El Salvador	940	2,000
Singapore	11,740	24,740	Thailand	1,520	2,000
Belgium	18,340	24,540	Guatemala	970	1,680
United Kingdom	16,220	24,430	Iran	2,590	1,680
United Arab Emirates	19,930	(NA)	Romania	1,720	1,670
France	19,860	24,090	Russia	(NA)	1,660
Ireland	11,960	22,660	Algeria	2,440	1,580
Canada	19,790	21,130	Bulgaria	2,260	1,520
Australia	17,590	20,240	Egypt	810	1,490
Italy	17,420	20,160	Kazakhstan	(NA)	1,260
Israel	10,860	16,710	Ecuador	970	1,210
Spain	11,790	15,080	Morocco	1,030	1,180
New Zealand	12,410	12,990	Philippines	740	1,040
Greece	7,770	11,960	Syria	940	940
Portugal	6,420	11,120	Sri Lanka	470	850
Slovenia	(NA)	10,050	China	320	840
South Korea	5,740	8,910	Ukraine	1,600	700
Argentina	3,190	7,460	Cote d'Ivoire	780	600
Saudi Arabia	6,620	7,230	Indonesia	620	570
Uruguay	2,870	6,000	India	390	450
Czech Republic	(NA)	5,250	Pakistan	390	440
Mexico	2,830	5,070	Vietnam	(NA)	390
Hungary	2,880	4,710	Bangladesh	280	370
Croatia	(NA)	4,620	Uzbekistan	(NA)	360
Chile	2,190	4,590	Nigeria	270	260
Venezuela	2,650	4,310	Congo (Kinshasa)	230	(NA)
Poland	(NA)	4,190	Ethiopia	160	100

Source: Statistical Abstract of the United States, U.S. Census Bureau, 2002, and World Development Indicators (Washington, DC: The World Bank, 1991).

Exhibit 2.5
Direct Foreign Investment by Region ($ million)

Region	1970	2000
Latin America & Caribbean	16,000	75,088
East Asia & Pacific	11,400	42,847
Europe & Central Asia	3,800	28,495
Africa	5,000	6,676
South Asia	400	3,093
Middle East	3,900	1,209
Total	40,500	1,167,337

Sources: Helen Hughes, "Debt and Development: The Role of Foreign Capital in Economic Growth," *World Development Report* 7, no. 6 (1979), 105 (with permission of Elsevier); and "Sustainable Development in a Dynamic World," *World Development Report* (2003), 240–241.

a history of very serious neglect by developed countries in locational decisions for foreign investment.

In contrast to Africa, Asia is more representative of a geographical construct of countries rather than a homogenous continent.[15] It is the largest and most populous of the continents, occupying 30 percent of the world's land area and serving as home for about 3.3 billion people, most of whom are inhabitants of China and India. This represents about half the human race. The continent's population has increased tremendously since the 1970s, when it was 2.2 billion.[16] Asia is also a continent of immense mineral resources, including reserves of coal, oil, natural gas, uranium, iron, bauxite, and other ores. Some 60 percent of the world's coal reserves and a like amount of the world's known oil and gas reserves are in Asia.[17]

In recent decades, a number of Asian nations have made impressive strides in all areas of modern technology. Several have a rather robust middle class, at least four have nuclear weapons or the capacity to produce weapons of mass destruction, and many of them produce goods that are commonplace imports of Western nations. The achievements of what are referred to as high-performing Asian economies such as Japan, South Korea, Taiwan, Hong Kong, Singapore, Malaysia, Thailand, and Indonesia bear note. These countries have seen relatively sustained economic growth and structural transformation in the last few decades. Their average annual growth in GDP during the periods 1970–1980 and 1980–1996 exceeded 7 percent and 6 percent, respectively. Manufacturing fueled the growth and exports grew at double-digit rates between 1980 and 1982.[18]

Similar to other Third World nations, however, the countries of Asia generally display common problems of underdevelopment, wrenching poverty, overpopulation, poor governance, civil strife, human rights violation, corruption, and the like.[19] Exhibits 2.2 and 2.4 essentially reveal the

Exhibit 2.6
Direct Foreign Investment in Third World Economies, Selected Countries ($ million)

Country	1980	1993	2000	Country	1980	1993	2000
China	0	25,800	38,399	El Salvador	6	16	185
Brazil	1,911	802	32,779	Madagascar	−1	30	176
Mexico	2,156	4,901	13,286	Sri Lanka	43	195	173
Argentina	678	6,305	11,665	Mozambique	0	30	139
Poland	10	1,715	9,342	Papua New			
Korea, Rep.	6	516	9,283	Guinea	76	450	130
Portugal	157	1,301	6,227	Lesothio	5	15	118
Venezuela	55	372	4,464	Kenya	79	2	111
Chile	213	841	3,675	Ghana	16	25	110
Thailand	190	2,400	3,366	Senegal	15	0	107
Colombia	157	850	2,376	Cote d'Ivoire	95	30	106
India	79	273	2,315	Paraguay	32	150	82
Philippines	−106	763	2,029	Zimbabwe	2	28	79
Hungary	0	2,349	1,692	Mali	2	1	76
Malaysia	934	4,351	1,660	Guinea-Bissau	0	0	63
Vietnam	0	300	1,298	Guinea	34	25	63
Egypt	548	493	1,235	Ethiophia	0	6	50
Nigeria	−740	900	1,082	Malawi	10	0	45
Dominican				Iran, Islamic			
Rep.	93	183	953	Rep.	0	−50	39
Tunisia	235	239	752	Cameroon	130	−81	31
Bolivia	47	150	733	Togo	42	0	30
Ecuador	70	115	710	Benin	4	10	30
Peru	27	349	680	Botswana	112	55	30
Panama	−47	−41	603	Chad	0	6	15
Jordan	34	−34	558	Rwanda	16	3	14
Jamaica	28	139	456	Congo	40	0	14
Costa Rica	53	280	409	Burundi	0	1	12
Pakistan	63	347	308	Burkina Faso	0	0	10
Uruguay	290	76	298	Morocco	89	522	10
Honduras	6	65	282	Algeria	349	15	10
Bangladesh	0	14	280	Cent. African			
Myanmar	0	4	255	Rep.	5	1	5
Nicaragua	0	39	254	Mauritania	27	1	5
Guatemala	111	149	230	Napal	0	6	4
Uganda	0	3	220	Sierra Leone	−9	35	1
Zambia	62	55	200	Yemen, Rep.	34	0	−201
Tanzania	0	20	193	Indonesia	180	2004	−4550

Sources: World Development Report (Washington, DC: The World Bank, 1995), 204–205; "Sustainable Development in a Dynamic World," *World Development Report* (Washington, DC: The World Bank, 2003), 240–241.

magnitude of such socioeconomic distress, as there is a tendency of Asian countries to predominate at the lower end of the GNP and GNP per capita world spectrum. While China, for example, experienced impressive growth in GNP and GNP per capita over the decade 1990 to 2000, GNP output stand-alone places the country among the higher GNP performers, but because of overpopulation, it is at the lower end of GNP per capita in the context of a world distribution of countries. Similar characteristics are displayed by India and other countries.

As in the case of Africa, Asian economic development has relied on direct foreign investment. In recent decades, however, Asia has received considerably more investment capital from developed countries than has Africa. Exhibit 2.5 shows that while capital flows to Africa have increased only slightly over time, comparatively capital flows to Asia have risen quite significantly. In fact, in 1970 direct foreign investment to Asia was only three times higher than Africa, but by 2000, the gap had increased nearly twelvefold. The robustness of economic growth in Asia—particularly regarding, for example, the "East Asian Miracle"—is in large part reflective of capital diffusion from developed countries.[20]

Exhibit 2.5 also reveals the disproportionate share of direct foreign investment to East Asia relative to Asia in general. South Asia has experienced relative neglect, and the comparatively greater degree of economic and social distress in South Asian countries generally evidences the extent of inattention by developed countries.

Joining Africa and Asia in the developing world schema is Latin America. It is descriptively a set of regions rather than a homogeneous continent, consisting of 20 countries. Its land surface is slightly larger than that of the United States and Canada combined and its population is around 540 million, up from about 300 million in the 1970s. The continent has vast natural resources, including petroleum and other minerals that provide substantial export earnings. Venezuela is the leading oil producer and a major oil exporting country. Mexico, Argentina, and Colombia are also major petroleum producers. Copper, lead, zinc, tin, and silver are produced in Latin America in substantial quantities. Chile is the principal copper producer, Mexico the leading zinc producer and a major producer of silver, and Bolivia is a major producer of tin. Further, a very significant portion of the world's bauxite comes from the region—Jamaica being the leading producer. The continent is also credited with having large deposits of iron ore, concentrated mainly in Brazil and Venezuela.[21]

Since World War II, Latin America has pursued economic modernization, and has made a strong effort to increase industrialization and to reduce the region's dependence on foreign exports. Industrialization, however, has not been achieved on a generally widespread basis, but has tended to be concentrated in a few centers of exceptional growth. Brazil, Mexico, and Argentina have enjoyed the most impressive industrial development among the Latin American countries, with Venezuela, Chile, and Colombia showing significant progress as well. Exhibits 2.2 and 2.6 show these countries as achieving the highest gross national product as well as receiving the highest levels of direct foreign investment in the Latin American region.

Despite efforts to modernize, Latin America has long had the most unequally distributed income and the highest skill differentials in the world.[22] The problem in many ways is connected to the level of high school graduates in Latin American countries. When the educational profiles of the adult population in Latin America are compared to Asia, for example, what is most apparent is the disproportionate number of university graduates in Latin America relative to adults with a high school education. In other words, there is a small number of adults with a high school education and a large proportion of university graduates. Between 1970 and 1985, both secondary and university education practically doubled in Asia, but university graduates increased twice as fast as high school graduates in Latin America.[23] Over time, the persistent emphasis on the university component has resulted in continued exacerbation of the income pyramid.

Further, income inequality in Latin America apparently has not been significantly impacted by direct foreign investment. Expectations are that direct foreign investment brings technology transfer that assists in raising the skill level of the general workforce, hence reducing income disparity. That Latin America's income distribution and skill differential are so out of balance, particularly with other developing regions, is especially noteworthy in the context of the data presented in Exhibit 2.5. For decades, Latin America has received the major share of direct foreign investment in the developing world. While this has not served to appreciably enhance skill development, Exhibit 2.7 suggests that direct foreign investment in the region generally has helped to improve the position of Latin American countries relative to others in the world as measured by GNP per capita. In the decade 1990 to 2000, Latin American countries experienced growth in GNP per capita to the extent that they were able to pull even or move ahead of other nations. For example, of the 74 countries represented, 12 are Latin American. With the exception of Brazil and Ecuador, all advanced in position relative to other countries. Peru, Chile, El Salvador, and Costa Rica experienced the highest movement up the GNP per capita ladder among Latin American countries.

Income distribution in the region remains out of sync with other developing areas, suggesting that capital flows have gone more to promote higher-end job development, presumably to support higher-quality export creation rather than lower-skill employment necessary to close the income gap. Clearly, Latin American education strategy has to be reexamined, but the diffusion of foreign capital on the continent in content and context deserves reassessment as well.

Exhibit 2.7

Gross National Product Per Capita, Selected Countries, Relative Position in 1990 by Comparison to 2000 ($)

	1990				2000	
Rank	Country	GNP Per Capita		Rank	Country	GNP Per Capita
1	Switzerland	33,510		1	Luxembourg	42,060
2	Luxembourg	31,350		2	Switzerland	38,140
3	Japan	27,100		3	Japan	35,620
4	Norway	25,490		4	Norway	34,530
5	Sweden	25,050		5	United States	34,100
6	Finland	24,890		6	Denmark	32,280
7	United States	23,440		7	Sweden	27,140
8	Denmark	23,430		8	Hong Kong	25,920
9	Germany	20,290		9	Finland	25,130
10	Emirates	19,930		10	Germany	25,120
11	France	19,860		11	Netherlands	24,970
12	Canada	19,790		12	Singapore	24,740
13	Netherlands	19,070		13	Belgium	24,540
14	Belgium	18,340		14	UK	24,430
15	Australia	17,590		15	Emirates	(NA)
16	Italy	17,420		16	France	24,090
17	UK	16,220		17	Ireland	22,660
18	Hong Kong	12,680		18	Canada	21,130
19	New Zealand	12,410		19	Australia	20,240
20	Ireland	11,960		20	Italy	20,160
21	Spain	11,790		21	Israel	16,710
22	Singapore	11,740		22	Spain	15,080
23	Israel	10,860		23	New Zealand	12,990
24	Greece	7,770		24	Greece	11,960
25	Saudi Arabia	6,620		25	Portugal	11,120
26	Portugal	6,420		26	Slovenia	10,050
27	Slovenia	(NA)		27	South Korea	8,910
28	South Korea	5,740		28	Argentina	7,460
29	Balarus	3,460		29	Saudi Arabia	7,230
30	Slovakia	3,340		30	Uruguay	6,000
31	Argentina	3,190		31	Czech Republic	5,250
32	South Africa	2,890		32	Mexico	5,070
33	Hungary	2,880		33	Hungary	4,710
34	Uruguay	2,870		34	Croatia	4,620
35	Czech Republic	(NA)		35	Chile	4,590
36	Mexico	2,830		36	Venezuela	4,310
37	Brazil	2,780		37	Poland	4,190
38	Croatia	(NA)		38	Lebanon	4,010
39	Venezuela	2,650		39	Costa Rica	3,810
40	Poland	(NA)		40	Slovakia	3,700
41	Lebanon	(NA)		41	Brazil	3,580
42	Iran	2,590		42	Malaysia	3,380
43	Algeria	2,440		43	Turkey	3,100
44	Malaysia	2,380		44	South Africa	3,020
45	Turkey	2,280		45	Belarus	2,870
46	Bulgaria	2,260		46	Peru	2,080

Exhibit 2.7 (*continued*)

1990

Rank	Country	GNP Per Capita		Country	GNP Per Capita
47	Chile	2,190		Peru	780
48	Costa Rica	1,790		Cote d'Ivoire	780
49	Romania	1,720		Philippines	740
50	Ukraine	1,600		Indonesia	620
51	Thailand	1,520		Sri Lanka	470
52	Colombia	1,180		India	390
53	Morocco	1,030		Pakistan	390
54	Guatemala	970		China	320
55	Russia	(NA)		Vietnam	(NA)
56	Kazakhstan	(NA)		Bangladesh	280
57	Ecuador	970		Uzbekistan	(NA)
58	El Salvador	940		Nigeria	270
59	Syria	940		Congo	230
60	Egypt	810		Ethiopia	160

2000

Rank	Country	GNP Per Capita	Rank	Country	GNP Per Capita
47	Colombia	2,020	61	Syria	940
48	El Salvador	2,000	62	Sri Lanka	850
49	Thailand	2,000	63	China	840
50	Guatemala	1,680	64	Ukraine	700
51	Iran	1,680	65	Cote d'Ivoire	600
52	Romania	1,670	66	Indonesia	570
53	Russia	1,660	67	India	450
54	Algeria	1,580	68	Pakistan	440
55	Bulgaria	1,520	69	Vietnam	390
56	Egypt	1,490	70	Bangladesh	370
57	Kazakhstan	1,260	71	Uzbekistan	360
58	Ecuador	1,210	72	Nigeria	260
59	Morocco	1,180	73	Congo	(NA)
60	Philippines	1,040	74	Ethiopia	100

Source: Statistical Abstract of the United States, U.S. Census Bureau, 2002; and *World Development Indicators* (Washington, DC: The World Bank, 1991).

All in all, the history of the developing world remains somewhat of a constant—developing. Africa emerged from colonialism in dire straits and remains so. Economic growth for the continent lags other developing regions and generally shows few signs of catching up. Asia has recorded the most significant progress with the sprouting of the East Asian Newly Industrializing Countries, achievements in South Korea, and efforts by China to move from a command to a market economy. Of course, Japan is the star performer, though obviously it is not a developing nation.[24] But much of the Asian complex remains mired in underdevelopment. Latin American countries have been free of colonial rule for nearly two centuries, yet not a single one has achieved the status of a developed country. This is particularly disappointing, as expectations were that several Latin American nations had the inherent capacity to at least advance to the doorstep of developed status.[25]

Ignition of African, Asian, and Latin American development certainly on any scale even closely approximating that of G8 nations may depend on their relationship with the multinational corporation. As the plight of developing countries continues in the vein of bridging the gap between developed and developing—First World and Third World—rich and poor, the multinational corporation is becoming increasingly viewed as a necessary actor in this sought-after transformation. Direct foreign investment, the multinational's trademark, has had an impact on this transformative process.[26] The history so attests; the future remains in question.

NOTES

1. Neil H. Jacoby, "The Multinational Corporation," in A. Kapoor and Phillip D. Grub, eds., *The Multinational Enterprise in Transition* (Princeton, NJ: The Darwin Press, 1972), 23.

2. Ibid., 24.

3. See David A. Heenan and Warren J. Keegan, "The Rise of Third World Multinationals," *Harvard Business Review* (1979), 101–102; See also D. Lecraw, "Direct Investment by Firms from Less Developed Countries,"*Oxford Economic Papers* 29, no. 3 (1977).

4. Gross national product is the total value of a nation's annual output of goods and services.

5. Richard J. Barnet and Ronald E. Muller, *Global Reach* (New York: Simon and Schuster, 1974), 15.

6. Ibid., 14–16 and 26.

7. B.R. Tomlinson, "What Was the Third World?" *Journal of Contemporary History* 38 no. 2 (2003), 307–321.

8. Andre Gunder Frank, "The Development of Underdevelopment,"*Monthly Review* (1966), 111–123.

9. George J. Coakley and Philip M. Mobbs et al., "The Mineral Industries of Africa," *U.S. Geological Survey Minerals Yearbook* (Washington, DC: Bureau of Mines, 2001).

10. Gross domestic product, like gross national product, is a measure of a nation's annual output of goods and services, but only for that which occurs within a nation.

11. Arne Bigsten and Anders Danielsson, "Is Tanzania an Emerging Economy?" *Emerging Africa* (Paris, France: OECD, 1999), 1; and Patrick Guillaumont, Sylviane Guillaumont Jeanneney, and Aristomene Varoudakis, "Economic Policy Reform and Growth Prospects in Emerging African Economies," *Technical Papers* (Paris, France: OECD Development Center, 1999), 15–17.

12. Per capita income here refers to GNP per capita, which is used as an indicator of a person's well-being, whereas GNP is an indicator of the well-being of a nation. GNP per capita is GNP divided by population.

13. Arne Bigsten and Anders Danielsson, ibid.

14. Rubens Ricupero, Secretary-General of UNCTAD, *Foreign Direct Investment in Africa: Performance and Potential* (Geneva: United Nations, 1999), Preface.

15. Ainslie T. Embree and Carol Gluck, eds., *Asia in Western and World History* (Armonk, NY: M. E. Sharpe, Inc., 1997).

16. *Demographic Yearbook 2002*, United Nations Department of Economic and Social Affairs, Issue 52, New York, 2002.

17. *The World Factbook 2003*, Central Intelligence Agency, Washington, DC, 2003.

18. K.S. Jomo, "Globalization, Liberalization, Poverty and Income Inequality in Southeast Asia," *Technical Papers* (Paris, France: OECD Development Center, 2001), 9.

19. Colin Mason, *A Short History of Asia* (New York: St. Martin's Press, 2000), 1–2; See also Leo Paul Dana, *When Economies Change Paths* (Singapore: World Scientific Publishing Co. Pte. Ltd., 2002).

20. The "East Asian Miracle" refers to the unprecedented economic growth experienced by Japan, South Korea, Taiwan, Hong Kong, Singapore, Malaysia, Thailand, and Indonesia in recent decades. See K.S. Jomo, ibid.

21. *The World Factbook 2003*, ibid.

22. Samuel A. Morley, "Distribution and Growth in Latin America in an Era of Structural Reform: The Impact of Globalization," *Technical Papers* (Paris, France: OECD Development Center, 2001), 8–16.

23. Ibid., 16.

24. Prodromos Panayiotopoulos and Gavin Capps, eds., *World Development*, (London: Pluto Press, 2001), xix–xxiv.

25. Victor Bulmer-Thomas, *The Economic History of Latin America Since Independence* (Cambridge: Cambridge University Press, 1995), 5; See also Nancy P. Appelbaum et al., eds., *Race and Nation in Modern Latin America* (Chapel Hill: The University of North Carolina Press, 2003).

26. December Green and Laura Luehrmann, *Comparative Politics of the Third World* (Boulder, CO: Lynne Rienner Publishers, Inc., 2003), 9.

CHAPTER 3

Multinational Corporations in the Economic Development of Black Africa: Some Problems that Affect an Equitable Relationship*

"Multinational Corporations in the Economic Development of Black Africa" records my early thinking on the involvement of multinational corporations in Third World development. The desire to join the dialogue and debate on the plight of Third World nations and the life choice constraints facing their peoples inspired this effort to engage critical analysis of issues and problems impinging the development process. Third World history, as provided in the preceding presentation, helps us to understand the need for such analysis. Because this article employs a regional perspective, it offers the opportunity to address the uniqueness of each Third World region and the special problems each presents to the analytical task. Africa's relationship with the multinational corporation provides a good analytical entrée to the assessment of Third World development because of its particularly low economic performance relative to other Third World regions, and its dire need for the kind of economic stimulus that the multinational corporation is capable of providing. In the rich country–poor country world order, African nations generally epitomize the poor country construct.

For black African nations, economic development has been slow and frustrating. Without some appreciable change in the rate of economic growth and development, a low standard of living, a problem to black Africa, as with the Third World in general, will persist and may worsen in light of the

*Reprinted with permission of Heldref Publications, www.heldref.org. Benjamin F. Bobo, "Multinational Corporations in the Economic Development of Black Africa," *Journal of African Studies* 9, no. 1 (March 1982).

world economic crisis. No doubt African leaders recognize that significant upward changes in their standards of living are predicated on achieving greater and greater advancement in economic development, which must be sustained over a long period of time if they are ever to achieve take-off. But economic development requires a lot of capital. Perhaps the best source of ready capital, without judging its merit here, is direct private foreign investment; the multinational corporation (MNC) is a vehicle commonly used for foreign direct investment purposes. Foreign investors tend to have objectives different from those of host nations; MNCs generally strive to maximize the value of shareholders' wealth, while host nations endeavor to upgrade the quality of life of their citizenry.

In the past, black Africa has turned to direct foreign investment as a means of financing development programs. A harmonious relationship has been difficult to establish because often multinational corporations and host African nations have opposing objectives, and have found it hard to reach agreement.

A withdrawal from African exploration by multinational corporations, or a complete rejection of multinational enterprise by black Africa would be difficult to reconcile, given that its needs are so great. With a population of around 350 million, its average GNP per capita is only about $260. This is not to say however, that industrialized nations do not reap tremendous benefits from the relationship. The developed world relies heavily on Africa's raw materials to sustain its relatively high standard of living. Africa, for example, contains a respectable share of the world's mineral resources, as can be seen in Exhibit 3.1.

Despite the apparent importance of Africa as a source of raw materials, some observers of international enterprise argue that today's direct foreign investors treat African investment opportunities with an attitude similar to that of their predecessors; the difference being that current direct investment is employed via a different form and structure. The late Kwame Nkrumah of Ghana characterized the form and structure as neocolonialist exploitation. This terminology, as Nkrumah applied it, refers to a nation-state that is, theoretically, independent and internationally sovereign, but where its economic system, and therefore its political system, is externally directed.[1] This concept has been descriptively explicated by Peter Berger as an exercise in growth without development and is couched in terms of foreign capital penetration of the Third World. As he put it:

"Growth without development" is based on the penetration of a Third World economy by foreign capital. This penetration results in a distortion of the economy, in the sense that it develops not in terms of international economic and social forces but in the interest of the foreign "metropolis" . . . The same "distortion" creates an essentially colonial structure for the benefit of the foreign capitalists. It is not quite the same structure as that of the old colonialism, which was largely extractive, taking out raw materials from the colony that were needed for industries

Exhibit 3.1
Africa's Share of World Mineral Resources

Resource	% of World Total
Coal	7.5
Petroleum	8.0
Natural Gas	12.0
Uranium	30.0
	(non-communist world)
Radium	Chief Source
Thorium	20.0
Iron Ores	3.0
Chromium	Nearly 100%
Cobalt	90.0
Copper	20.0
Lead	8.0
Zinc	5.0
Tin	15.0
Bauxite	27.0
Titanium	Largest known deposits
Antimony	7.0
Gold	50.0
Platinum	40.0
Tantalum	80.0
Germanium	Bulk of world reserves
Lithium	Largest deposits of any other continent
Phosphates	Over half of world reserves
Diamonds	Bulk of world reserves

in the home country. The new colonialism promotes industrialization, but of a very peculiar kind. Generally it is capital-intensive rather than labor-intensive, thus actually creating unemployment in the "developing" country . . . Allocation of scarce resources to this kind of industrialization actually prevents development in other sectors of the society . . . "Neocolonialism," therefore, implies increasing impoverishment and ever-greater dependency on foreign forces. In Andre Gunder Frank's graphic phrase, it means "the development of underdevelopment"![2]

This perception, and perhaps truth, has created an atmosphere of discontent in the Third World. Poor nations are becoming more and more disposed to the idea that there can be no equitable reciprocity between the rich and the poor. As a Third World entity, black Africa must decide whether its objectives can be realized without the know-how, capital and technology that multinational corporations offer. This decision is made even more difficult by the possibility that hosting direct private foreign investment may harbor potential for further "development of underdevelopment." The degrees of freedom available to black Africa in making such a decision are limited. It is an unlikely proposition, as some observers of the African situation purpose that black Africa will be able to arouse any significant economic growth and development[3] without the kind of assistance multinationals can offer. But whether black Africa will elect to maintain and/or expand the presence of multinational corporations in its economies may well depend on how successful it is in finding solutions to several problems that have emerged from its recent relationship with multinational firms. This paper discusses the nature of selected problems relating to technology transfer, transfer pricing, taxation, and corporate ethics. With no specific intent to offer solutions to these problems, we explore the prospects of the New International Economic Order doctrine as providing bases for a general resolution of problems existing between multinational corporations and host African nations.

PROBLEMS LIMITING MNC PRESENCE

Because students and practitioners of economic development know that underdevelopment is neither predestined nor incurable, they hold the conviction that economic development can be stimulated and sustained by pursuing certain courses of action and applying certain inducements. Although black African nations have been very serious in their attempts to take action on matters relevant to the development process, they have been unable to apply necessary inducements to bring development objectives to fruition. Attempts to induce growth in capital formation, for example, perhaps the most formidable ingredient of the development process, have met with little success. Historically, capital creation and accumulation have presented major obstacles to African economic development. Improvements in other components of the development process, e.g. balance of payments, planning and economic management, agriculture, and education, are seldom possible without some increase in the stock of capital. Hence, the role of capital may be the central issue and capital accumulation may be regarded as the core process upon which all other aspects of growth depend.

The multinational corporation can be an important facilitator in African economic development, particularly as it relates to capital creation. The MNC has the ability to mobilize enormous amounts of capital for development throughout black Africa. Injection into African economies of what in many cases amounts to crucial "seed" capital supported by the kinds of technological know-how and marketing skills that MNCs possess can provide the necessary stimulus to economic development. To some extent this is taking place in Africa. But problems with establishing an equitable relationship between MNCs and host African countries have made Africans skeptical about the presence of multinational corporations. Until solutions to several crucial problems are found, the MNC may be relegated to a very limited role in the economic development of black Africa.

TECHNOLOGY TRANSFER

Many observers of the MNC-black Africa relationship feel that technology transfer is one of the most important areas of interaction. Indeed, black African nations feel that sufficient and appropriate technology transfers from developed countries to developing ones must take place to support development objectives. The quantity and quality of technology transfer to developing countries have been the subject of considerable controversy, and unfortunately, have damaged and even severed some relationships. Coca Cola and IBM of India are examples of cases in which certain technology transfers, i.e., disclosures of details of their technologies, were not permitted by the companies and thus resulted in the closure of Indian operations. This raises a question of why MNCs restrict the flow of technology to developing countries, which in some instances leads to a break in relations with host countries. A brief examination of what is involved in technology transfer might provide some clues.

With respect to multinational enterprise, *technology transfer* has been defined as the transmission, absorption and assimilation of technology. *Technology* includes the physical capital and those technical and managerial skills or software needed to operate, maintain, and service that physical capital and effectively tie its output into a marketing and distribution system.

Further, two types of technology may be identified insofar as the enterprise is concerned: embodied and disembodied. That technology which is engineered into physical capital and into an organization in the form of knowledge is said to be embodied. Until these processes are complete, certain aspects of the technology remain disembodied.[4]

R. Hal Mason states that technology transfer remains incomplete until indigenous personnel employed by the firms in the host or receiving nation are able to operate, maintain and repair the physical capital. Installing a foreign produced machine in a host country factory, for example, does not involve a complete transfer of technology because it (the technology) has been absorbed by the indigenous work force. Historically, receiving countries have had to rely upon expatriate personnel to operate and service physical capital. This was necessary because the transfer only amounted to a "technology transplant," which is essentially the emplacement of technology, which has not been transmitted to and absorbed by indigenous workers. To be sufficiently complete, a technology transfer must involve one-to-one complementarities between physical and human capital—the human capital being derived from the indigenous work force.[5]

In the black Africa–MNC relationship, Africans have relentlessly pressed for complete technology transfer, particularly as it has been elucidated above. Apparently MNCs feel that one-to-one complementarity between physical capital and indigenous human capital puts them in an over-whelmingly compromising position in many instances.

Perhaps an understanding of the MNC's attitude can be ascertained if one views the multinational enterprise as being endowed with certain competitive advantages which are inherent in its ability to internalize a unique set of resources, and as a matter of prerogative it can elect to restrict or even refuse access by other enterprises to these resources. This gives the firm a monopoly power, thus enabling it to appropriate economic rents, i.e. demand a premium for its technology, by controlling access to its unique capabilities. Of course, in a perfectly competitive market, the enterprise could not singularly appropriate economic rents for its capabilities because individually differentiated competitive strengths would not arise.[6]

Unique capabilities and comparative advantages allow enterprises to appropriate rents. But the degree of rent appropriation depends upon how well enterprises can control access to proprietary technological know-how. And this depends upon the difficulty or cost of duplicating the technology. The higher the cost of duplication, the more restrictive are the barriers to entry and hence the less formidable is competition. Under such conditions the greater will be the incentive to the supplying firm to limit access to the technology. On the other hand, the easier it is for another firm to duplicate the technology, the more inclined will be the supplying firm to sell the technology outright, which may involve a complete technology transfer to the receiving country.[7]

The premium that a supplying firm can get for its technological advantages is usually constrained by the presence of competitors offering near substitutes, or by the threat of new entrants. Thus economic rent appropriation or price setting is typically oligopolistic. MNCs often find themselves at the oligopolistic side of the spectrum (as represented above) but over time may gradually approach the more competitive side. Because of this, MNCs use a variety of institutional arrangements to supply and apply technology. The arrangement used depends upon the degree of control the supplying firm can exercise over access to its technology. The institutional arrangements commonly used are:[8]

1. Direct Foreign Investment (wholly owned)
2. Joint Ventures
    a. Foreign only (two or more foreign firms)
    b. Majority foreign
    c. Minority foreign
    d. Equally foreign and local

3. Contractual Agreements
   a. Licenses and franchises
   b. Technical aid agreements
   c. Management contracts
   d. Engineering and consulting contracts
   e. Turnkey plants
   f. Supply contracts
   g. Resource concessions
4. Debt financing
5. Combinations of the above.

The greater the technological advantage possessed by the supplying firm, the more likely it is to opt for technology transfer via a wholly owned subsidiary. This of course gives the supplier full ownership and control of the facility. It is, however, important to distinguish between ownership and control and to recognize that it is control that matters. This is not to minimize the importance of ownership, but control of the entity would likely mean that the technology transfer is sufficiently complete, thus giving indigenous participants the ability and opportunity to operate and maintain productive facilities.

Historically, black African nations have been unable to exercise control over productive processes because of their weaknesses in the area of technology and technological innovation. Selected weaknesses on the part of black African nations, of which supplying firms take advantage are:[9]

(1) Black African nations frequently lack the ability to decide what to produce, and generally lack the capacity to prepare a project properly from the preliminary study to the economic and technological feasibility study and then to the engineering study.

(2) Of the various inputs into the project, one is technology. In the last analysis it is likely to be the crucial one, but along with technology many other items may be missing. Furthermore, in addition to lacking the technology, the seeker is generally ill-informed of the alternative sources thereof.

(3) There is a lack of capital, which is frequently offered by the technology supplier as a contribution to the equity, as local capital or in the form of suppliers' credits.

(4) Management ability is lacking or limited.

(5) Specific skilled personnel are not available.

(6) There is a lack of knowledge and skilled ability to purchase other inputs such as raw materials, components, equipment, etc.

(7) Black Africa needs access to the market of the technology supplier as an outlet for the product to be produced (in the case of exports).

(8) Even where there is a world market, i.e., many potential outlets, African enterprise lacks the marketing skills.

Until black Africa is able to overcome such weaknesses it is unlikely to be able to control productive processes to any large degree, though it may command ownership. Black African countries are almost entirely "buyers" and only very rarely sellers of technology. They are proportionately far more dependent on external sources of new technical knowledge than industrialized countries, a dependency that puts them in a compromising position insofar as technology transfer is concerned.

TRANSFER PRICING

Transfer pricing—the pricing of goods and services traded among units of the same multinational corporation has presented major problems for African host countries in their relationship with MNCs. The difficulty largely relates to the inability of African governments to investigate and monitor transfer pricing of commodity trade by multinational corporations. Numerous difficulties African host nations have experienced in this regard arise from four factors in particular: conceptual issues in defining appropriate transfer prices; an imbalanced or uneven incidence of transfer pricing across different industries and by different firms; internal and external problems in gathering data relevant to checking and monitoring intra-firm pricing; and, management and procedural problems in monitoring transfer pricing and detecting improper conduct.[10]

Underlying problems with data collection, monitoring and detection is the fact that MNCs have tremendous autonomy in pricing goods and services traded among their affiliates. In a transaction involving intra-unit transfer or sale of goods, a corporation may assign to those goods whatever price it prefers, within limits.[11] The limits on transfer pricing tend to be only moderately restrictive because of a desire by African host nations to show a liberal and welcoming attitude to foreign direct investment. Consequently, transfer-pricing policies are largely designed and applied at the discretion of the MNC.

Although transfer pricing policies appear to vary[12] from company to company, transactions with controlled units abroad seem to be governed by three basic approaches. These are:

(a) all domestic and foreign units are permitted to act as separate financial entities, with the result that transfer prices are set at levels that yield a reasonable profit to both the selling and the buying units; (b) profits are allocated in proportion to the value added (excluding profits) by the various units or the functions performed in producing and marketing the products in question; (c) the gross margin or per-centage mark-up is divided between the producing and the marketing units, on the basis either of value added (excluding profits), of assets employed or of costs incurred, or on whatever may be considered an equitable basis.[13]

A particular MNC may use one or all of these approaches in transactions with foreign affiliates. The approach used depends on the type of product involved in intra-firm transactions.[14] Notably, transfer pricing also occurs in inter-firm trade. Under- or over-invoicing of openly traded goods have been observed in a number of countries.

Pricing policies are a key element of corporate development strategy. Several advantages may be gained by the manipulation of transfer prices, the benefits of which help a company expand its growth and market power. The following tend to be the most influential in the decision to manipulate transfer prices: "(a) the attainment or maintenance of market power or the penetration of new markets; (b) lessening the impact of price controls; (c) minimizing taxes and other payments to governments; and (d) circumventing exchange controls and hedging against currency changes."[15]

The ability to expand market powers and market penetration is enhanced by a company's ability to manipulate transfer prices. The more capable an MNC is in manipulating transfer prices, the better able it is in obtaining a competitive edge in the market place. Low transfer prices in intra-unit transactions can be used to strengthen the competitive position of the parent company or the foreign affiliate. Relatively high prices to unrelated buyers would eventually discourage new entrants, thereby providing more opportunity for existing firms. Those multinationals which are successful at the game are perhaps those in vertically integrated industries where dominant market power at the raw material or semi-processed material stages make possible the setting of prices at levels which tend to result in the bulk of profits being realized at the final processing and marketing stages.[16]

The advantage gained by manipulating transfer prices to avoid the negative impact of price controls is straightforward. Price controls that limit mark-ups on ex-factory or imported prices, for example, induce MNCs to inflate the cost of imports of the final product or raw materials. In such instances, a corporation can increase the margin of profit after accounting for, say, higher import duty payments. Further, the advantage gained by manipulating transfer prices to minimize taxes and other payments also produces a higher profit margin. MNCs often attempt to minimize their over-all tax burden in an effort to increase profits globally. To do so, they engage in transfer price manipulation to raise profits in low-tax-rate countries and to reduce them in high-tax-rate countries.[17]

In regard to exchange controls and currency changes, MNCs have been able to protect cash flows via transfer price manipulation. When faced with an impending devaluation, for example, profits and cash balances will be, if possible, shifted out of a country via the transfer pricing mechanism. Another interesting point is that multinationals use transfer prices to reinforce normal leads and lags in intra-corporate payments. This is done for hedging or speculative purposes, and to minimize outstanding payment in a weak currency. An interesting example of how intra-firm leads and lags may be employed and utilized, and cash balances managed is described by an executive:

One of our Danish subsidiaries had excess cash, which it lent to another Danish subsidiary that was receiving goods from the Swedish subsidiary. The Danish company prepaid its account with the Swedish subsidiary, and this money financed the movement of Swedish products into the Finnish subsidiary. What did the maneuver accomplish? If Finland had been required to pay for the goods, it would have had to borrow at about 15 percent, the going Finnish rate. If the Swedish subsidiary had financed the sale, it would have had to borrow at about 9 per cent. But cash in Denmark was worth only 5 per cent to 6 per cent. Moreover, Danish currency was weak in relation to the Swedish; by speeding up payments to Sweden we not only obtained cheaper credit, we hedged our position in Danish Kroner as well.[18]

A product's degree of 'specificity' essentially determines how easily transfer prices can be manipulated. Transfer prices that differ from the open market prices of products more generally traded, and less specific, have a greater chance of being detected by government officials. Product 'specificity' has several aspects, which have been ably described by Sanjaya Lall as follows:

(i) A product may be specific in the highest degree when it is an intermediate traded only within a particular TNC. Here there are no open market prices available for reference, and the potential for arbitrary pricing is at its maximum.

(ii) A product may be highly specific when it is produced only by one TNC, but is sold both to affiliates and to third parties. Here arm's length prices may be established by a host government with reference to prices charged to unrelated buyers, but with two problems: first, the prices charged to buyers in different countries may be secret; and, second, these prices may incorporate a high degree of monopoly rent, and they may vary from case to case, so that a particular reference price may be misleading or unsatisfactory. This raises problems of monopoly power in trade more generally.

(iii) A product which is sold on a discontinuous basis (like tailor-made capital equipment) will be highly specific, because prices of identical products elsewhere would be very difficult, or impossible, to obtain.

(iv) A product, which is made up of large numbers of component parts (an extreme example being a turnkey plant), would be fairly specific, unless such products required a standardized and well-diffused technology.

(v) A product, which was highly differentiated from its competitors, because of promotion (for consumer goods), or because of performance, quality, specifications and delivery times (for producer goods), would be fairly specific.[19]

Abuse, defined as the difference between intra-firm and arm's length prices, of transfer pricing, tends to be greatest in industries in which intra-firm trade and monopoly power are high.[20] Abuse is also higher in industries with highly specific products than in those with standardized products. The pharmaceuticals industry is reported to have the highest incidence of large price differentials between transfer and arm's length prices, thus making it the heaviest abuser of transfer pricing. This has been confirmed by evidence from Latin America, Iran, Sri Lanka, the United Kingdom, and elsewhere.[21]

The ability of MNCs to manipulate or abuse transfer pricing depends to some extent on how well they can establish transfer prices. In this regard a number of methods may be used, but multinationals primarily rely on the "cost-based" and the "market-price based" methods of transfer price determination. Under the cost-based method, a transfer price is determined by adding a certain percentage mark-up to the calculated cost of production. Determination of a transfer price via the market price based method, which is also called the discount method, is done by discounting an established selling price (market price) of a product. Multinationals argue that discounting is necessary because an affiliated buyer makes product modifications or bears the operating costs of advertising and marketing not usually performed or assumed by outside buyers.[22]

Evidencing its importance to MNCs, transfer-pricing decisions are usually made at the highest corporate levels. In fact, such decisions are accorded higher importance than market price decisions. The person responsible for setting transfer prices has a corporate rank of treasurer or higher. In most cases, however, this responsibility is assigned to the financial vice-president or comptroller. Interestingly, MNCs regard a decision on transfer pricing as the most critical short-run decision.[23]

TAXATION

Multinational corporations pose unique problems for taxing governments, and thus face tax problems that are unique to multinationals. Tax problems in this context seem to be almost entirely related to income taxation and particularly corporation income taxation. Because of its ubiquitous nature, the taxation of corporate income is encountered by MNCs worldwide. The reason for this is perhaps obvious: with the exception of customs duties, the corporate income tax is the most widely used of any major tax. Tax problems do not derive necessarily from ubiquity, but primarily from the lack of uniformity. Tax policies vary from country to country, both in regard to levels of tax rates, and in the definitions of taxable profits, net royalties, interest, and other taxable items. Further, there is a lack of uniformity in the allocation of a firm's global income among the taxing jurisdictions in which it operates. Allowances made for host country taxes by home countries are not systematic.[24]

As a result of the lack of uniformity, a large number of possible different tax outcomes is faced by each multinational firm. This situation creates an equally large number of more or less legal patterns from which a multinational firm can choose, in an attempt to minimize its worldwide tax obligation. Hence, multinational corporations and taxing governments find that the sheer complexity of the matter may cause them to be in an unfavorable tax situation.[25]

CONDUCT AND ETHICS

In their quest for market expansion and increased profits, international corporations have been party to business dealings that have involved questionable ethics. The past several years have witnessed public revelations of unethical practices ranging from payments to foreign officials and politicians, with the objective of obtaining business advantages and special privileges, to simply using their enormous size and skills to over-compete with host country entrepreneurs.

The conduct of multinational corporations in foreign locales has become the subject of on-going discussion and debate in recent years. This attention is primarily a reflection of the growing power and visibility of multinationals in world affairs. Not only are they key participants in international economic relations, but their importance has grown in recent years at nearly twice the growth rates of the industrialized nations, and more rapidly than world trade in general. MNCs can facilitate economic development in black Africa through their ability to accumulate, direct and employ massive sums of direct private investments. Their managerial and marketing skills, and advanced technology can be and have been put to the service of development.[26]

However, the global strategies of MNCs do not always reflect sufficient consideration for the national objectives of host African nations. This, along with the possibility that MNC affiliates could escape national policies, control essential resources, and conceal transfers of funds, caused sharp apprehension among many African countries. Revelations of corrupt practices and incidents of political interference contribute to an atmosphere of mistrust. Indeed, there is considerable mistrust, particularly on the part of host governments, which has led to widespread conflict between government and corporation. The consequence, in numerous instances, has been government takeovers and nationalization of assets. In light of this, all parties concerned have become aware of the need to reconcile conflict, while at the same time provide a stable and encouraging investment climate in which the positive contributions of MNCs can be enhanced and their undesirable effects minimized or eliminated.[27]

Past conflict between MNCs and host African countries has prompted the realization of a need for the development of ground rules for foreign direct investments, which would establish a code of conduct for multinational enterprise. To this end, the United Nations and the Organization for Economic Cooperation and Development (OECD) have been prime movers. The U.N. General Assembly, as early as December 1975, approved by consensus a resolution which:

condemns all corrupt practices, including bribery by transnational and other corporations, their intermediaries, and others involved in the violation of the laws and regulations of the host countries; calls upon both home and host governments to take all necessary measures which they deem appropriate, including legislative measures, to prevent such corrupt practices and to take subsequent measures against the violators; and, calls upon government to collect and exchange information on such corrupt practices.[28]

In 1975, a Committee on International Investment and Multinational Enterprises was established by the twenty-four-nation OECD to draft a proposed code of conduct for multinationals.[29] Among other things, the OECD code "opposes the payment of bribes by multinational corporations to foreign officials—as well as the solicitation of bribes; calls on business firms not to make political contributions to candidates for public office or to political parties or political organizations, unless legally permissible; and, directs enterprises to abstain from any improper involvement in local activities."[30]

The significance of the OECD code of conduct guidelines becomes apparent upon the realization that the OECD nations account for sixty percent of world industrial production, receive eighty percent of world investment, and serve as the home countries for over ninety percent of the world's multinational enterprises.[31]

Not all aspects of corporate behavior abroad can be regulated by governing bodies. But controversy surrounding the matter has brought about a new sense of awareness in recent years, so much so, that various international and other multinational codes of conduct have been created or are in the process of formulation by host countries and MNCs to regulate multinational corporations.[32]

PROSPECTS FOR IMPROVING THE RELATIONSHIP

Multinational corporations have a special contribution to make to African economic development. They provide capital, in addition to managerial, technical and marketing skills that cannot be supplied through aid mechanisms or through foreign trade. This undoubtedly makes the MNC attractive to black African nations. But the equity issue looms large in the minds of black Africans and must be satisfactorily addressed by the MNC before a harmonious and prolonged relationship can be established. The MNC's reluctance and in many cases outright refusal to engage in complete technology transfer, to develop pricing policies that allow host African nations to share equitably in revenues, and to adopt accounting practices and procedures that show true and actual revenues and expenses, are viewed by Africans as deliberate efforts by multinational enterprise to exploit African nations. Because this behavior is often so severe, many Africans fear that a relationship with multinationals will invariably lead to the "development of underdevelopment."

Recognizing in part that the MNC can be a moving force in the economic development of black Africa, African nations have joined other Third World countries in a call for a New International Economic Order (NIEO). If any prospects for improving the relationship between multinational corporations and black African nations exist, a Third World coalition may provide the necessary platform from which differences can be resolved. In a declaration of principles set forth by the coalition of Third World nations, three items are especially noteworthy.[33] The Third World body called for:

Just and equitable relationship between the prices of raw materials, primary products, manufactured and semi-manufactured goods exported by developing countries and the prices of raw materials, primary commodities, manufactures, capital goods and equipment imported by them, with the aim of bringing about sustained improvement in their unsatisfactory terms of trade and the expansion of the world economy;

Securing favorable conditions for the transfer of financial resources to developing countries;

Giving to the developing countries access to the achievements of modern science and technology, and promoting the transfer of technology and the creation of indigenous technology for the benefit of the developing countries in forms and in accordance with procedures which are suited to their economies.

If Third World governments maintain a unified front in their effort to bring about changes in MNC conduct, these principles may well serve as a foundation upon which to erect an equitable and sustaining relationship between MNCs and host African countries. There is little doubt that until problems centering on technology transfer and transfer pricing are resolved, few prospects exist for preventing further "development of underdevelopment" in black African nations. Moreover, until the development of underdevelopment can be minimized, there can be no real harmony between black African and multinational corporations, and furthermore, any significant expansion of MNC involvement in African economic development processes will likely be resisted by black African policymakers.

NOTES

1. Richard D. Steade (1978). Multinational Corporations and the Changing World Economic Order, *California Management Review, 21*(2), 6.

2. Ibid., and Peter L. Berger (1974). *Pyramids of Sacrifice.* New York: Basic Books, 48–49.

3. Growth and development are occasionally used synonymously in economic discussion. This is true of this discussion. As a point of information, economic growth means more output, while economic development implies both more output and changes in the technical and institutional arrangements by which it is produced and distributed. In the early stages, any economy that grows is likely to develop. But Robert Clower has presented an exception to this notion. In his study of the Liberian economy, he described the rapid rise in exported primary commodities owned primarily by foreign concessions and noted the absence both of structural changes to induce complementary growth in other economic sectors and of institutional changes to diffuse gains in real income among all sectors of the population. See Robert Clower (1966). *Growth Without Development.* Evanston, Illinois: Northwestern University Press, 6. For a more explicit explication of the growth and development issue, see Charles P. Kindleberger and Bruce Herrick (1977). *Economic Development.* New York: McGraw-Hill Book Company, 1–4.

4. See R. Hal Mason (1978). Technology Transfers: A Comparison of American and Japanese Practices in Developing Countries. Paper prepared for the Japan Society's Business Educational Program Workshop, Graduate School Management, UCLA, 9. In the report, as here, the terms embodied and disembodied are used somewhat differently than they generally are in the literature. In the literature, embodied refers to that which is engineered into physical capital, while disembodied is human capital and knowledge. As Mason argues, one can view organizations as having knowledge engineered into them just as does equipment. Thus, technology is not fully embodied, or more directly, is disembodied until a one-to-one complementarity between physical and human capital is created, which is required for its assimilation. See also *Handbook on the Acquisition of Technology by Developing Countries* (1978). UNCTAD, E. 78.II.D.15, 5–6.

5. R. Hal Mason, Ibid., 7–9.

6. Ibid., 9–10. Only Ricardian rents can exist under perfect competition, i.e. rents from superior land, superior location, and so forth, which are not consciously created by the firm itself. Generally, economic rent appropriation is possible under the following conditions: (1) When the supplying firm has appropriated a major technological innovation which enables it to disregard the constraining influence of its competitors in the oligopoly. This happens from time to time in the markets for some highly specialized technical services, particularly where there are economies of scale or other barriers to entry: e.g. in the supply of some specialized oil-field services, in some specialist engineering activities for the chemical industry or in cases where a basic engineering group captures a new process. It also happens when machinery suppliers make a major breakthrough. (2) Where

markets are dominated by a very few giant firms which are able to achieve a geographical division of the world market. This, however, is comparatively rare; (3)
when external conditions restrict competition between suppliers. The most obvious case in the developing countries is where new investments are financed by
tied aid, which obliges the purchaser of technology to buy from firms in the aid-
giving country. For this and further comment, *see Handbook on the Acquisition of
Technology by Developing Countries* (1978) UNCTAD, 6.

7. R. Hal Mason, Technology Transfers, 10.

8. Ibid., 11–12.

9. See *Handbook on the Acquisition of Technology by Developing Countries*, ibid., 12.

10. Sanjaya Lall (1979). Transfer Pricing and Developing Countries: Some Problems of Investigation, *World Development*, 7, 59.

11. Under such pricing practices, the traditional theory of pricing in competitive, oligopolistic or monopolistic markets ceases to apply. This is so because in
transactions between unrelated firms on the open market, the buyers and sellers
are trying to benefit at each other's expense, while in an intra-firm transaction the
price is essentially an accounting device.

12. Variations in transfer pricing policies among different corporations depend
on corporate organizational structure, i.e., centralized or decentralized, and intra-
corporate relations on dependency resulting from such factors as vertical integration, product specialization and market arrangements.

13. Dominant Positions of Market Power of Transnational Corporations: Use of
the Transfer Pricing Mechanism (1978). UNCTAD, 6. See also, J. Greene and
M. Duerr (1970). *Intercompany Transactions in the Multinational Firm*. New York: The
Conference Board, 5–12.

14. Ibid. Irrespective of the approach used, corporations argue that established
transfer prices are for the most part arm's length prices. In intra-firm transactions,
the term arm's length is generally used to indicate the prices that would prevail if
the two parties were unrelated. However, the term does not necessarily imply that
such prices are established under competitive market conditions or that they are
fair prices.

15. Ibid.

16. Ibid., 7.

17. Ibid. Further, an MNC may elect to establish an international base company
as an intra-firm trade intermediary in a tax haven. The objective here would be to
accumulate profits in that company. Tax havens are most often located in low-
tax-rate countries and frequently exempt from taxes all or most income generated
from foreign sources. Examples of countries that serve as good tax havens are the
Bahamas and Bermuda, which provide tax exemption on all corporate earnings.

18. Ibid. Also, the description of how intra-firm leads and lags may be utilized,
as reported in the above listed source, is taken from an interview reported in
Financial Times (1969). London, September 12, 1969.

19. Sanjaya Lall, Transfer Pricing, 63.

20. Examples to the contrary are high marketing industries where intra-firm
trade is significant but the potential for profit sharing is low, e.g., textiles. There
are also some high technology industries where intra-firm trade is high but the
products are sold in a finished form, e.g., computers, thus making comparisons
with open market prices fairly easy.

21. See Lall, Transfer Pricing, 63.

22. See Dominant Positions of Market Power of Transnational Corporations: Use of the Transfer Pricing Mechanism, 10.

23. Ibid., 11. See also J.S. Arpan (1972). *International Intracorporate Pricing: Non-American Systems and Views.* New York: Praeger, 111; and J.S. Arpan (1972). International Intracorporate Pricing: Non-American Systems and Views. *Journal of International Business Studies,* 7.

24. See Carl S. Shoup (1974), Taxation of Multinational Corporations. In *The Impact of Multinational Corporations on Development and on International Relations. Technical Papers: Taxation* (United Nations, Department of Economic and Social Affairs, STE/SA/11), 3–4.

25. Ibid., 4–5.

26. Klaus A. Sahlgren (1977). A View from the United Nations. *California Management Review,* 20(1), 84–5.

27. Ibid., 84–5.

28. John Sparkman, Economic Interdependence and the International Corporation, *California Management Review,* 20(1), 88.

29. The OECD Committee drafted principles of behavior regarding MNCs that were adopted by the OECD foreign ministers on June 21, 1976, and entitled, *Declaration of OECD Member Governments on International Investment and Multinational Enterprises,* including an annex on 'Guidelines for Multinational Enterprises.'

30. John Sparkman, Economic Interdependence, 89.

31. Carl Nisser and Don Wallace, Jr. (1978). National Treatment for Multinational Enterprises: Will the OECD Governments Meet the Challenge? *Columbia Journal of World Business,* 14.

32. For selected codes of conduct, see a report to the U.S. Department of State, prepared by Ronald E. Muller and David H. Moore (undated), entitled *Inter-American Relations and Latin American Investment by U.S. Multinational Corporations: Exploration of an Emerging New Harmony,* see Appendix A, 66–75. For additional input, see Coney T. Oliver (1972). The Andean Foreign Investment Code: A New Phase in the Quest for Normative Order as to Direct Investment. *American Journal of International Law,* 66; Organization of American States, *Transnational Enterprises,* AG Doc. 1003/78, June 30, 1978; ECOSOC, Centre on Transnational Corporations, Document E/C.10/17, July 1976; ECOSOC, Corrupt Practices, Particularly Illegal Payments in International Commercial Transactions, Resolution 2/22 (63); Action on the Problem of Corrupt Practices (1978). *The CTC Reporter,* 1(4); ILO: Draft on Transnationals Ready for Approval (1977). *The CTC Reporter,* 1(2). UNCTAD: Code of Conduct on the Transfer of Technology, *The CTC Reporter,* 1(2); OECD: Guidelines for Multinational Enterprises (1972). *The CTC Reporter,* 1(2); *Guidelines for International Investment.* Paris: International Chamber of Commerce.

33. See Declaration on the Establishment of a New International Economic Order (1974). United Nations, 2229th plenary meeting, 1 May 1974.

CHAPTER 4

Issues in North–South Relations and the New World Order*

Issues presented by the multinational corporation in the economic development of Africa essentially reflect similar concerns throughout the Third World. Redress of the life-choice constraints issue and development problems on the whole requires assessment of a host of broader concerns impinging Third World development. The North-South arrangement of countries, as well as problems of inequality, wealth disparity, and debt servicing, and tariff restrictions, among others, hold enormous implications for Third World development. These concerns have led to a call for a new world order and are paramount in the debate on the plight of Third World nations and how they can achieve the level of development that will lead to sustained enhancement of life-choice decisions. This chapter attempts to promote a greater understanding of the broader parameters of Third World development and the linkage between the multinational corporation and the development process.

SUMMARY

The inequality gap between rich and poor nations has persisted over time. Poor nations, primarily located in the Southern Hemisphere, are calling for a new world order in which a reallocation of resources among the world's communities is requisite. This task would be accomplished, as

*Benjamin F. Bobo and Lawrence S. Tai, "Topicos Sobre Las Relaciones Nort-Sur y El Nuevo Ordern Mundial [Issues in North–South Relations and the New World Order]," *Revista de Contablidad Y Auditoria* 25, 95–118. Published in Spanish, reprinted in English with permission.

poor nations suggest, through a process of wealth redistribution from the more affluent Northern Hemisphere countries to the less endowed nations in the South. Important to the process would be the development of policies and practices that include more sensitive direct foreign investment policies, debt relief, sovereignty over natural resources, commodity agreements, preferential tariffs and technology transfer. Inattention to these concerns would prolong the economic disparity between North and South and potentially destabilize their already strained relations.

As the future unfolds, conflict between two worlds—one rich, one poor—remains unresolved. Among the rich, are the advanced industrialized nations including the United States, Japan, United Kingdom, Canada, Germany, France and Italy. The poor, commonly referred to as the Third World, comprises a majority of nations around the globe including Peru, Mali, India, Pakistan, Thailand, Bangladesh, Ethiopia, Chad, Dominican Republic, Zaire, Zambia, Brazil, to name a few. Observers of conditions in Third World countries often lament that some only need time and technology to build modern, developed economies for they are for the most part wealthy in mineral resources. Others, it is felt, require significant financial assistance to spur self-sustaining economic growth. And in the worst cases, we are told, there is need for massive foreign aid to uplift them from degradation and abject poverty.[1] What we appear to be more convinced of is that much of the emerging conflict is an outgrowth of incongruent and nonconverging objectives that underlie aspirations of Third World leaders to emulate Western society in enhancing the standard of living of their people, and the conquest of the multinational corporation (MNC) to exploit Third World resources in pursuit of stockholder wealth maximization.

Many multinationals, by any standards of comparison, possess far greater financial, technological and physical resources than most developing economies. Consequently, they oftentimes exact and obtain derogations of municipal law and receive special privileges, which are not in the best interest of Third World people. On the other hand, however, leaders in host countries have been known to conduct dubious and deceptive business dealings with corporate investors; the general outcome has revealed serious mistrust on both sides.

With confused programs and opposing objectives, the seriousness of increasingly poor relations between guest corporations and host countries cries out for new direction. Clearly, the relationship between multinational corporations and host countries is experiencing marked changes and undergoing strong adjustments in role-playing, thus producing dangerous tension and ill feeling. A withdrawal from Third World exploration by multinationals, or a complete rejection of multinational presence by the Third World would be difficult to reconcile, given that the need of Third World people is so great. The extent and depth of this need is clearly suggested by Exhibit 4.1. Some 100 countries had an average gross

Exhibit 4.1
Issues in North-South Relations and the New World Order
Third World Population and GNP Per Capita, 1991

	Africa	
Nonaligned Nations	*Population*	*GNP Per Capita ($)*
Angola	10,280,000	1,550
Benin	4,900,000	370
Botswana	1,300,000	2,530
Burundi	5,700,000	210
Cameroon	11,900,000	850
Cape Verde	390,000	923
Central African Republic	3,100,000	890
Chad	5,800,000	210
Comoros Islands	540,000	400
Congo	2,400,000	1,120
Equatorial Guinea	360,000	480
Ethiopia	52,800,000	120
Gabon	1,200,000	3,780
Gambia	870,000	350
Ghana	15,300,000	400
Guinea	5,900,000	460
Guinea-Bissau	1,000,000	180
Ivory Coast	12,400,000	690
Kenya	25,000,000	340
Lesotho	1,800,000	580
Liberia	2,700,000	510
Madagascar	12,000,000	210
Malagasy Republic	7,700,000	170
Malawi	8,800,000	230
Maldives	218,000	460
Mali	8,700,000	280
Mauritania	2,000,000	510
Mauritius	1,100,000	2,410
Mozambique	16,100,000	80
Niger	7,900,000	300
Nigeria	99,000,000	340
Rwanda	7,100,000	270
Sao Tome & Principe	120,000	2,000
Senegal	7,600,000	720
Seychelles	67,000	5,720
Sierra Leone	4,200,000	210
Somalia	7,900,000	230
South Africa	38,900,000	2,560
St. Lucia	151,000	1,690
Sudan	25,800,000	150
Swaziland	780,000	840
Tanzania	25,200,000	100

Exhibit 4.1 (*continued*)

Africa

Nonaligned Nations	Population	GNP Per Capita ($)
Togo	3,800,000	410
Uganda	16,900,000	170
Upper Volta	6,200,000	80
Zaire	36,600,000	250
Zambia	8,300,000	480
Zimbabwe	10,100,000	650

Asia

Nonaligned Nations	Population	GNP Per Capita ($)
Afghanistan	16,400,000	990
Bangladesh	110,600,000	220
Bhutan	1,500,000	180
Burma	31,200,000	90
Cambodia	8,300,000	292
China	1,148,177,000	356
India	866,500,000	330
Indonesia	181,300,000	610
Laos	2,400,000	100
Malaysia	18,200,000	2,520
Nepal	19,400,000	180
North Korea	22,000,000	390
Pakistan	115,800,000	400
Sri Lanka	17,200,000	500
Vanuatu	159,900	1,020
Vietnam	68,100,000	38

Latin America and the Caribbean

Nonaligned Nations	Population	GNP Per Capita ($)
Argentina	32,700,000	2,790
Bahamas	260,000	8,733
Barbados	260,000	6,488
Belize	185,300	2,135
Bolivia	7,300,000	650
Colombia	32,800,000	1,260
Cuba	11,094,300	3,540
Djibouti	416,000	600
Ecuador	10,800,000	1,000
Grenada	91,000	2,312
Guyana	1,040,000	110
Jamaica	2,400,000	1,380
Nicaragua	3,800,000	460
Panama	2,500,000	2,130
Peru	21,900,000	1,070
Suriname	404,000	4,000
Trinidad and Tobago	1,300,000	3,670

Exhibit 4.1 (*continued*)

Mideast, Mediterranean and Europe

Nonaligned Nations	Population	GNP Per Capita ($)
Algeria	25,700,000	1,980
Bahrain	530,000	7,350
Cyprus	740,000	7,760
Egypt	54,600,000	540
Iran	57,700,000	2,170
Iraq	20,000,000	8,732
Jordan	3,700,000	1,050
Kuwait	2,200,000	11,170
Lebanon	3,000,000	1,420
Libya	4,700,000	5,270
Malta	355,000	6,580
Morocco	25,770,000	980
Oman	1,500,000	7,360
People's Republic of Yemen	11,000,000	1,060
Qatar	510,000	14,471
Saudi Arabia	15,400,000	7,820
Syria	12,500,000	2,100
Tunisia	8,200,000	1,500
United Arab Emirates	1,631,000	20,640
Yemen Arab Republic	6,900,000	120
Yugoslavia	23,900,000	1,250

Sources: World Development Report (1993). World Bank, New York: Oxford University Press; and *The World Economic Factbook* (1993). London: Euromonitor.

national product (GNP) of less than $2,200 per capita in 1991. When the Mid-east oil producers are excluded, the figure drops to less than $1,400 per capita. With such a low output of goods and services, a drastic infusion of technology and investment that multinationals can offer is all but imperative.

In view of the fact that the Third World comprises nearly three-fourths of the world's population and produces an impressively sizeable portion of the world's natural resources, it seems essential that we make a concerted attempt to fully understand Third World aspirations for economic development if we are to maintain and indeed increase our trade relations with this sector of the international arena. With intent to enhance this understanding, we will explore several related issues highlighting MNC-Third World involvement including the matter of sovereignty with control; the North-South concept; the issue of inequality; wealth redistribution, as it relates to new world order precepts; US direct foreign investment policy; the extent to which the MNC has helped or hindered economic progress in the South; and, given the influence of these matters, future prospects for MNC presence in the South.

SOVEREIGN BUT CONTROLLED

There is a widely held view that MNCs jeopardize the sovereignty and independence of nation-states. As the argument goes, MNCs exert "external control" in its affairs, "exploits" labor and natural resources, realizes "excessive" profits and fails to reinvest significantly in Third World development. On the other hand, it is argued that nation-states exact and impose harsh restrictions on foreign investment. These arguments appear to suggest that these parties are locked into a relationship with no recourse.

But these parties can take independent actions. When a government feels that corporate exploitation is simply intolerable, it nationalizes or expropriates the assets of the foreign companies. Similarly, a corporation that feels overly restricted simply pulls back capital investments and employs them in more lucrative and pleasing alternatives.

Many observers purport that past decades have witnessed major atrocities committed by MNCs upon the sanctity of Third World nations. If it were possible to have a replay of the events and alter the course of history, perhaps much of the current conflict between MNCs and the Third World would not occupy volumes of thought in the literature today. But what happened—happened. The rational thinker has long arrived at this realization. There is, however, another side to the MNC-Third World controversy that leads one to conclude that what happened continues to happen, though with a somewhat different form and structure.

The late Kwame Nkrumah of Ghana characterized the form and structure as neocolonialist exploitation. This terminology, as Nkrumah applied it, referred to a nation-state that is, theoretically, independent and internationally sovereign, but where its economic system, and therefore its political system, is externally directed.[2] This concept has been descriptively explicated by Peter Berger as an exercise in growth without development and is couched in terms of foreign capital penetration of the Third World. As he put it:

'Growth without development' is based on the penetration of a Third World economy by foreign capital. This penetration results in a distortion of the economy, in the sense that it develops not in terms of international economic and social forces, but in the interest of the foreign 'metropolis.' . . . The same 'distortion' creates an essentially colonial structure for the benefit of the foreign capitalists. It is not quite the same structure as that of the old colonialism, which was largely extractive, taking out raw materials from the colony that were needed for the industries in the home country. The new colonialism promotes industrialization, but of a very peculiar kind. Generally it is capital-intensive rather than labor-intensive, thus actually creating unemployment in the 'developing' country. . . . Allocation of scarce resources to this kind of industrialization actually prevents development in other sectors of the society. . . . 'Neocolonialism,' therefore, implies increasing impoverishment and ever-greater dependency on foreign forces. In Andre Gunder Frank's graphic phrase, it means 'the development of underdevelopment'![3]

THE NORTH-SOUTH CONCEPT

At the conclusion of World War II, two major blocs of industrialized nations emerged on an East-West axis. The Western bloc came to be known as the First World and included the advanced industrialized nations of Europe, North America and Asia. This bloc was characterized by essentially capitalistic, market-oriented economies. The Eastern bloc, in turn, was called the Second World, and included the centrally planned communist-run nations. Countries not included in the two major blocs were those that had not achieved modern developed economies. For the most part, they either had natural resources but lacked ample technology with which to develop them, or had neither natural resources nor technology. Such countries, located mainly in Latin America and the Caribbean, Southern Asia, and Africa, were classified as the Third World.[4]

Third World countries are considered nonaligned and are shown in Exhibit 4.1. Although the terms are used interchangeably and refer to the same group of countries, there is a distinguishing mark. Third World connotes economically disadvantaged and industrially poor. Whereas, technically speaking, nonaligned refers to those nations with no formal military ties with the Western or Eastern superpowers. They may, however, have close military links with one side or the other. For example, Iraq, Syria, Angola, Mozambique and Cuba abound with Russian influence. Contrastingly, Saudi Arabia, Egypt, Kenya and Kuwait, for example, are tilted toward the West. The nonaligned movement grew out of the US-Soviet cold war and dates back to a meeting of African and Asian nations in Bandung, Indonesia, in April, 1955.[5] Out of subsequent nonaligned meetings emerged an international philosophy of Third World nations that was couched in terms of self-determination and premised on the need to develop their own industrial capacity. Reacting to sovereign power interference from the West and the East, poorer nations have sought ways to protect themselves from economic and political encroachment by the superpowers. Their quest for self-determination and internally controlled economic growth perhaps fueled the demise of the East-West axis. This arrangement was replaced by a North–South axis— the "have-nots" in the South and the "haves" in the industrialized North.[6] Both geopolitical and economic in nature, this arrangement largely identifies a chasm of economic inequality between wealthier nations in the northern hemisphere and poorer ones in the southern hemisphere. Concern that inequality is on the rise or at least that it has not declined relatively in recent years has become a major issue in North-South relations.

THE ISSUE OF INEQUALITY

In the context of global political economy, rising global interdependence alongside increasing inequality between and within nations is difficult to reconcile especially for those who find themselves among the "have-nots." Four major alternative approaches to the study of the global political economy have been advanced as relevant theses from which the equity issue can be explored. Exhibit 4.2 identifies these approaches.[7]

Each approach espouses a particular belief about how inequality is engendered in the world economy and corrective action necessary to resolve the problem. In American political economy literature, liberalism remains the leading approach to the study of international political economy[8] and has been most fully developed and applied in the field of economics. As a distinguishing character, liberalism assumes that "domestic inequality" is independent of both economic growth and inequality among nations. More specifically, proponents of liberalism argue that, under conditions of underdevelopment, an accumulation of greater aggregate wealth must precede the alleviation of domestic disparities. By contrast, proponents of economic nationalism, internationalism and dependency theory contend that economic development and wealth accumulation must follow or at least move simultaneously with the promotion of social equity.[9]

With liberalism taking the position that the give-and-take of the market provides maximum growth and a tendency toward an equalization of incomes, it might be interpreted that over time the "gap" between rich and poor countries would close and eventually disappear. Prior to World War II, liberal economists predicted a reduction in the gap predicated on the assumption that the terms of trade for Third World countries would become increasingly more beneficial to them. Unfortunately, the actual trend has been in the opposite direction.[10] Perhaps liberalism is not fully to blame. Liberalism prescribes that nations should avoid market interventions since such actions will only make matters worse. Many, if not most, Third World countries pursue socialist policies in social and economic development. By definition, socialism obstructs the operation of the free market mechanism. It may be that this action more than anything is responsible for difficulties experienced by liberalism in the Third World marketplace.

Exhibit 4.2
Approaches to the Analysis of Inequality Between and Within Nations

	Key Assumptions	Prescription	
		Among Nations	*Within Nations*
Liberalism	The give-and-take of the market provides maximum growth and a tendency toward an equalization of incomes.	Nations should avoid market interventions since such actions will only make matters worse.	Resolution of domestic disparities in poor nations must be postponed until the generation of greater aggregate wealth.
Economic Nationalism	A liberal capitalist world-economy acts to preserve or increase existing inequalities.	Poor nations should intervene in markets in order to protect the domestic economy from foreign domination.	Measures to promote social equality should be taken simultaneously with economic growth and development.
Internationalism	Same as that of economic nationalism.	Effective international organizations are needed to act on the behalf of Third World countries.	Same as that of economic nationalism with added emphasis on national planning.
Marxist and Independency Theory	A capitalist world economy (liberal or otherwise) will continue to breed inequality.	Third World countries must withdraw from the global capitalist system if they are to achieve genuine national development.	Revolution and socialism only feasible path to achieve social equity.

Source: Deepa Ollapally (1993). The South Looks North: The Third World in the New World Order, *Current History, 92*(573), 175–179. © 2005 Current History Inc. Don Walleri (1978). The Political Economy Literature on North-South Relations. *International Studies Quarterly, 22*(4), 589.

Despite the plausibleness of this rationale, Third World countries are calling for an immediate reversal of the widening gap between rich and poor nations.

NEW WORLD ORDER: THE REDISTRIBUTION DOCTRINE

Towards improving equality and closing the economic gap between North and South, Third World nations have put forth what amounts to a doctrine of redistribution. In terms of a broad and encompassing international policy measure, these nations are advancing the notion of a new world order. What they want includes wealth redistribution, debt relief, sovereignty over natural resources, a code of conduct for multinational corporations, agreements on commodities and prices, preferential tariffs and a more substantive and quicker transfer of technology.[11] These are viewed as necessary arrangements to bring closure to the inequality "gap."

WEALTH REDISTRIBUTION

The Third World sees a redistribution of wealth between rich and poor countries as its overall primary objective. Many observers of foreign trade interpret this as a call for economic parity between North and South. The South is seeking increased foreign aid donations and a larger share of advanced countries' GNP for development support.

This issue of wealth redistribution is clearly two-sided, both of which must be dealt with if world economic peace is to transpire. On one side, there is the question of how the North would effect a redistribution of wealth between North and South. At present, the free market system is viewed as an apparatus capable of acting as a change mechanism with the capacity to push the two economies toward economic parity. In conventional wisdom, industrialized nations, particularly major Western powers, would invest and reinvest accumulated surpluses in weak economies. Under conditions of world economic expansion, strong economies would purchase increasingly greater amounts of exports from Third World countries. In the process, prices of exports relative to imports for these nations should rise substantially. Over time, this should create the kind of economic momentum in the South that would bring about greater parity with the North.

The other side of the issue relates to balanced wealth redistribution among Third World countries. Latin American countries receive the largest share of US investment as revealed in Exhibits 4.3 and 4.4. Two-thirds of American investment in the less developed world is located there, with book value equaling $77 billion in 1991. Mexico and Brazil had a combined stock of more than $27 billion in US investment at the end of

Exhibit 4.3
U.S. Direct Foreign Investment in All Industries in Developing Countries: 1980–1991 ($ billions)

Year	Latin America	Other Developing Areas
1980	38.8	14.4
1985	28.3	24.5
1988	53.5	26.6
1989	62.7	29.4
1990	71.6	30.7
1991	77.3	34.3

Source: Statistical Abstract of the United States (1993). Washington, DC: Bureau of Statistics.

Exhibit 4.4
U.S. Direct Investment Position Abroad, 1991

Country/Region	$ Billions	% of Total
Canada	68.5	15.2
Europe	224.6	49.9
Africa	5.4	1.2
Latin America	77.3	17.2
Middle East	4.7	1.0
South Asia	25.2	5.6
East Asia and Oceania	41.3	9.2
Others	3.2	0.7
Total	450.2	100.0

Source: Statistical Abstract of the United States (1993). Washington, DC: Bureau of Statistics.

1991, making the stake of American companies in those two countries greater than in France and almost equal to that in Germany, though considerably less than in Britain or Canada.

There is some resentment among Third World nations concerning the apparent preferential treatment given to selected members by industrialized countries. Latin America has clearly been the target of US foreign investment, receiving predominantly more investment in all industries than other developing countries. This disparity is further underscored in Exhibit 4.4. Latin America received 14 times more than Africa, 16 times more than the Middle East and three times more than South Asia. A similar scenario can be constructed for East Asia and Oceania relative to Africa, the Middle East and South Asia. This raises one very important question that the South must address: How are foreign investments to be allocated and distributed among member nations effectively and efficiently so as to produce full equity and equality? This of course presupposes that the North would be amenable to establishment of an allocation system.

DEBT RELIEF

The debt burden of Third World nations is becoming increasingly overwhelming. Under current economic conditions there is little doubt that affected nations lack the capacity to service even a reasonable portion of the debt. Exhibit 4.5 shows the external public debt of developing countries. In a four-year period, total outstanding debt more than doubled, rising from $74 billion in 1970 to $151 billion in 1974. With dramatically increased costs brought on significantly by the oil crisis, which began around 1973–74, the debt soared to $1,388 billion by 1990. Of this hefty sum, Brazil and Mexico have $110 billion and $108 billion, respectively. But other countries are also heavily debt burdened: Argentina owes $52 billion;

Exhibit 4.5
External Public Debt of Developing Countries

Year	Total Debt Outstanding at End of Year ($ billions)
1970	74
1971	87
1972	101
1973	122
1974	151
1980	572
1981	670
1982	753
1983	819
1984	855
1985	952
1986	1,047
1987	1,176
1988	1,156
1989	1,166
1990	1,388

Sources: Roger D. Stone & Eve Hamilton (1991). *Global Economics and the Environment: Toward Substainable Rural Development in the Third World.* New York: Council on Foreign Relations Press, 19; Sidney Weintraub (1979). The New International Economic Order: The Beneficiaries. *World Development,* 7(3), 251 (with permission from Elsevier); *World Bank Annual Report* (1976). Washington, DC: World Bank, 101.

Venezuela, $34 billion; the Philippines, $34 billion; Egypt, $44 billion and Nigeria, $23 billion. Of the more than $1 trillion owed in total by the Third World, Latin American countries have about 34 percent and African countries 22 percent.[12]

Can such an enormous debt obligation ever be satisfied? Poorer countries would simply like to erase the slate and start anew. It is, however, uncertain whether relaxing or canceling the debt is the appropriate solution. Relaxation of debt absent of serious plans for stimulating economic growth and development would merely have the short-term effect of reducing debt to some practical serviceable level or eliminating it in total. But without necessary economic expansion, debt financing would remain a pre-condition to economic survival. In the long run, that familiar debt burden would simply reappear.

SOVEREIGNTY OVER NATURAL RESOURCES

Third World nations hold an impressive share of some of the world's highly demanded resources, as indicated by Exhibit 4.6. The magnitude of these figures lends well to the thesis that many poor countries are only poor in a financial sense. In the new world order ideology, the feeling is that emerging nations must have full sovereignty over their natural resources and economic activity if economic parity between North and South is to be realized.

Exhibit 4.6
Natural Resource Reserves of Third World Countries

Region	Resource	% of World Total
Africa	Industrial diamonds	74
	Chromium	68
	Manganese	53
	Phosphates	53
	Gold	51
	Aluminum	29
Asia	Rubber	78
	Tin	30
Latin America	Bauxite	48
	Copper	20
Middle East	Oil	53

Source: Jim Norwine and Alfonso Ganzalez (1988). *The Third World: States of Mind and Being.* Boston: Unwin and Hyman, 62 and 64. Reproduced by permission of Routledge/Taylor & Francis Books, Inc.

CODE OF CONDUCT FOR MULTINATIONAL CORPORATIONS

The argument that many multinational corporations demand and receive special privileges which are not in the best interests of the host country lead to a call for an international code of ethics to govern the operations of MNCs. Many Third World nations are at the mercy of MNCs and are simply unable or incapable of warding off excessive demands or unfair practices.

The Organization for Economic Cooperation and Development (OECD) has adopted a voluntary "code of conduct." While some MNCs are making increasing use of the code, many have not yet become fully attentive to the voluntary standards. The code includes standards for information disclosure, employee relations, taxation and national treatment.[13]

Apart from poorer nations' conflict with MNC ethics, the US too has had problems with MNC conduct in host countries. Inaccurate record keeping of foreign transactions brought MNCs under close scrutiny by the US government and resulted in the passage of the Foreign Corrupt Practices Act of 1977. In part, the act prohibits the use of an instrumentality of interstate commerce (such as the telephone or the mails) in furtherance of a payment, or even an offer to pay "anything of value," directly or indirectly to any foreign official with discretionary authority or to any foreign political party or foreign political candidate, if the purpose of the payment is the corrupt one of getting the recipient to act (or to refrain from acting) in such a way as to assist the company in obtaining or retaining business for or with or directing business to any person. Violation of the act can result in substantial fines to the violating party.[14]

COMMODITY AGREEMENTS, PRODUCER CARTELS AND PRICE STABILITY

One of the most emphasized elements of the new world order ideology involves primary commodity prices. Essentially, poorer countries are demanding worldwide commodity agreements, including producer cartels to stabilize commodity prices, with prices indexed to the cost of industrial imports from industrialized countries. Price stabilization, if possible, is one area where real gains can be achieved. But the perceived distributional effects lead one to doubt whether the benefits will accrue to the very poor nations.

Exhibit 4.7 provides some notion of who the beneficiaries would be under price stabilization. What we find is that when taking into consideration primary commodity exports of developing countries, under conditions of price stability the principal gainers are likely to be wealthier Third World countries. Those with per capita income in excess of $1,000 have average net exports of $450 million while those under $1,000 show a trade

Exhibit 4.7
Mean Exports and Imports for Third World Countries, 1991 ($ millions)

Grouping by Per Capita Income	Number of Countries	Exports	Imports	Net Exports
Under $1,000	31	5,175	5,277	(102)
Over $1,000	24	522	7,072	450

Source: International Financial Statistics Yearbook (1993). Washington, DC: International Monetary Fund.

deficit. This suggests that the poorer Third World countries lack the capacity to produce exports at a competitive level with wealthier ones and would therefore receive a disproportionate share of any benefits accruing from price stabilization.

PREFERENTIAL TARIFFS

The doctrine of redistribution also serves as a platform for demanding preferential tariffs in industrialized countries for manufactured products from the Third World. As in the case of price stabilization, here too we must inquire about the real likelihood of the very poorest countries realizing any substantial benefit from preferential tariffs. Liberalization of tariffs would benefit most those developing countries that are in a position to export goods and services, which tend to be primarily the wealthier Third World nations. Under the new world order precepts, the master plan apparently calls for a trickling down of potential benefits to the poorer nations.

Trade liberalization, however, can potentially provide enormous benefits to the Third World in general. Benefits from the elimination of tariff and non-tariff barriers in the developed countries could increase the export earnings of developing countries by billions of dollars a year. Exhibit 4.8 shows a distribution of the benefits. Of an estimated $39 billion in increased earnings, the poorer nations would receive an additional $6 billion in export earnings, with the wealthier nations receiving $33 billion.

TECHNOLOGY TRANSFER

A transfer of more technology and productive facilities to the Third World is also highly regarded in the new world order. The demand for more technology essentially breaks down to a demand for several types of technologies that are germane to the planning, design and implementation of an industrial project: planning and proposal preparation; design and

Exhibit 4.8
Additional Developing Country Exports Resulting from the Elimination of
Trade Barriers 1991 ($ billions)

Country Grouping	Manufactures	Commodities	Total
Poorer Nations	4	2	6
Wealthier Nations	23	10	33
Total	27	12	39

Note: Earnings are estimates based on 1991 export data for developing countries.

Source: International Financial Statistics Yearbook (1993). Washington, DC: International Monetary Fund.

construction of plant; start-up of plant; value engineering to achieve cost-effectiveness and quality control; product adaptation and modification; external support from research standards associations to assure dependability and quality; and project/product evaluation.[15] These technologies are most valuable to the Third World when transferred in such a manner that the local labor force can intellectually internalize the technology, replicate and improve upon it, and market it to the outside world. Only then will Third World nations realize control of their sovereign powers.

US DIRECT FOREIGN INVESTMENT POLICY: MARKET FORCES

The new world order platform presents an interesting challenge to industrialized nations. Success of income redistribution, to be sure, depends heavily upon foreign investment and international trade policies observed by countries in the North and how willing they are to adapt their policies to the new philosophy. The US, itself a major recipient of foreign direct investment, will likely play a role in any address of new world order demands. Since the US puts its faith in the free market system and thus develops and conducts foreign investment and trade in accord with the free market model, success of new world order demands will not come easy, primarily because it calls for interventionist policies.

Interventionism flies counter to the US preference of having international comparative advantage and market forces determine the location of economic activity and wealth redistribution. Throughout the postwar period, US policy toward the development aspects of foreign direct investment has been premised on the neoclassical view that it generally promotes welfare in both the home and host country. Such investment has been viewed as helping development in the recipient countries, and at the same time supporting US economic objectives. In this vein, a fundamentally non-interventionist relationship is sought between the US government and the private investor—whether US or foreign.[16]

NEW WORLD ORDER: THE MNCS' ROLE

Multinational corporations have a special contribution to make to Third World development. As the vehicle for US direct foreign investment, MNCs broaden the capacity of American foreign policy. They provide capital in addition to managerial, technical and marketing skills that cannot be supplied through aid mechanisms or through foreign trade. Notwithstanding pejorative impacts of past MNC policies and behavior in the Third World, and recognizing that future relations between MNCs and Third World nations will involve conflict from time to time, the fact that MNCs are the major suppliers of technology and managerial capability to the Third World will essentially govern the quality of the climate for MNCs in that part of the world in future decades. This is true even in view of potential changes that are likely to appear as a result of the impending new world order. Third World policymakers should recognize that what they seek in terms of wealth redistribution and development objectives and the pace at which they aspire to achieve their objectives may be vastly facilitated by MNC. But there are trouble spots that must be reconciled.

While it is certainly true that MNCs have necessary resources to facilitate Third World economic growth objectives, there are however two reasons why MNCs may not add to capital formation in the host country, and thus may not support economic development and growth to the fullest extent possible. These factors are of great concern to Third World nations. First, rather than bring new capital into the country, MNCs may borrow locally, thus reducing the amount of funds available to indigenous firms. We might refer here to the argument that foreign firms receive preferential treatment from host country lenders. In addition to this, MNCs may monopolize the best local investment opportunities, thereby forcing indigenous capitalists to seek lucrative ventures abroad.[17]

Secondly, to control inflation Third World governments (as elsewhere) restrict credit markets. Under such conditions, foreign subsidiaries tend to receive a more generous ration of loans for corporate expansion than do domestic firms. Further, foreign subsidiaries tend to receive more sympathetic service than their domestic counterparts in periods of economic contraction, particularly when financial institutions are hesitant to roll over the loans of businesses that are in danger of bankruptcy.

Also, income distribution from foreign investment may be adversely affected if the foreign investment is more capital-intensive than is appropriate for local conditions. Recall that under the neoclassical assumption of full employment, foreign investment increases the efficient use of host country resources (whether capital-intensive or labor-intensive) and frees the labor it may displace for more productive activity elsewhere in the economy. However, if there is chronic or permanent unemployment, or underemployment in the host country, a capital-intensive foreign investment may bid up the wages for a domestic skilled labor elite. As this type of labor is frequently in short supply in the host country, a wider gap between the skilled and unskilled will be perpetuated.[18]

Clearly, American firms face increasingly more challenging conditions for doing business in the Third World. The call for a new world order is part of a dynamic process that has yet to fully unfold. It is certain that the old rules of doing business in the Third World are fast disappearing and will never apply again. Unmistakably, MNCs must heed the warnings of the marketplace. Although the South, despite its large membership, cannot be considered a "bloc" at present, we must recognize that the existence of relevant ingredients (and clearly they do exist) pertinent to the formulation of such a coalition makes it a very real and very near future possibility.

Let's not appear insensitive and irresponsible, and further, let's not be caught off guard by the fact that their interests are too varied and self-serving, their nationalism too intense and individualistic, and their suspicions of each other too innate to allow them to coalesce and act in concert on a range of issues. Be mindful of how allies unite in time of war and act in concert to challenge the enemy. Is not a transfiguration of this model possible in time of peace?

Does it not sound reasonable that an economic crisis is sufficient inducement to cause affected nations to put aside individualism and selfish interests, overlook suspicions, and unite for the common good? MNCs would be well advised to be cautious in their future exploitative behavior and realize that the days of wine and rose are relics of the past. Survival of the MNC in the Third World may very well depend on its ability to reverse the widening inequality "gap," and further, on how willing it is to accept a limited presence in the Third World on a project-by-project basis. Length of stay based on a reasonable rate of return on invested capital and time required to return invested capital to the investor may become the *modus operandi* in North-South relations. Future harmony among nations may depend on it.

NOTES

1. See Hans W. Singer and Javed A. Ansari (1988). *Rich and Poor Countries: Consequences of International Disorder*, 4th ed. Boston: Unwin and Hyman; and Poor vs. Rich: A New Global Conflict (1975). *Time*, December 22, 1975, 34–35.

2. Diane Elson (1988). Dominance and Dependency in the World Economy. In Ben Crow, Mary Thorpe et al., (eds.), *Survival and Change in the Third World*. New York: Oxford University Press, 264–287; and Richard D. Steade (1978). Multinational Corporations and the Changing World Economic Order. *California Management Review*, 21(2), 6.

3. Ibid. and Peter L. Berger (1974). *Pyramids of Sacrifice*, New York: Basic Books, 48–49.

4. In some instances the literature identifies five worlds. The First and Second are as described above. The third is comprised of countries that require time and technology to build modern, developed economies. Generally, they have both financial wealth and natural resources. The Fourth World includes those countries that have natural resources but lack financial and technological capability. The Fifth World includes those nations that require massive foreign aid in all categories to uplift them from poverty. For a more in depth description, see Allen H. Merriam (1988). What Does 'Third World' Mean? In Jim Norwine and Alfonso Gonzalez (eds.). *The Third World: States of Mind and Being*. Boston: Unwin and Hyman, 15–22; Poor vs. Rich: A New Global Conflict, ibid.; and Richard D. Steade, ibid., 7.

5. The first official nonaligned meeting was held in Belgrade in 1961. See Sheikh R. Ali (1989). The Third World Debt Crisis and U.S. Policy. In Sheikh R. Ali (ed.). *Third World at the Crossroads*. New York: Praeger, 193–204.

6. Richard D. Steade, ibid., 6.

7. Deepa Ollapally (1993). The South Looks North: The Third World in the New World Order, *Current History, 92*(573), 175–179; and R. Dan Walleri (1978). The Political Economy Literature on North-South Relations, *International Studies Quarterly, 22*(4), 587–588.

8. See for example, Cristobal Kay (1993). For a Renewal of Development Studies: Latin American Theories and Neo-liberalism in the Era of Structural Adjustment. *Third World Quarterly, 14*(4), 691–702; Jacob Abadi (1993). India's Economic Policy Since Nehru: The Failure of Democratic Socialism and the March Toward Free Trade. *Journal of Third World Studies. 10*(2), 12–35; Nora Hamilton and Eun Mee Kim (1993). Economic and Political Liberalization in Mexico and South Korea. *Third World Quarterly, 14*(1), 109–136; F. Stewart (1985). The Fragile Foundations of the Neoclassical Approach to Development. *Journal of Development Studies, 21*(2), 282–292; D. Blake and R. Walters (1976). *The Politics of Global Economic Relations*. Englewood Cliffs, NJ: Prentice-Hall; D. Calleo and B. Rowland (1973). *America and the World Political* Economy: Atlantic Dreams and National Realities. Bloomington: Indiana University Press. R. Gilpin (1995). U.S. Power and the Multinational Corporation: The Political Economy of Foreign *Direct Investment*. New York: Basic Books. G. Meier, ed. (1970). *Leading Issues in Economic Development*, New York: Oxford University Press.

9. R. Don Walleri, ibid., 590. See also Deepa Ollapally, ibid.; and W.F. Kuhn (1970). *The Evolution of Economic Thought*. Chicago: South-Western Publishing Co.

10. See Cristobal Kay, ibid. See also R. Don Walleri, ibid.; K. Hoisti (1975). Underdevelopment and the 'gap' theory of International Conflict. *American Political Science Review, 69*, 827–839; and Ward, B. Runnalls and L. D'Anjou, eds. (1971), *The Widening Gap: Development in the 1970s*. New York: Columbia University Press.

11. For additional comment see Hans W. Singer and Javed A. Ansari, ibid., 231–237 and Richard D. Steade, ibid., 8.

12. See Sheikh R. Ali, ibid., 196.

13. For discussion of how host countries have attempted to develop a policy environment to boost the impact of MNC investment, see Hans W. Singer and Javed A. Ansari, ibid., 250–252.

14. For a thorough explanation of the act, see George C. Greanias (1982). The Foreign Corrupt Practices Act: Anatomy of a Statue. Lexington, Mass: Lexington Books.

15. Hans W. Singer and Javed A. Ansari, ibid., 252–261 and W.A. Dymsza (1972). *Multinational Business Strategy*, McGraw Hill.

16. Sheikh R. Ali, ibid., 195–196.

17. Hans W. Singer and Javed A. Ansari, ibid., 252–261.

18. Ibid. and David Wield and Ed Rhodes, Divisions of Labour or Labour Divided? In Ben Crow, Mary Thorpe et al., eds. (1988). *Survival and Change in the Third World*. New York: Oxford University Press, 288–309.

CHAPTER 5

MNC–Third World Relations: A Comparative Study of Policymakers' Attitudes and Perceptions*

The inequality gap between rich and poor countries is clearly a source of considerable tension that places two worlds at odds with potentially catastrophic implications. In hindsight, factors giving rise to September 11, 2001 loom large on this horizon. Since the foregoing discussion has explored numerous broader parameters of MNC–Third World development, this chapter provides strategic information on how key decision makers on both sides of the aisle view very specific factors underpinning this relationship that could be useful to development of a prescription for redress of the inequality gap. "MNC–Third World Relations: A Comparative Study of Policymakers' Attitudes and Perceptions" reports the results of an international survey of decision makers in multinational corporations and Third World countries. This information provides enlightenment on perceptions of MNC–Third World relations with implications for promoting harmonious change in the Third World environment, thus setting the stage for a unified assault on the inequality gap.

The pursuit of business objectives by multinational corporations in the Third World is often at odds with development objectives of these nations. With new world order precepts creating new perceptions of the MNC–Third World engagement, the relationship is experiencing

*Reprinted with permission. Benjamin F. Bobo and Lawrence S. Tai, "MNC–Third World Relations: A Comparative Study of Policymakers' Attitudes and Perceptions," *12th Annual Meeting: Association of Third World Studies, Inc., ATWS Proceedings* (Williamsburg, VA: ATWS Pub., 1994), 45–53.

marked changes and undergoing significant adjustments in role playing, thus producing dangerous tension and ill-feeling. There is a pressing need for identification of the current problem areas and prospects for resolving the tension, given the constantly changing social, economic and political environment. The primary objective of this paper, through a comparative analysis, is to examine the issues surrounding the engagement between MNCs and countries in the Third World and also to investigate whether there is some "happy medium" within which these players can interact viably in a long and continuous relationship, particularly with respect to recent changes in the world geo-political makeup. The paper will attempt to assess what the terms of such a relationship should be through examination of a wide range of factors impinging on the MNC-LDC [less-developed country] relationship.

Aspects of the MNC–Third World relationship have been extensively examined in the literature.[1] What has been discovered that is perhaps key to the understanding of international business operation is that in many ways it is a constantly changing and dynamic process. It must be continually appraised to afford intelligent decision-making about needed changes and modifications so as to promote greater harmony among actors in the international business game.

To accomplish any appreciable success with respect to, for example, the New World Order, it would seem that there exists a real need for a compilation of broad-based strategic information that would permit the rationalization and development of broad ground rules yet specific enough to make possible the operationalization of New World Order precepts. But should the policies of all MNCs be the same toward all Third World nations, and vice versa. Crookell has suggested that Third World nations should differentiate between types of foreign investment based on whether the firm is oriented toward exports or toward engaging in local market development.[2] Given the complexity of international investment and negotiating processes, differentiation decisions could conceivably require matrix analysis in some cases. What this means essentially is that the complexity of international business enterprise may be too enormous to allow desirable specificity in any single empirical examination of the MNC–Third World relationship: specific policies would have to be developed on a case by case and country by country basis.

But a broad-based empirical exploration of major issues surrounding direct private foreign investment in developing countries particularly as related to improving the relationship between multinational corporations and Third World nations could provide a premise for generating intelligent overall policy guidelines to govern MNC–Third World relations, as well as specific policies as the need arises. With this in mind, an MNC–Third World mail survey was conducted during two periods of time, 1980 and 1994, to ascertain attitudes about and perceptions of the interaction of multinational corporations and Third World nations and to determine whether time has affected these attitudes and perceptions. Further, since popular beliefs in the marketplace may encourage misconceptions about foreign enterprise, these surveys offer a useful means of assessing the perceptions of top-level government and corporate leaders, the decision-makers who give final approval on direct foreign investment policies. This allows us to separate fact from innuendo and focus on legitimate issues and concerns. We can also discern whether there is consensus on the importance of these issues.

METHODOLOGY AND MEASUREMENT

Approximately one hundred questions were asked in each survey concerning joint ventures, method of ownership, and Third World preference for origin of direct foreign investment, efforts toward reciprocity, participants in investment selection decision-making processes, political risk, institutional impacts, cultural factors, location of MNC subsidiaries, and the New World Order. This range of topics provides ample bases for examining the interaction between multinational corporations and Third World nations.

The data obtained are based on the responses of 180 participants in the two surveys. Questionnaires were sent to chief executive officers of Fortune 500 companies, heads of state, ambassadors and congressional leaders. The study sample comprises, therefore, leaders of large industrial corporations with extensive international experience that in the aggregate account not only for a substantial share of U.S. direct investment in the Third World but also for a sizeable proportion of direct foreign investment in developing countries by industrialized nations. It also includes political leaders who have the ultimate responsibility for setting international business-related policy. Thus the significance of the responses is rather profound. Impressions gathered are from many of the world's key policymakers who not only formulate policies, but serve as supreme overseers of their implementation.

For measurement purposes, a variation of the semantic differential technique[3] has been employed in these MNC–Third World surveys. In fact, the technique used here is more akin to the Staple scale,[4] a scaling procedure used in sample survey which provides a way of introducing a "qualitative" dimension in the development of questionnaires that probe latent variables, such as attitudinal set.[5]

The Staple scale has been selected, though modified here, because of its proven effectiveness in attitude research and because it enabled the quantification and aggregation of responses as applied to this study. While the Staple scale is a 10-point non-verbal rating scale ranging from +5 to −5 which measures direction and intensity simultaneously,[6] such a scale can have any number of positions, although usually it is an odd-numbered position scale.[7]

Generally, semantic differential type scales consist of a series or set of descriptive (phrases or adjectives) polar-opposite rating scales, each assumed to be an equal-interval ordinal scale.[8] The Staple scale, however, tests adjectives separately rather than using pairs of contrasting adjectives, such as stable-unstable, honest-corrupt, etc., as poles of a single scale.[9] A similar procedure is also employed in this study. For our purposes, individuals were generally asked to respond to a series or set of phrases that describe attitudes about various aspects of MNC–Third World interaction. To rate the responses, the Staple scale was modified to incorporate a verbal rating scale ranging from such verbal measurements as strongly agree to strongly disagree, strongly reduce to strongly increase, extremely important to never important, and extremely positive to extremely negative. In some cases, no opinion or no impact was included as part of the scale range. When responses were coded for data analysis, verbal ratings were assigned numerical ratings, e.g., strongly agree = 1, agree = 2, no opinion = 3, disagree = 4, strongly disagree = 5. "No opinion" is assigned a location between agree and disagree because (a) it is generally standard procedure in semantic differential type analysis, and (b) "no opinion" is neither a positive nor negative response, nor is it equivalent to a "no" response; therefore, it logically fits between agree (which is positive) and disagree (which is negative). Thus, in such case the numbers 1 and 2 are interpreted as positive responses, 3 as neutral or uncertain, and 4 and 5 as negative responses. The responses for each verbal measurement were summed for all of the respondents and multiplied by the respective verbal rating. A weighted average rating was then computed for each question. Since the sample included four independent categories of policymakers, the weighted average is not distorted by views expressed by any single category.

Further, the weighted average ratings for each area of inquiry in the two surveys were ranked and the Spearman rank correlation coefficient was computed. This coefficient is a measure of the degree of correspondence between the ranks of two sample observations. In this case the observations occurred in 1980 and 1994. A significant coefficient indicates that there is consensus among the policymakers between 1980 and 1994 in each area of inquiry.

COMPARATIVE ATTITUDE PROFILES

When the weighted average ratings of the individual responses to each attitude scale are computed, the result is an "attitude profile" that shows the representative attitudes of the policymakers toward various issues related to direct foreign investment in the Third World. Attitude profiles are presented Exhibits 5.1 through 5.4. A range of attitudinal responses is portrayed for each area of inquiry.

Exhibit 5.1
Comparative Attitude Profile
Impact of Joint Ventures on MNC-LDC Relations
Weighted Average Rating and Ranking

Factors	Rating		Ranking	
	1980	*1994*	*1980*	*1994*
Reducing national resentment felt towards MNCs	2.50	2.03	3	1
Creating an aura of greater reciprocity among MNCs & LDCs	2.31	2.14	2	2
Legitimizing MNCs' activities	2.72	2.49	4	4
Less threatening to LDCs	2.21	2.37	1	3
Shifting control from MNCs to LDCs	3.09	2.98	5	5
Trading off efficiency for equity	3.23	3.02	6	6

JOINT VENTURES

Participants were asked to respond to a list of statements about the relationship of multinational corporations and less-developed countries (LDCs) concerning joint ventures. As Exhibit 5.1 indicates, the question engendered a range of responses. Overall, the respondents regard joint ventures as having a positive influence on the creation of greater reciprocity among MNCs and developing countries. This perception holds true for both 1980 and 1994. However, there seems to be a small amount of uncertainty about whether joint ventures result in trading off efficiency for equity suggesting that this form of direct foreign investment may be somewhat problematic for the multinational corporation. But since the weighted average ratings of 3.23 and 3.02 in the two respective surveys only indicate a very minor problem, there is no strong justification for a rejection of equity positions for foreign nationals. Further, because the other factors weigh rather substantially in favor of joint ventures, the efficiency issue becomes even less a factor in the MNC's decision to undertake this form of investment.

The role of joint ventures in creating a greater spirit of reciprocity appears to be quite significant. It has the highest consensus ranking among the factors. The weighted average ratings of 2.31 and 2.14 for 1980 and 1994 indicate that over time the policymakers are in fairly strong agreement on this matter. The general attitude in the marketplace is that joint ventures offer host countries an opportunity to more directly influence MNC operations. As such, host countries apparently are more inclined to welcome direct foreign investment as revealed by the policymakers' responses.

On the matter of legitimizing MNC activities, the policymakers tend to agree that joint ventures have a positive impact. This was their impression in both 1980 and 1994 when this factor was ranked fourth in both years in terms of overall importance. The weighted average ratings of 2.72 and 2.49 in the two respective surveys might however suggest a small amount of uncertainty. This perhaps should be expected since joint ventures particularly in Latin America have not been necessarily effective in reducing suspicion of illegitimate practices or indeed illegitimate practices by multinational corporations, whichever may be the case. Latin America has had a more extensive and complex history of involvement with MNCs than other Third World regions; it is the primary recipient of direct foreign investment. Expropriation of foreign assets there has been more striking than elsewhere in the Third World. The less than full agreement among the policymakers is perhaps a reflection of Latin America's experiences with such multinationals as ITT [International Telephone and Telegraph Corporation] and Anaconda.

Generally, the respondents agree that joint ventures are less threatening to developing countries. But they are not as certain that control is shifted to the host country as a result of joint ventures. However, since the weighted average ratings show reasonable agreement that joint ventures have a positive impact on these factors, the relationship between MNCs and LDCs is well served by sharing ownership. The rankings of these factors clearly indicate that the policymakers feel that the former has greater impact on the relationship than the latter.

This finding was evident in both surveys. Finally, policymakers view joint ventures as an important means of reducing national resentment towards MNCs. A weighted average rating of 2.03 for 1994 indicates that this factor is far more significant in the relationship in recent time than it was earlier. This is also confirmed by its first place ranking. The overall significance of the results can be gleaned from the relative importance attached to the factors by the policymakers for the two different periods in time. Notably, there is considerable consensus between the two sample groups as indicated by the Spearman rank correlation coefficient, which was computed to be .7714. This is significant at the 5 percent level. Thus, the general implication here is that joint venture arrangements work to the advantage of both the multinational corporation and the less-developed country and should be used as a means of establishing positive perceptions of both parties.

METHOD OF OWNERSHIP

As a matter of policy and practice, MNCs tend to show a strong preference for the retention of full ownership and control of direct foreign investment. At least this is the impression one gets from casual observation of international enterprise. The resistance multinationals have shown towards sharing equity in direct investment with host country entrepreneurs has made ownership and management control perhaps the most controversial issue in the MNC–Third World relationship. It is responsible to a large degree for much of the resentment felt towards multinational corporations by developing countries. The host country constantly faces the arduous task of balancing aspiration for greater equity and control with efforts to maintain as many as possible of the benefits that accrue from direct private foreign investment. Local officials perhaps fear that the practical reality of the matter is that benefits to the host country may be directly related to MNC control. In other words, the greater the control of local ventures by MNCs, the greater the benefits to local interests. But there appears to be a great deal of uncertainty on this issue. Many Third World nations argue that there is an inverse relationship between corporate control and benefits accruing to the host country. In fact they often cite this as a major contributor to the "inequality gap" between rich and poor countries.

The survey results on the ownership issue are very interesting. Participants were given a list of methods of ownership in direct foreign investment (see Exhibit 5.2) and asked to indicate whether the method of ownership would increase or reduce resentment felt towards MNCs by host countries. In terms of overall response, participants in both surveys felt that majority ownership by the host country would serve to reduce resentment more so than any other item listed. However, this was far more evident in 1980. The weighted average rating of 1.69 for that period

Exhibit 5.2
Comparative Attitude Profile
Method of Ownership and Resentment Towards MNCs by LDCs
Weighted Average Rating and Ranking

Factors	Rating		Ranking	
	1980	*1994*	*1980*	*1994*
Majority ownership by LDCs	1.69	2.47	1	1
Minority ownership by LDCs	2.71	2.95	6	6
Majority ownership by MNCs	3.63	3.48	7	8
Minority ownership by MNCs	2.41	2.73	2	3
Sole ownership by MNCs	4.21	3.27	8	7
Equal ownership by MNCs and LDCs	2.50	2.68	4	2
Joint ownership by LDCs and MNCs from Other LDCs	2.42	2.87	3	5
Joint ownership by LDCs, MNCs from other LDCs, and MNCs from DCs [Developed Countries]	2.51	2.82	5	4

suggests that the preference for majority ownership by LDCs was virtually at the center of thought on this issue. Multinational as well as host country leaders were apparently in very close concurrence on the importance of LDC majority ownership in the not too distant past. Though this feeling has subsided to some extent, the weighted average rating of 2.47 in 1994 suggests that there remains reasonably strong agreement among the multinational and host country leaders. This is further underscored by the first place ranking of this factor for both periods.

Two of the methods of ownership are perceived as having a negative effect on MNC–host country relations: majority ownership by the MNC and sole ownership by the MNC. These methods were ill advised in 1980 and remain so today. They are ranked last among the method of ownership factors in both surveys. Minority ownership by MNCs and equal ownership by MNCs and LDCs are perceived to be as effective in reducing resentment based on their weighted average ratings for 1980 and 1994. The rankings suggest that these methods of ownership could be readily substituted for the higher ranked option particularly in cases where the ownership issue involves stringent negotiation.

Consensus on the method of ownership issue between the policymakers in 1980 and 1994 was quite high. The Spearman rank correlation coefficient was computed to be .8571, which is significant at the 1 percent level. Policymakers in the two surveys attach major importance to the method of ownership used in the MNC–host country relationship. While they prefer majority ownership by the host country, they would be content with equal ownership particularly in today's environment.

GOVERNMENT CODES AND BUSINESS PRACTICES

Efforts to improve MNC-LDC relations must place significant focus on government codes and business practices. There are numerous factors that must be considered to achieve necessary restructuring of codes and practices. Policymakers were asked to rate 15 factors in terms of degree of importance in improving MNC-LDC relations. The results are presented in Exhibit 5.3. Several results are noteworthy. Policymakers felt that four factors in particular weigh rather heavily in improving the relationship. Creation of a more favorable investment climate, liberalization of foreign exchange regulations, removal of barriers to capital flows, and enactment of codes that enable MNCs to know their legal status were given high marks in both surveys. In fact, the results for 1980 and 1994 for all practical purposes are mirror images of each other. The weighted average ratings ranging from 1.49 to 1.70 in 1980 and 1.44 to 1.64 in 1994 suggest a heavy emphasis on policies that address these factors. The rankings of these factors above all of the others considered evidence their tremendous importance to the MNC-LDC relationship.

Exhibit 5.3
Comparative Attitude Profile
Government Codes and Business Practices
Weighted Average Rating and Ranking

Factors	Rating		Ranking	
	1980	*1994*	*1980*	*1994*
Removal of barriers to capital flows by LDCs	1.59	1.58	3	3
Creation of more favorable investment climate	1.49	1.44	2	1
Enactment of codes that enable MNCs to know their legal status	1.60	1.64	4	4
Liberalization of foreign exchange regulations	1.70	1.46	5	2
MNCs conform to local business practices	1.81	2.14	6	8
Identifying the interest of MNCs with the interest of LDCs	2.23	2.05	10	6
Disclosure of MNCs' costs and profits to LDCs	2.92	2.63	13	12
Disclosure of MNCs' economic benefits to LDCs	2.20	2.34	9	9
Decentralization of authority to LDC national management	2.01	2.53	7	10
Performance of research and development in LDCs	2.31	2.61	11	11
Programs for increasing LDCs' national personnel into the management of joint ventures	1.40	2.10	1	7
Listing of MNCs' securities for trading in LDCs	3.31	3.19	15	14
Establishing stock-ownership loans for LDC employees	2.90	3.42	12	15
Increased receptivity to form joint ventures	2.18	1.98	8	5
Association with the Center for the Settlement of Investment Disputes	3.02	2.76	14	13

In two instances the policymakers accorded little importance to efforts that might be regarded as useful in improving MNC-LDC relations. They were not favorably disposed to establishing stock-ownership loans for LDC employees nor the listing of MNCs' securities for trading in LDCs. These were not important issues in 1980 nor are they important today. One explanation for this finding may be that since capital markets are not well developed in Third World countries or lack the sophistication necessary to accommodate the broad needs of multinational corporations, security trading is not a priority particularly in the context of other more pressing issues. It is, however, rather striking that so little importance was attached to the establishment of stock-ownership loans for local employees. Conceivably, this would be beneficial to both the corporation and the employees. On the one hand, stock ownership would tend to improve employee loyalty and increase productivity. Yet at the same time, employees would be able to share the prosperity of the corporation. But policymakers show little concern in this regard. These factors are ranked at the bottom of the list. Surprisingly, disclosure of costs and profits to LDCs is also viewed as rather unimportant to the relationship by policymakers. This is quite perplexing since MNCs have long been accused of transfer pricing improprieties. Disclosure of costs and profits is central to any efforts geared toward monitoring transfer-pricing practices.

Consensus between the sample groups on the wide range of factors affecting government codes and business practices was remarkably high. The Spearman rank correlation coefficient was computed to be .8286, which is significant at the 1 percent level. The findings offer a clear indication of what factors should be emphasized in structuring government codes and business practices that promote better business relations between MNCs and LDCs.

LABOR RELATIONS AND PERSONNEL TRAINING

Host countries accuse MNCs of being insensitive to the needs and dynamics of the local labor market. They argue that expatriate labor is paid considerably higher salaries than indigenous employees; training programs are mostly inadequate; MNCs have tended to resist forming joint ventures and have avoided complete technology transfer; and many MNCs often introduce inappropriate technology. Further, according to host countries the sheer size and sophistication of MNCs enable them to monopolize local markets and appropriate rents thereby discouraging local entrepreneurship. Policymakers in the surveys were asked to rate a number of factors which have been identified as important in ameliorating these vexing issues. The resulting comparative attitude profile is presented in Exhibit 5.4. The policymakers in both surveys indicate that increased local employment resulting from MNC presence has had a more positive effect on host country receptivity than any of the other factors listed. As expected, employment is always a top priority issue and the results for 1980 and 1994 confirm that this is indeed the case. The level of employment in Third World countries has increased substantially as a result of direct foreign investment. Providing labor training is also viewed as engendering a very favorable opinion of multinationals. Consistent with the training of the general labor force is the finding that management training for local personnel is an important objective.

Survey results also indicate that the introduction of inappropriate technology damages the MNCs' image in the Third World and has a very negative impact on the receptivity of multinationals by the indigenous population. Weighted average ratings of 3.89 and 3.66 in the two respective surveys clearly underscore this finding. This factor was ranked last

Exhibit 5.4
Comparative Attitude Profile
Labor Relations and Personnel Training
Weighted Average Rating and Ranking

Factors	Rating		Ranking	
	1980	*1994*	*1980*	*1994*
Increase LDC employment	1.61	1.41	1	1
Provide labor training in LDCs	1.79	1.46	3	2
Promote labor relations in LDCs	2.30	1.86	7	7
Improve labor communications in LDCs	2.31	1.98	8	8
Improve labor benefits in LDCs	2.00	1.67	5	4
Provide management training in LDCs	1.90	1.61	4	3
Provide MNC management expertise	1.71	1.82	2	6
Opening of international–communication channels	2.21	1.72	6	5
Introduction of inappropriate technology by MNCs	3.89	3.66	11	11
MNCs' effect on local economic policy	2.81	2.47	9	9
MNCs' effect on economic control	3.49	3.02	10	10

among those listed in both 1980 and 1994 further punctuating its pejorative influence on the relationship.

The findings also suggest that the policymakers take a dim view of any impingement on local economic policy or control of internal development by multinationals. The rating and ranking of these factors in both surveys clearly disclose the importance of maintaining control of the local economy by the host country. Any serious infringement by the multinational in this regard would damage the MNC–host country relationship.

The policymakers in both surveys were in close agreement on the impact of the employment and personnel training factors on MNC-LDC relations. The Spearman rank correlation coefficient was computed to be .9091, which is significant at the 1 percent level. With employment and labor related factors being tremendously important to the host country, relations between the host country and the multinational will invariably improve when these factors are given top priority.

CONCLUSION

This study was conducted with hopes of assisting MNCs and Third World policymakers in formulating strategies that promote reciprocity and harmony between multinationals and host countries. The high level of consensus between the sample groups regarding the wide range of factors considered important in improving the MNC–host country relationship lend well to this objective. The results will hopefully serve as a basis for developing new policies, modifying those that do not meet current expectations and expunging altogether ineffective ones.

With ever changing attitudes about risk and return on the MNC's part and inequitable sharing in the benefits of direct foreign investment on the host country's part, the potential for dispute is ever present. Staying abreast of the evolving relationship between multinational corporations and Third World countries is essential to the promotion of long standing harmony in the global marketplace.

NOTES

1. For empirical studies specifically relating to multinational enterprise and the Third World, see European Round Table of Industries (1993). *Survey on improvement of conditions for investment in the developing world.* Brussels, Belgium: European Round Table of Industrialists; Franklin R. Root (1968). Attitudes of American executives toward foreign government and investment opportunities. *Economic and Business Bulletin,* 20, 15–23; Ashok Kapoor and James E. Cotten (1972). *Foreign investments in Asia.* Princeton, New Jersey: The Darwin Press; and Ashok Kapoor (1975). *Foreign investments and the new Middle East.* Princeton, New Jersey: The Darwin Press.

2. H. Crookell (1975). Investing in development—a corporate view. *Columbia Journal of World Business.*

3. See Donald S. Tull and Gerald S. Albaum (1973). *Survey research: A decisional approach.* New York: Intext Educational Publishers, 120–123; and E. Laird Landon, Jr. (1971). Order bias, the ideal rating, and the semantic differential. *Journal of Marketing Research,* 8, 375–378.

4. See Irving Crespi (1961). Use of a scaling technique in surveys. *Journal of Marketing,* 25, 69–72.

5. Ibid., 69.

6. Ibid., 70.

7. See Donald Tull and Gerald Albaum, ibid., 121.

8. Ibid.

9. See Irving Crespi ibid., 70.

CHAPTER 6

Multinationals in the Third World: Reciprocity, Conflict Resolution and Economic Policy Formulation*

This chapter is essentially an extension of Chapter 5. They are very closely aligned in purpose, and the content in the first half of the two presentations is essentially replicated, except that Chapter 5 reflects both 1980 and 1994 survey results. This chapter benefits from an added dimension resulting from questions regarding whether specified activities are being practiced and to what extent. Further, this presentation is expanded to include review and analysis of a wider range of issues, using 1994 survey results throughout, to provide more extensive insight into the relationship between multinational corporations and Third World nations. The underlying desire here continues to be development of a perspective on how an assault on the inequality gap might be orchestrated through MNC–host country relations.

INTRODUCTION

The pursuit of business objectives by multinational corporations in the Third World is often at odds with development objectives of Third World nations. With New World Order precepts[1] calling for new arrangements in MNC–Third World business relations, roles traditionally played by both parties will likely undergo significant adjustment. Reaching common ground upon which to build future relations will be problematic

*Reprinted with permission. Benjamin F. Bobo and Lawrence S. Tai, "Multinationals in the Third World: Reciprocity, Conflict Resolution and Economic Policy Formulation," *Journal of the Third World Spectrum* 3, no. 1 (Spring 1996).

and, if ill conceived, will occasion perhaps avoidable conflict. There is a pressing need for identification of problem areas and prospects for conflict resolution, given the constantly changing social, economic and political environment.

Aspects of the MNC–Third World relationship have been extensively examined in the literature.[2] What has been discovered that is perhaps key to understanding the relationship is that in many ways it is dynamic and constantly changing. It must be continually appraised to afford intelligent decision-making about needed changes and modifications so as to promote greater harmony between the corporation and the host government.

Accomplishing even reasonable success in addressing, for example, the New World Order attitude, will require an ongoing compilation of broad-based strategic information that permits the rationalization and development of broad ground rules yet specific enough to make possible the operationalization of New World Order precepts. At the very basis of this initiative is the development of foreign investment policies that are fully reciprocating and sensitive to the full range of needs of both the multinational and the host country.

But should the policies of all MNCs be the same toward all Third World nations, and vice versa? Crookell (1975) has suggested that Third World nations should differentiate between types of foreign investment based on whether the firm is oriented toward exports or toward engaging in local market development.[3] Given the complexity of international investment and negotiating processes, differentiation decisions could conceivably require matrix analysis in some cases. What this means essentially is that the complexity of international business: enterprise may be too enormous to allow desirable specificity in any single empirical examination of the MNC–Third World relationship; specific policies would have to be developed on a case by case and country by country basis.

But a broad-based empirical exploration of major issues surrounding direct private foreign investment in developing countries particularly as related to improving the relationship between multinational corporations and Third World nations could provide a premise for generating intelligent overall policy guidelines to govern MNC–Third World relations, as well as specific policies as the need arises. With this in mind, an MNC–Third World survey was conducted to ascertain current attitudes about and perceptions of the interaction of multinational corporations and Third World nations. Further, since popular beliefs in the marketplace may encourage misconceptions about foreign enterprise, this survey offers a useful means of developing informed opinion through assessing the perception of top-level government and corporate leaders, the decision makers who give final approval on direct foreign investment policies.

METHODOLOGY AND DATA COLLECTION

One hundred and four questions were asked concerning factors germane to improving the MNC–Third World relationship. It is hoped that the wide range of matters addressed will help bring us closer to the creation of a harmonious international business environment.

The primary data presented here are based on the responses of 62 participants in the survey conducted during 1994. Questionnaires were sent to chief executive officers of Fortune 500 companies, heads of state, ambassadors and congressional leaders. The study sample comprises, therefore, leaders of large industrial corporations with extensive international experience that in the aggregate account for a substantial share of U.S. direct investment in the Third World. It also includes political leaders who have the ultimate responsibility for setting international business policy. Thus, while the number of responses may appear small it is important to recognize that the respondents are among the world's key policymakers and power brokers and therefore are expressing more than mere opinion, but the desire and ability to change existing policies and policymaking processes which they actually undertake in the real world. So the real significance of these respondents can be seen in the fact that they not only talk about what can be done, but also directly influence and set forth what is done.

The respondents were asked to indicate the significance of each survey question in the context of the MNC–Third World relationship. Often this type of survey research is one-dimensional in that it is limited to obtaining only the degree of significance with little or no indication of what is actually taking place in the real world. This study offers an added dimension by asking the respondents whether the various activities as indicated by the questions are being practiced and moreover, to what extent. This will enhance the policy maker's ability to formulate strategies that encourage greater reciprocity between the multinational corporation and the host government by adding policies that don't exist, improving those that fall short of expectations or deleting altogether undesirable ones.

DATA MEASUREMENT AND ANALYSIS

The survey instrument was segmented into 12 areas of inquiry each designed to elicit views on a range of issues concerning the MNC–Third World relationship. Respondents were given a series of phrases that describe attitudes about various aspects of the relationship. To rate the responses, a verbal rating scale ranging from such verbal measurements as strongly agree to strongly disagree, strongly reduce to strongly increase, extremely important to never important, extremely positive to extremely negative, and much practice to some practice. In some cases, no opinion, no influence or no impact was included as part of the scale range. When responses were coded for data analysis, verbal ratings were assigned numerical ratings, e.g., strongly agree = 1, agree = 2, no opinion = 3, disagree = 4, strongly disagree = 5. "No opinion" is assigned a location between agree and disagree because (a) it is generally standard procedure in descriptive rating scales type analysis, and (b) "no opinion" is neither a positive or negative response, nor is it equivalent to a no response; therefore, it logically fits between agree (which is positive) and disagree (which is negative). Thus, in such case the numbers 1 and 2 are interpreted as positive responses, 3 as neutral or uncertain, and 4 and 5 as negative responses. This technique measures direction and intensity simultaneously. The responses for each verbal measurement were summed for all of the respondents and multiplied by the respective verbal rating. A weighted average rating was then computed for each question. Since the sample included four independent categories of policymakers, the weighted average is not distorted by views expressed by any single category.

Further, in most cases respondents were asked whether certain activities are being practiced and to what extent. To rate these responses, a verbal rating scale using much, some and little was employed and converted to a numerical rating scale of 1, 2 and 3, respectively. Here again a weighted average rating was computed.

ATTITUDE PROFILE

When the weighted average ratings of the individual responses were computed, the results produced profiles that show the representative attitudes of the policymakers regarding direct foreign investment, economic policy formulation and conflict resolution. Attitude profiles are presented in Exhibits 6.1 through 6.9.

JOINT VENTURES

Participants were asked to respond to a list of statements, about the relationship of multinational corporations and less-developed countries (LDCs) concerning joint ventures. As Exhibit 6.1 indicates, the question engendered a range of responses. Overall, the respondents regard joint ventures as having a positive influence on the creation of greater reciprocity among MNCs and developing countries. However, there seems to be a small amount of uncertainty about whether joint ventures result in trading off efficiency for equity suggesting that this form of direct foreign investment may be somewhat problematic for the multinational corporation. But since the weighted average rating of 3.02 only indicates

Exhibit 6.1
Attitude Profile
Impact of Joint Ventures on MNC-LDC Relations
Weighted Average Rating

Factors	Extent of Agreement
Reducing national resentment felt towards MNCs	2.03
Creating an aura of greater reciprocity among MNCs and LDCs	2.14
Legitimizing MNCs' activities	2.49
Less threatening to LDCs	2.37
Shifting control from MNCs to LDCs	2.98
Trading off efficiency for equity	3.02
Making MNCs more socially responsible	2.71

a very minor problem, there is no strong justification for a rejection of equity positions for foreign nationals. Further, because the other factors weigh rather substantially in favor of joint ventures, the efficiency issue becomes even less a factor in the MNC's decision to undertake this form of investment.

The role of joint ventures in reducing national resentment towards MNCs and also in creating a greater spirit of reciprocity appears to be quite significant. The weighted average ratings of 2.03 and 2.14, respectively, indicate that the policymakers are in fairly strong agreement on these matters. The general attitude in the marketplace is that joint ventures offer host countries an opportunity to more directly influence MNC operations. As such, host countries apparently are more inclined to welcome direct foreign investment as revealed by the policymakers' responses.

On the matter of legitimizing MNC activities, the policymakers tend to agree that joint ventures have a positive impact. The weighted average rating of 2.49 might however suggest a small amount of uncertainty. This perhaps should be expected since joint ventures particularly in Latin America have not been necessarily effective in reducing suspicion of illegitimate practices or indeed illegitimate practices by multinational corporations. Latin America has had a more extensive and complex history of involvement with MNCs than other Third World regions; it is the primary recipient of U.S. direct foreign investment.[4] Expropriation of foreign assets there has been more striking than elsewhere in the Third World. The less than full agreement among the policymakers is perhaps a reflection of Latin America's experiences with such multinationals as ITT [International Telephone and Telegraph Corporation] and Anaconda.

Generally, the respondents agree that joint ventures are less threatening to developing countries than other forms of direct foreign investment. But they are not as certain that MNCs are more socially responsible or that control is shifted to the host country as a result of joint ventures. However, since the respective weighted average ratings of 2.37, 2.71 and 2.98 show reasonable agreement that joint ventures have a positive impact on these factors, the relationship between MNCs and LDCs is well served by sharing ownership.

METHOD OF OWNERSHIP

As a matter of policy and practice, MNCs prefer to retain full ownership and control of direct foreign investment. The multinationals have shown resistance towards sharing equity in direct investment with the host country, which has made ownership perhaps the most controversial issue in the MNC–Third World relationship. It is responsible to a large degree for much of the resentment felt towards multinational corporations by developing countries. The host country faces the unenviable task of balancing aspirations for greater equity and control with efforts to maintain as many as possible of the benefits that accrue from direct foreign investment. Local policymakers fear that the practical reality of the matter is that benefits to the host country may be directly related to MNC control. In other words, the greater the control of local ventures by MNCs, the more inclined they are to, for example, engage in state-of-the-art technology transfer. But there appears to be mixed emotions on this issue. Many Third World nations argue that there is an inverse relationship between corporate control and benefits accruing to the host country. In fact they often cite this as a major contributor to the "inequality gap" between rich and poor countries.

The survey results on the ownership issue are very interesting. Participants were given a list of methods of ownership in direct foreign investment (see Exhibit 6.2) and asked to indicate whether the method of ownership would increase or reduce resentment felt towards MNCs by host countries. In terms of overall response, participants felt that majority ownership by the host country would serve to reduce resentment more so than any other item listed. However, since majority ownership by the host country would tend to discourage full technology transfer and other benefits that the MNC has to offer, the host country is faced with making necessary tradeoffs between benefits and ownership. Majority ownership by the host country invariably dampens the corporation's desire to fully engage the direct investment process.

Two of the methods of ownership are perceived as having a negative effect on MNC–host country relations: majority ownership by the MNC and sole ownership by the MNC. The displeasure that host countries hold for these methods of ownership appears not to be abated by the willingness of the MNC to provide greater benefits in return for ownership control.

Exhibit 6.2
Attitude Profile
Method of Ownership and Resentment Towards MNCs by LDCs
Weighted Average Rating

Factors	Extent of Practice	Degree of Impact
Majority ownership by LDCs	1.94	2.47
Minority ownership by LDCs	2.04	2.95
Majority ownership by MNCs	1.62	3.48
Minority ownership by MNCs	2.27	2.73
Sole ownership by MNCs and LDCs	2.04	3.27
Equal ownership by MNCs and LDCs	2.36	2.68
Joint ownership by LDCs and MNCs from other LDCs	2.60	2.87
Joint ownership by LDCs, MNCs from other LDCs, and MNCs from DCs [Developed Countries]	2.52	2.82

Minority ownership by MNCs and equal ownership by MNCs and LDCs are perceived to be about equally effective in reducing resentment.

Respondents were also asked to indicate whether the methods of ownership are practiced and to what extent. For the most part, majority ownership by MNCs is the prevailing practice. But since it is perceived as increasing resentment by the host country (weighted average rating of 3.48), this form of ownership will likely persist as a source of dissension between the multinationals and local policymakers. Interestingly, there is some majority ownership by LDCs. But this perhaps mostly involves sensitive natural resources, telecommunications or national security ventures. The policymakers agree that equal ownership by MNCs and LDCs would reduce resentment, but this form of ownership is little practiced.

CONTRIBUTIONS, EXPECTATIONS
AND SOURCES OF CONFLICT

Undoubtedly MNCs have much to contribute to economic growth and expansion in developing nations. Indeed much is expected by host countries in this regard. Matching the contributions made by multinationals with expectations held by host countries will surely evolve as a source of conflict between the two parties. To expand our perspective on this matter, policymakers were given a list of statements regarding contributions made by MNCs and expectations of LDCs including problem areas that are sources of conflict and asked to indicate the extent to which they agree on each statement.

In a positive vein, several statements received high marks, as reported in Exhibit 6.3, in terms of their reduction of conflict in the MNC-LDC relationship. When asked if MNCs and LDCs can resolve friction and co-exist in a manner conducive to the mutual satisfaction of both parties, the weighted average rating of 1.80 indicates that there is indeed a general feeling that the interaction between these parties can be harmonious and successful. It is very likely that this view leads to a strong attraction of MNCs to LDCs. In fact, when asked if LDCs are attracting MNCs, policymakers responded very positively. This attraction has been aided by the willingness of multinationals to pursue joint venture arrangements in host countries. Such arrangements are believed to have moderated the tendency by host countries to nationalize MNC assets. This is supported by the policymakers' very positive response to the statement that joint ventures are moderating economic nationalist pressures in LDCs. Further, MNCs are expected to be facilitators in creating new modes of interaction within which advancements in investment policies and practices can be made. This view is fully shared by the policymakers in responding quite affirmatively that MNCs are initiators of change in the MNC-LDC relationship.

Even though MNCs are viewed as initiators of change, there have been some questions about whether the MNC–host country relationship largely adjusts on its own to evolving market conditions. Policymakers were asked if the MNC-LDC relationship is a self-adjusting mechanism that readily adapts in response to market changes. The survey results revealed a weighted average rating of 2.84, indicating that there was a measure of uncertainty about this issue. This might suggest that while there is an impression among the policymakers that there are self-adjusting forces operating in the Third World environment, these forces are not sufficiently strong to do the job alone; hence, the feeling that MNCs must assist the process as change agents.

It is helpful to recognize here that multinational executives, as a segment of the survey respondents, are "free market" oriented. As such they view the interaction of business and society as largely a self-adjusting mechanism, vis-à-vis the operation of market forces. Therefore, they expect market forces to signal the need for necessary changes in MNC operating policies and practices in the Third World. In this respect, the survey result should not be surprising since corporate executives perhaps do not feel as strongly about their role as independent change agents as Third World policymakers would expect.

Several issues in the survey met with considerable disagreement by the policymakers. When confronted with the statement that MNCs threaten the national security of the host country, they responded with a weighted average rating of 3.87, the highest in this segment of the survey. This clear rejection of any threat by MNCs to host country security can be presumed a statement of unwavering support for the presence of multinational

Exhibit 6.3
Attitude Profile
Contributions, Expectations and Sources of Conflict
Weighted Average Rating

Factors	Extent of Agreement
LDCs prefer MNCs from other LDCs over MNCs from DCs	3.51
Investments by MNCs from LDCs are less threatening to the host LDC than investments by MNCs from DCs	3.42
The MNC-LDC relationship is a self-adjusting mechanism that readily adapts in response to environmental changes	2.84
The local portion of a joint venture feels more LDC governmental pressure than the MNC portion	2.89
Foreign investments are natural compliments to foreign government aid programs	2.93
Divestment agreements prior to investment created greater harmony between MNCs and LDCs	2.56
Joint ventures are moderating economic nationalist pressures in LDCs	2.31
Foreign investors are becoming more politically nonpartisan	2.76
MNCs assist LDCs in pursuing their national goals	2.61
MNCs have stimulated a revolution among LDCs toward acceptance of MNCs	2.84
There is a harmonization of policies of taxation, trade, antimonopoly, labor and regulatory laws of LDCs with the more developed countries	2.80
The harmonization is from LDC influence	3.05
The harmonization is from MNC influence	2.44
MNCs' investment selection would be better made if LDCs had more input into the decision-making and selection process	2.96
The lack of provision of relevant data on operations and activities of MNCs create resentment by national LDC businesses	2.69
LDCs are attracting MNCs	1.96
National political risk insurance programs are aiding in creating greater faith among MNCs and LDCs	2.33
MNCs and LDCs can resolve friction and co-exist in a manner conducive to the mutual satisfaction of both parties	1.80
LDCs would expect economic stagnation without MNCs	2.76
LDCs would experience greater political instability without MNCs	3.17
More MNC facilities should be located in rural rather than urban areas	2.74
The degree of subsidiary control is more important than the degree of subsidiary ownership	2.56
MNCs are initiators of change in MNC-LDC relationships	2.31
MNCs threaten the national security of the host country	3.87
Discouragement of local entrepreneurship	3.70
Creation of oligopoly patterns in small national markets	3.06

enterprise in Third World countries. Their disagreements with the statement that multinationals discourage local entrepreneurship was also resounding. Contrary to popular belief, multinationals encourage local entrepreneurship through creating a demand for local supply of parts and services used by multinationals in the production process.

The policymakers also disagreed strongly with the proposition that Third World countries prefer multinationals from other developing countries to multinationals from developed countries. This response should not be unexpected since rationality would suggest that a preference should be shown for the multinationals that can better support the goals and objectives of the host country. Is it not the case that multinationals from developed countries on the whole are far more financially and economically able to promote economic growth and development in Third World countries than those from developing countries? Interestingly, the policymakers also disagreed substantially that investments by multinationals from developing countries are less threatening than investments by multinationals from developed countries. With considerable emotional fervor against developed countries in the Third World sector, one might question this response. But in reality all firms seek to maximize shareholders wealth. Why then would a firm from a developing country be any less inclined to pursue every opportunity available to achieve this objective than one from a developed country? Apparently the policymakers take this more academic approach to addressing the statement. Of course it is recognized that the emotional perspective should be taken into consideration in that host countries feel a greater degree of comfort with those countries with which they are more familiar.

GOVERNMENT CODES AND BUSINESS PRACTICES

Notwithstanding the views of policymakers on the independent role of corporate executives as change agents, there are numerous factors that may be helpful in bringing about changes in the conduct of international enterprise. Policymakers were asked to rate 17 factors in terms of degree of importance and extent of practice in improving MNC-LDC relations. The results are presented in Exhibit 6.4. Selected results are noteworthy. Policymakers felt that four factors in particular weigh rather heavily in improving the relationship. Creation of a more favorable investment climate, liberalization of foreign exchange regulations, removal of barriers to capital flows, and enactment of codes that enable MNCs to know their legal status were given high marks. Their weighted average ratings are 1.44, 1.46, 1.58 and 1.64, respectively. The importance of these factors is also underscored by the extent to which they are being practiced in the Third World marketplace. The weighted average ratings in this category, ranging from 1.40 to 1.66, suggest a heavy emphasis on policies that address these matters.

Exhibit 6.4
Attitude Profile
Government Codes and Business Practices
Weighted Average Rating

Factors	Extent of Practice	Degree of Impact
Removal of barriers to capital flows by LDCs	1.40	1.58
Creation of more favorable investment climate	1.44	1.44
Enactment of codes that enable MNCs to know their legal status	1.66	1.64
Application of uniform rules to both domestic corporations and MNCs	1.94	2.02
Liberalization of foreign exchange regulations	1.58	1.46
MNCs conform to local business practices	1.69	2.14
Identifying the interest of MNCs with the interest of LDC	1.95	2.05
Disclosure of MNCs' costs and profits to LDCs	2.08	2.63
Disclosure of MNCs economic benefits to LDCs	1.90	2.34
Decentralization of authority to LDC national management	2.19	2.53
Performance of research and development in LDCs	2.29	2.61
Programs for increasing LDCs' national personnel into the management of joint ventures	1.94	2.10
Listing of MNCs' securities for trading in LDCs	2.34	3.19
Establishing stock-ownership loans for LDC employees	2.49	3.42
Increased receptivity to form joint ventures	1.84	1.98
Association with the Center for the Settlement of Investment Disputes	2.35	2.76
MNCs undertake initiatives to protect the environment	2.09	2.29

In two instances, the policymakers accorded little importance to efforts that might be regarded as useful in improving MNC-LDC relations. They were not favorably disposed to establishing neither stock-owner-ship loans for LDC employees nor the listing of MNCs securities for trad-ing in LDCs. Since capital markets are not well developed in Third World countries or lack the sophistication necessary to accommodate the broad needs of multinational corporations, security trading apparently is not a priority particularly in the context of other more pressing issues. It is, however, rather striking that so little importance was attached to the establishment of stock-ownership loans for local employees (weighted average rating of 3.42). Conceivably, this would be beneficial to both the corporation and the employees. On the one hand, stock ownership would tend to improve employee loyalty and increase productivity. Yet at the same time, employees would be able to share the prosperity of the corporation.

LABOR RELATIONS AND PERSONNEL TRAINING

Host countries have accused MNCs of being insensitive to the needs and dynamics of the local labor market. They have voiced many concerns in support of their accusation. For example, host countries charge that expatriate labor is paid considerably higher salaries than indigenous employees; training programs are mostly inadequate; MNCs have tended to resist forming joint ventures and have avoided complete technology transfer; and many MNCs often introduce inappropriate technology. Further, according to host countries, the sheer size and sophistication of MNCs enable them to monopolize local markets and appropriate rents thereby discouraging local entrepreneurship. Policymakers in the survey were asked to rate a number of factors, which have been identified as important in improving receptivity of MNCs by host countries. The resulting attitude profile is presented in Exhibit 6.5.

The policymakers indicated that increased local employment resulting from MNC presence has had a more positive effect on host country receptivity than any of the other factors listed. The level of employment in developing countries has increased substantially as a result of direct foreign investment. Providing labor training is also viewed as engendering a very favorable opinion of multinationals. This is being practiced a great deal in the host country. Consistent with the training of the general labor force is the finding that management training for local personnel is an important objective and is being practiced to some extent.

Exhibit 6.5
Attitude Profile
Labor Relations and Personnel Training
Weighted Average Rating

Factors	Extent of Practice	Degree of Impact
Increase LDC employment	1.41	1.41
Provide labor training in LDCs	1.53	1.45
Promote labor relations in LDCs	1.95	1.86
Improve labor communications in LDCs	1.87	1.98
Improve labor benefits in LDCs	1.71	1.67
Provide management training in LDCs	1.86	1.61
Provide MNC management expertise	1.53	1.82
Opening of international communication channels	1.88	1.72
Introduction of inappropriate technology by MNCs	2.45	3.66
MNCs' effect on local economic policy	2.11	2.47
MNCs' effect on economic control	2.42	3.02

Survey results also indicate that the introduction of inappropriate technology damages the MNCs image in the Third World and has a very negative impact on the receptivity of multinationals by the indigenous population. A weighted average rating of 3.66 clearly underscores this finding. Fortunately, according to the survey results, this is not widely practiced among multinational corporations.

TECHNOLOGY TRANSFER, INDUSTRIAL INFRASTRUCTURE AND IMPORT SUBSTITUTION

Technology transfer is arguably as important to the host country as that of jobs and training of local personnel. In fact, the policymakers indicated that the introduction of new products and new production methods by MNCs has a very positive impact on the MNC-LDC relationship. Moreover, the results presented in Exhibit 6.6 show a substantial emphasis on such investment practices as revealed by a weighted average rating of 1.76. This is consistent with the survey finding that MNCs seldom introduce inappropriate technology.

Through their emphasis on technology transfer, MNCs have been able to foster import substitution in the host countries, as the findings reveal, thereby lessening balance-of-payments problems so prevalent in the Third World. In the process, industrial infrastructure has undergone measurable improvement as multinationals have found it necessary to support efforts to modernize ports and expand ground transport and communication facilities to accommodate their production and distribution needs. The results from the survey strongly support the importance of technology transfer, import substitution and infrastructure development as means of introducing direct foreign investment and promoting harmony between MNCs and host countries. These findings are particularly interesting

Exhibit 6.6
Attitude Profile
Technology Transfer, Industrial Infrastructure and Import Substitution
Weighted Average Rating

Factors	Extent of Practice	Degree of Impact
MNC introduction of new products and new production methods and processes	1.76	1.63
MNCs materially add to LDCs' industrial infrastructure	1.93	1.54
MNCs help in increasing exports and import substitution	1.67	1.51
LDCs provide incentives and concessions to MNCs	1.86	1.72
LDCs adopt measures to cut red tape	2.22	1.70

because of their implications for overall economic growth in the host country. Industrial infrastructure improvement, for example, not only provides an upward lift to industrial growth but to commercial and agricultural expansion as well.

CULTURAL FACTORS AND SOCIAL RELATIONSHIPS

Familiarity with the host country's culture and social norms can be invaluable to multinational corporations. Such factors as language, religious beliefs, cultural values, and rate of literacy can in some cases actually determine the success of a direct foreign investment venture. The multinational must be sensitive to a range of conditions and peculiarities that may be unique to the local marketplace. Products manufactured for the local market may require special adaptation. Local customs may require work schedules not ordinarily followed in other corporate settings. The labor force may be inadequately trained to support labor requirements. Language barriers may impede the rate of project development in the short run and increase the cost of operations. Cultural values may preclude the application of certain management practices or the successful marketing of certain products. The structure of local social organizations may require adaptation to social norms unlike those found in the corporate organization or in the home country.

Policymakers were presented with a set of cultural factors as shown in Exhibit 6.7 and asked to indicate what effect MNC knowledge of them would have on improving the MNC-LDC relationship. Using a scale from 1 to 10 and 10 being an extremely positive effect, they felt that an understanding of cultural values and the social organization would be most helpful in developing a harmonious relationship. Both factors received a weighted average rating of 7.89, indicating that one is as important as the other in the context of MNC-LDC interaction. The importance of education and literacy to the success of direct foreign investment projects was

Exhibit 6.7
Attitude Profile
Cultural Factors and MNC-LDC Relationships
Weighted Average Rating

Factors	Extent of Practice
Language	7.63
Aesthetics	6.04
Education level	7.78
Religious beliefs	5.85
Cultural attitudes and values	7.89
Social organization and relationships	7.89

also highly valued by the policymakers. This was followed closely by knowledge of the host country's language as being helpful in encouraging a cooperative spirit. Interestingly, familiarity with local religious beliefs by corporate executives was viewed as having the least positive effect on MNC-LDC relations.

POLITICAL INFLUENCE AND DOMESTIC POLICY FORMULATION

There is much speculation in the marketplace about the influence of MNCs and, in a larger context, the U.S. government on domestic policy formulation in developing countries. To shed light on this matter, policymakers were asked to rate a list of factors associated with the general perspective of political influence and domestic policy formulation. The resulting weighted average ratings, as reported in Exhibit 6.8, indicate that joint venture arrangements and negotiated investment incentives are most often sources of positive influence by multinational corporations. This suggests that joint ventures and investment incentives that are highly regarded by host governments tend to encourage them to enact domestic policies that accommodate the desires of multinational corporations. However, popular belief is that multinationals tend to use their enormous power to influence domestic policy formulation when negotiating investment incentives and joint venture arrangements. Through the give-and-take of negotiations, host governments, it is said, are often persuaded to enact domestic policies that favor direct foreign investment. In other words, submitting to joint venture arrangements by MNCs might

Exhibit 6.8
Attitude Profile
Political Influence and Domestic Policy Formulation
Weighted Average Rating

Factors	Extent of Practice	Degree of Impact
MNC-LDC negotiated investment incentives	1.96	1.98
MNC stated investment incentives	1.90	2.40
Joint venture arrangements	1.94	2.06
Contributions to political campaigns	2.47	3.39
Philanthropic activities	2.14	1.98
Covert activities	2.54	3.75
United States government pressure	2.34	3.32
United States foreign aid	2.38	2.31
United States government negotiations	2.35	2.67

require local governments to, for example, liberalize foreign exchange regulations or eliminate corporate disclosure requirements.

There is further speculation that multinationals and the U.S. government influence domestic policy formulation through covert activities, political campaign contributions and government pressure. The policymakers quite adamantly agree that if such activities exist they would exert a very negative influence on domestic policy formulation. Covert activities received the highest weighted average rating of 3.75, which suggests that policymakers soundly renounce this approach as a means of promoting direct foreign investment. Contributions to political campaigns and U.S. government pressure are also ill advised as foreign investment promotion tools and are seen as destabilizing to the MNC-LDC relationship. On a positive note, such activities tend to be frowned upon by multinationals and the U.S. government as judged by their extent of practice.

NIEO AND THE NEW WORLD ORDER

New International Economic Order (NIEO) precepts have been the subject of debate over the past decade. There is some concern that the issues considered important in the NIEO doctrine have lost their appeal. Policymakers in the study were given a list of issues that were considered important in the earlier years and asked to indicate how important they are today. In the aggregate, the policymakers feel that past issues remain very important in the context of MNC–host country involvement. Not surprisingly, all of the issues were rated quite highly ranging from a weighted average rating of 2.04 to 2.63 as reported in Exhibit 6.9. At the top of the list was the dissolution of Third World debt. For quite some time, the general presumption in the marketplace has been that poor countries would like to have the enormous debt forgiven and start anew.

Exhibit 6.9
Attitude Profile
NIEO and the Present
Weighted Average Rating

Factors	Extent of Practice
A redistribution of world's wealth	2.40
The dissolution of Third World debt	2.04
An end to neo-colonialism	2.63
Equal decision-making powers in international economic bodies	2.56
An alteration of world trade, technology transfers and investments which would be more advantageous to LDCs	2.12

Today, Third World debt stands at more than one trillion dollars.[5] Clearly, this burden is so overwhelming that most developing countries are simply incapable of servicing it.

Further, the policymakers are quite sensitive to the issue concerning an alteration of world trade, technology and investments that would be more advantageous to LDCs. This response is consistent with our expectation since this issue involves worldwide commodity agreements, price stabilization, preferential tariffs, trade liberalization, and expansion of productive facilities, which are all matters of deep concern in the Third World. Any one of these, and certainly some combination, if arranged in favor of the LDCs, could assist enormously with debt abatement.

Highly rated too is the policymakers perception that the NIEO continues to call for a redistribution of the world's wealth. This too has generated considerable debate. Points of contention surround two questions: how will the industrialized world accommodate wealth redistribution, and how will the Third World conduct an equitable allocation of foreign investments among its member nations? Of the more than $ 100 billion of U.S. direct foreign investment in developing countries, two-thirds of it has gone to Latin America. If this trend continues, it will become very problematic for the Third World in terms of developing a process of real-locating the investment dollars on a fair share basis.

While wealth redistribution will clearly command a great deal of attention in future MNC-LDC interaction, interest surrounding the matter of equal decision-making powers in international economic bodies will also occupy much of the ongoing debate. A system of decision-making differentiated by wealth, status, political and economic power, and productive capability has emerged and is entrenched in the world economic order. Poorer nations are less able to influence major decisions about how the world economy is to function. And for that matter, the operation of local economies is often affected by decisions made in developed countries.

Policymakers were asked whether equal decision-making powers in international economic bodies remains a high priority among Third World countries. Based on a weighted average rating of 2.56, it appears that this matter is still highly regarded as a significant factor in direct foreign investment. But Third World participation in the making of major decisions concerning international investment selection can be a sensitive matter, especially for multinational corporations. Major decisions establish corporate policy wherein lies the control mechanism. Because MNCs are such a dominant force in the international marketplace, their corporate policy effectively controls the heartbeat of the world economy. Perhaps it is simply the case that if the relationship is to survive and prosper, the Third World must be an active part of the control mechanism. The current conditions of the world market may be the best rationalization for this.

CONCLUSIONS AND SUGGESTIONS
FOR FUTURE RESEARCH

Staying abreast of the evolving relationship between multinational corporations and Third World countries is essential to the promotion of long standing harmony in the global marketplace. Efforts by poor countries to close the "inequality gap" between them and developed countries place enormous pressure on MNCs not only to resolve the inequality problem but to do it at perhaps a far too unrealistic pace. At the same time, the multinational is predisposed to achieving its single most important objective, maximizing shareholders' wealth. These interests are characteristically nonconverging thereby occasioning conflict and disharmony in the MNC–host country relationship. With constantly changing attitudes about risk and return on the MNC's part and inequitable sharing in the benefits of direct foreign investment on the host country's part, the potential for dispute is ever present.

This study was conducted with hopes of updating information on the MNC–Third World relationship and assisting MNCs and Third World policymakers in formulating strategies that promote reciprocity and harmony between multinationals and host countries. The results will hopefully serve as a basis for developing new policies, modifying those that do not meet current expectations and expunging altogether ineffective ones.

In concluding the survey, policymakers were asked to share their specific thoughts about issues related to the MNC–Third World relationship that would serve as useful topics for future research. Many more than expected were suggested. The following are a few of the more frequently mentioned ones: sound central bank with a freely convertible currency; clear set of rules and regulations backed by an honest judicial system; systematic laws that promote direct foreign investments; job security, worker benefits and pensions; adequate definition of property rights; political corruption and economic liberalization.

NOTES

This research received the financial support of Loyola Marymount University, which is gratefully acknowledged. Stephanie Swanson provided research assistance, which enabled the timely completion of this work. As an extension of this research, the authors are planning an edited volume on MNC–Third World conflict resolution.

1. Towards closing the economic gap between developed countries and Third World nations, a New World Order has been proposed that calls for wealth redistribution, debt relief, sovereignty over natural resources, a code conduct for multinational corporations, agreements on commodities and prices, preferential tariffs and a speedier transfer of technology. For discussion of the New World Order doctrine, see Benjamin F. Bobo & Lawrence S. Tai (1994). Issues in North-South

Relations and the New World Order, paper presented at the 1st Annual Conference on Multinational Financial Issues. Camden, New Jersey: Rutgers University, June 2–4, 1994. See also Deepa Ollapally (1993). The South Looks North: The Third World in the New World Order. Current History, 92 (2), 175–179.

2. For empirical studies specifically relating to multinational enterprise and the Third World, see *Survey on Improvements of Conditions for Investment in the Developing World* (1993). Brussels, Belgium: European Round Table of Industrialists; Franklin R. Root (1968). Attitudes of American Executives Toward Foreign Government and Investment Opportunities. *Economic and Business Bulletin, 20*(2), 15–23; Ashok Kapoor and James E. Cotton (1972). *Foreign Investments in Asia.* Princeton, New Jersey: The Darwin Press; and Ashok Kapoor (1975). *Foreign Investments and the New Middle East.* Princeton, New Jersey: The Darwin Press.

3. H. Crookell (1975). Investing in Development—A Corporate View, *Columbia Journal of World Business.*

4. Two-thirds of American direct foreign investment in less developed countries is located in Latin America with book value equaling $77 billion in 1991. See Bobo and Tai, ibid., 16.

5. Bobo and Tai, ibid., 19–21. See also Roger D. Stone and Eve Hamilton (1991). *Global Economics and the Environment: Toward Sustainable Rural Development in the Third World.* New York: Council on Foreign Relations Press, 19; Sidney Weintraub (1979). The New International Economic Order: The Beneficiaries. *World Development, 7*(3), 251; and *World Bank Annual Report.* (1976). Washington, DC: World Bank, 101.

CHAPTER 7

Multinationals, the North and the New World Order: Objectives and Opportunities*

This chapter continues the dialogue on MNC–Third World relations using the international survey results to further deliberate the inequality gap issue. Importantly, this article formally initiates a discussion of specific prescriptive measures I believe are necessary to launching a direct assault on the inequality problem, hence the rich country–poor country dilemma. Various objectives of the new world order agenda are outlined in the context of articulating a set of important opportunities that could play a key role in tackling the problem of inequality. At this point, precise reference is made to the multinational as the change agent necessary to promote new world order objectives, and to two particularly prescriptive approaches to inequality remediation—a power sharing arrangement between MNC and host, and the *profit satisficing* approach to profit making.

In some circles, suggestion that multinational corporations and countries in the South continue to do business in a climate of disharmony is treated with less than a receptive ear. The cessation of the cold war between the superpowers, improvements in communications owing to advancements in information technology and greater access by all nations to world capital markets have supposedly brought about a very much

*Reprinted with permission. Benjamin F. Bobo,"Multinationals, the North and the New World Order: Objectives and Opportunities." *Proceedings of the International Management Development Association*, Fifth World Business Congress, 17–21 July, 1996, 107–114.

improved business environment within which the MNC and the Southern host interact. No doubt many positive changes have taken place in the global geopolitical climate and paths to the financial markets are more easily traveled than in the past. But the South, a composition of Third World nations, remains desperately in need of economic stimulus. The multinational corporation, having done business there for decades, has been unable to master this feat as expected by host nations. Though the multinational has not viewed its role with such magnanimity, the expectations of Third World hosts cannot be ignored. With their large natural resource reserves and tremendous consumer market potential, these nations conceivably hold the key to future market expansion by the multinational hence a source of job creation and export earnings for the North.

The disharmony referred to here stems not so much from what the multinational has done in its business pursuits in the Third World but what it has left undone. Clearly we can point to a host of contentious issues that punctuate the ongoing relationship; transfer pricing practices, ownership methods, taxing policies, technology transfer, and asset nationalization, among others. In a broader sense, however, disharmony stems from the failure of the MNC–Third World partnership to tackle a disturbingly persistent problem in the Third World—Poverty. By World Health Organization standards, upwards of two-thirds of the world's population are caught up in some stage of poverty with the most gripping and debilitating conditions found in the Third World (Meier, 1995, p. 3). Though the cure has been elusive, Third World nations are displeased with what they see as the multinational's ineffectiveness in fostering a course of change and adopting clear directives that produce desired results. While this may carry high expectations on the part of Third World nations, not surprisingly many observers of the situation see the multinational corporation as a force of change with the know-how and financial capacity to bring some semblance of parity between rich and poor. Indeed the corporate sector has played a very important and strategic role in upgrading living standards around the globe. But the Third World argues that it must do much more.

Third World nations are expressing their displeasure with the pace of poverty abatement through what is popularly termed the New World Order. Under this precept, they have put forth essentially a doctrine of redistribution. Their aim is to bring closure to the "inequality gap" between rich and poor nations and they believe that a redistribution of wealth must be the primary motivation of all players in the global economy particularly the multinational corporation. The inequality gap between rich and poor nations is a formidable obstacle to business relations and occasions an atmosphere of disharmony. Rising aspirations and expectations of the Third World must be taken seriously if any long-term relationship between the corporation and the host nation is to materialize.

With wealth redistribution at the top of the Third World agenda, a lack of serious initiative on this issue will not go unnoticed.

The multinational is in a unique position to provide needed leadership in facilitating wealth redistribution. It may be in the multinational's best interest to assume such a role for an especially important and obvious reason. Emerging Third World markets will be the source of lucrative future business opportunities, the successful cultivation of which will depend on the multinational's image in Third World nations. A serious promotion of wealth redistribution by multinationals would place them in a favorable light in the Third World community. But taking a leadership role will require the multinational to address a number of objectives that underlie the Third World's doctrine of redistribution and also pursue important opportunities available to it that will further promote the New World Order agenda.

OBJECTIVES

To speed the pace of achieving parity between rich and poor nations, Third World leaders have outlined a series of objectives that reveal their perception of how it may be accomplished. These include a program to relieve the huge debt that Third World nations have accumulated over time; an agreement by industrialized countries to provide preferential tariffs for Third World products; arrangements to stabilize commodity prices; technology transfer that accommodates the intellectual capacity of the local labor force with a timetable for full technology adaptation; and sovereignty over natural resources. The likelihood of redistributing the world's wealth and bringing closure to the inequality gap without firm commitment to these objectives is viewed by the Third World as highly improbable.

The need to pursue Third World objectives is perhaps best underscored by examining, for example, the U.S. direct investment position abroad. Exhibit 7.1 shows that the nineties began with more than sixty-five percent of U.S. direct foreign investment going to Europe and Canada. In 1991 alone, the United States placed nearly three hundred billion dollars in the European and Canadian sectors with only about half as much going to the rest of the world. This is particularly noteworthy since the data reveal a far greater emphasis on the industrialized community than on the developing world where the need is decidedly more acute and the population is infinitely larger. Such investment paucity in the Third World suggests that multinationals and the general investor community as well feel that investment opportunities there carry significantly higher risk than those elsewhere. Without challenging the validity of such behavior, fear of investing in the Third World can be abated and might well begin with efforts to address Third World debt. This is a primary objective of the

Exhibit 7.1
U.S. Direct Investment Position Abroad, 1991

Country/Region	$ Billions	% of Total
Canada	68.5	15.2
Europe	224.6	49.9
Africa	5.4	1.2
Latin America	77.3	17.2
Middle East	4.7	1.0
South Asia	25.2	5.6
East Asia and Oceania	41.3	9.2
Others	3.2	0.7
Total	450.2	100.0

Source: Benjamin F. Bobo & Lawrence S. Tai (1994). Topicos Sobre Las Relaciones Norte-Sur
Y El Nuevo Order Mundial (Issues in North-South Relations and the New World Order).
Revista de Contabilidad Y Auditoria, 25, 106; and *Statistical Abstract of the United States* (1993).
Washington, DC: Bureau of Statistics.

wealth redistribution agenda and if successfully tackled would do much
to change the perception of risk associated with Third World investment.

The external debt of Third World nations is becoming increasingly
overwhelming. The pattern of debt accumulation is rather striking,
increasing from $74 billion in 1970 to $151 billion in 1974 to $572 billion in
1980 to $952 billion in 1985 to $1388 billion in 1990. Though reasons for
such voluminous expansion in Third World debt are numerous, several
are particularly noteworthy in the context of this discussion (Nafziger,
1990, p. 379).

1. The international balance on goods and payments for Third World countries
   rose from a number of successive global shocks, including oil price increases
   from 1973 to 1974 and 1979 to 1980 which caused non–oil-producing Third
   World countries' terms of trade to decline, and the 1980 to 1983 OECD recession which exhibited dramatically falling commodity prices, reduced export
   expansion and increased OECD protectionism.
2. Restrictions on international trade and payments and overvalued domestic
   currencies contribute to capital flight from Third World countries, worsening
   the current account deficit and external debt problems.
3. Third World governments are required by international lenders to guarantee
   private debt, increasing public debt service.
4. Third World debt servicing has been exacerbated by the denomination of debts
   in U.S. dollars particularly when their appreciation or increased value relative
   to other major currencies increased the local and non-dollar currency cost of
   servicing the debt.

Many problems and conditions such as these over which Third World countries have no control severely restrict their capacity to service their debt. Leaders in the Third World want this taken fully into account in efforts to actualize the wealth redistribution agenda.

A part of Third World demands for a new world order include changes in the international trading system. Third World countries are focusing on tariffs as a further means of balancing world wealth. Invariably discussion on tariffs invoke the doctrine of comparative advantage. Theory underlying comparative advantage states that world welfare is maximized when each country exports products whose comparative costs are lower at home than abroad and imports goods whose comparative costs are lower abroad than at home. Comparative advantage may be based on technological advantage whereby a new product or production process gives a country a temporary monopoly in the world market until other countries absorb the technology and are able to imitate. This is supported by the product cycle model, which indicates that technology subsumed in higher skilled labor in the beginning of a product cycle is later transferred to less skilled labor as markets grow and techniques become common knowledge. As such, a good becomes standardized so that less-sophisticated countries can produce the product with less skilled labor. Consequently, advanced economies have a comparative advantage in the production of non-standardized goods and developing countries are said to have a comparative advantage in the production of standardized goods (Nafziger, 1990; Meier, 1995; Krugman, 1986).

The comparative advantage doctrine has not represented well the participation of Third World countries in world markets. Success has come in only a few cases and then for limited product categories. Even when Third World nations are able to produce standardized goods, penetration of the markets of advanced economies by products manufactured in the Third World is often compromised by tariff barriers. Tariff rates are much higher on labor-intensive goods in which developing countries are more likely to have a comparative advantage. These restrictions produce the usual price effects making Third World products uncompetitive in world markets. This is the prevailing result even under the operation of the Generalized System of Tariff Preferences (GSP), adopted by the developed countries in the late 1960s, by which tariffs on selected imports from developing countries are lower than those offered to other countries. The GSP has been rather ineffective owing to its limited nature. For the European Community, the GSP covers a little more than 20 percent of the total value of merchandise imports from developing countries; for the United States it is around 12 percent (low-income countries account for only about 1.0 percent); and for all OECD countries it hovers around 7 percent (Nafziger, 1990). E. Wayne Nafziger comments, "Thus far GSP benefits have been modest, but expanding the scheme could make for more rapid LDC industrial export growth. . . . LDCs were hurt by renewed DC protectionist policies during the 1980 to 1982 international recession and in subsequent years. The increased tariffs and other trade restrictions DCs used to divert demand to domestic production especially hurt LDC primary and light manufacturing export expansion" (Nafziger, 1990, p. 404).

As a counter measure, Third World nations are demanding expanded preferential tariffs in industrialized countries for manufactured products from the Third World. They want the Generalized System of Tariff Preferences modified to place a broader emphasis on merchandise imports from developing countries with a greater volume of activity. Tariff restraint and special tariff policies that assist the competitive ability of Third World products in world markets will produce a significant change in the international trading system and make a serious contribution to the wealth redistribution agenda. Without special tariff policies, and not just of a limited nature, any hope of substantively sharing the tremendous wealth of markets in developed countries may be lost to the Third World.

Further change in the international trading system is seen as necessary by poorer countries to foster wealth redistribution and they have targeted commodity price stabilization. Of primary interest are worldwide commodity agreements, including producer cartels to stabilize commodity prices, with prices indexed to the cost of industrial imports from industrialized countries. In the area of primary commodity prices, an integrated program for commodities advanced by UNCTAD [United Nations Conference on Trade and Development] may serve as a model for commodity price stabilization. This program consists of international buffer stocks, a common fund, compensatory financing, and output restrictions. Hence, international agreements might provide for funds and storage facilities to operate a buffer stock to stabilize prices. Under such an arrangement, prices may be maintained within a certain range by buying and accumulating goods when prices are low and selling when prices are high. Financing of buffer stock agreements may be done most cost effectively through a common fund by taking advantage of lower borrowing terms for volume accounts, supporting new international commodity agreements, and so on. The program may also include compensatory financing, such as provided by the IMF's compensatory financing facility, that would be used to finance a temporary shortfall in domestic supplies or in export earnings (Nafziger, 1990). In the presence of trade barriers against primary products, these measures may hold some long range potential for stabilizing product prices and increasing Third World export earnings. No doubt substantial gains from such efforts will be necessary to produce a noticeable impact on wealth redistribution.

Also high on the Third World's list of wealth redistribution objectives is a transfer of more technology and productive facilities that accommodate the intellectual capacity of the local labor force with a timetable for full technology adaptation. The prevailing mood is that sufficient and appropriate technology transfers from developed countries to developing ones must take place to support development objectives with an underlying purpose of fully enabling the indigenous laborer to become technologically proficient. This would mean the transmission, absorption and assimilation of technology through providing the physical capital and those technical and managerial skills needed to operate, maintain, and service that physical capital and effectively tie its output into a marketing and distribution system (Bobo, 1982). This clearly is not an overnight task but the many years of involvement in Third World business activity by multinational firms with little one-to-one complementarity between physical capital and indigenous human capital is difficult to reconcile by host countries. Understandably the multinational wants to control access to proprietary technology and know how, but if the wealth redistribution objective is to be realized technology transfer is a clear and essential avenue.

The remaining objective, sovereignty over natural resources, holds deep meaning for Third World countries. Natural resources can be a formidable bargaining tool because of their value not only to local economic development but also to advanced economies. The Third World holds an impressive share of some of the world's highly demanded resources (see Exhibit 7.2). The importance of resources such as these to economic

Exhibit 7.2
Natural Resource Reserves of Third World Countries

Region	Resource	% of World Total
Africa	Industrial diamonds	74
	Chromium	68
	Manganese	53
	Phosphates	53
	Gold	51
	Aluminum	29
Asia	Rubber	78
	Tin	30
Latin America	Bauxite	48
	Copper	20
Middle East	Oil	53

Source: Benjamin F. Bobo & Lawrence S. Tai (1994). Topicos Sobre Las Relaciones Norte-Sur Y El Nuevo Order Mundial (Issues in North-South Relations and the New World Order). *Revista de Contabilidad Y Auditoria, 25,* 106; and Jim Norwine & Alfonso Ganzalez (1988). *The Third World: States of Mind and Being,* Boston: Unwin and Hyman, 62 and 64. Reproduced by permission of Routledge/Taylor & Francis Books, Inc.

development has been the subject of some debate. Simon Kuznets has suggested that economic growth "is unlikely to be inhibited by an absolute lack of natural resources" (Nafziger, 1990, p. 165; Kuznets, 1955).

Some economists have argued that natural resources are fixed factors and thus unrelated to growth (Nafziger, 1990; Meade, 1961). Support for these views has come from Japan, Switzerland and Israel which have developed at a rather fast pace in the absence of any measurable quantity of natural resources. On the other hand, Kuwait and the United Arab Emirates have some of the world's highest per capita incomes, and Saudi Arabia and Libya have per capita incomes higher than those in other developing countries. That these nations are supported almost fully by oil production suggests that natural resources do indeed play a role in the development process (Nafziger, 1990).

Actions by the United States, for example, further exemplify the importance of natural resources to economic development. Through the instrumentality of the multinational corporation and pressures on host governments, the U.S. has assured its access to sources of raw materials to fuel economic growth and expansion (Gilpin, *U.S. Power and the Multinational Corporation*, 1975). It would be difficult to imagine what the state of the American economy would be without the wide array of natural resources used to support its growth. Third World nations are fully aware of the importance of their natural resources to the outside world and are demanding the right to independently determine their use and value. Plainly put, the Third World wants to control supply and price without outside influence. This would considerably advance the wealth redistribution objective.

OPPORTUNITIES

From an overall perspective, the combined strength of the targeted objectives if pursued rigorously by the North could potentially set into motion forces that would ultimately contribute significantly toward transforming the international trading system into a mechanism of wealth redistribution. But these are not the only initiatives that can be taken to achieve a balance of world wealth. There are important opportunities yet available to the North that could assist the advancement of the wealth redistribution agenda. As an instrument of government policy and indeed an agent of shareholder interests, the multinational is in a unique position to capture these opportunities and turn them into positive gains in terms of endearment and improved long-run relations with the Third World. The nature of these opportunities may be gleaned from a recent survey of corporate executives and Third World policymakers about what policies and practices work best in creating greater harmony between the multinational and the host country, and how these may lead to greater wealth redistribution between North and South (Bobo and Tai, 1996). Exhibit 7.3

Exhibit 7.3
Attitude Profile
Importance of Selected Factors in Improving MNC-LDC Relations
Weighted Average Ratings*

Factors	Degree of Importance
Importance of joint ventures in reducing national resentment felt towards MNCs	2.03
Importance of joint ventures in making MNCs more socially responsible	2.71
Equal ownership of local subsidiaries by MNCs and LDCs	2.68
Joint Ventures moderate economic nationalist pressures in LDCs	2.31
MNCs' investment selection would be better made if LDCs had more input into the decision making and selection process	2.96
MNCs and LDCs can resolve friction and co-exist in a manner conducive to the mutual satisfaction of both parties	1.80
MNCs are initiators of change in MNC-LDC relationships	2.31
Identifying the interest of MNCs with the interest of LDCs	2.05
Decentralization of authority to LDC national management	2.53
MNC introduction of new products and new production methods and processes	1.63
A redistribution of world's wealth	2.40
The dissolution of Third World debt	2.04
An alteration of world trade, technology transfers and investments which would be more advantageous to LDCs	2.12

*Responses were coded for data analysis assigning numerical ratings to verbal ratings, i.e., strongly agree = 1, agree = 2, no opinion = 3, disagree = 4, strongly disagree = 5.

presents a summary of the survey results from which several deductions can be obtained.

It is apparent from the findings that MNCs and host countries see their engagement as being impacted by a number of factors that are clearly pertinent to the well being of their business relations. MNC market entry strategy through joint venture arrangements in the views of corporate and Third World policy makers reduce takeover pressures from host country special interest groups and give the MNC an appearance of being more socially responsible. Placing greater authority for local corporate operations in the hands of indigenous management would greatly enhance the working relationship between MNC and host. And, the MNC is perceived to be the initiator of change in the Third World development process. The introduction of new products along with new production methods and processes by the multinational create economic change so necessary to the process of Third World development.

Perhaps more importantly, the policy makers felt that a stronger identification of the MNC's interests with the host country's interests would be a tremendous asset in the relationship. In the past, much criticism has been cast upon the MNC by host countries for placing MNC interests above those of the host. In their view, this posture has led to inappropriate exploitation of natural resources, improper business practices, and uneven economic development. Further criticism of the MNC has pointed to their virtually closed corporate decision making process. The host country has had little or no direct input into investment decisions that affect local economic development. In the study, policy makers felt that the multinational's investment selection would be better made if the host country had more input into the decision-making and selection process.

Our familiarity with the MNC–host country relationship coupled with the study's findings provide an indication of directions for future initiatives by the MNC in addressing Third World wealth redistribution concerns. Unavoidably, the MNC must formally and officially recognize that, conditioned by the desire to maintain sovereignty over their natural resources and local economic development, host countries must be allowed direct input into decision making processes that govern policies and practices of multinationals in the Third World. Participation in policy making would enable them to better originate and influence New World Order initiatives particularly as they relate to foreign direct investment.

But there is no mechanism in place to make possible direct input. In fact, Robert Gilpin's models of world economic interdependence and MNC–host country interaction attach no significant power or decision-making role to the Third World host (Gilpin, 1975a). In all candor, the rather benign role of the host developing country is not by accident. Gilpin's models, sovereignty-at-bay, dependencia, and mercantilist characterize a virtual incapacitation of the Third World host by the powers of the multinational corporation (Gilpin, 1975a). The sovereignty-at-bay thesis regards the multinational as the embodiment of the liberal ideal of an interdependent world economy in which "national economies have become enmeshed in a web of economic interdependence from which they cannot easily escape . . ." (Gilpin, 1975a, p. 40). Placing an inseparable reliance on foreign direct investment, sovereignty-at-bay confides that "No government would dare shut out the multinational corporations . . ." (Gilpin, 1975a, p. 40).

In a similar fashion, the dependencia model also conveys a highly restricted capacity by Third World countries to influence or control forces that determine their course of development. Dependencia depicts a world of economic interdependence in which the host developing country is little more than a stepchild of ". . . a regime of North Atlantic Multinational Corporations that centralize high-level decision making . . . in a few key cities in the advanced countries . . . and confine the rest of the world to lower levels of activity and income . . ." (Gilpin, 1975a, p. 43). Dependencia and sovereignty-at-bay cast a dark shadow upon world economic inter-dependency particularly from a Third World perspective. The mercantilist thesis, however, offers hope in that it accords the host developing country with the decision-making capacity to act independently and outside the confines of an international economic web. But this may be more in theory than in practice.

Essentially, the mercantilist model emphasizes national interests rather than corporate interests as the primary determinants of the future world economic order. Under this approach ". . . each nation will pursue eco-nomic policies that reflect domestic economic needs and external political ambitions without much concern for the effects of these policies on other countries or on the international economic system as a whole" (Gilpin, 1975a, p. 46). Theoretically this approach may be possible, but practically speaking it carries little weight in view of the world economic order. If the mercantilist thesis were implementable, developing countries would have adopted it long ago. In reality, developing countries simply do not have the necessary resources to mount such an independent effort. With the expansive inequality gap between industrialized nations and the Third World, what possible chance could a lone developing country have in suc-cessfully undertaking the mercantilist approach?

It is apparent that the Gilpin models provide no power sharing oppor-tunity for Third World nations in determining the construct of the interna-tional economic system. The decision making process is limited to input from advanced economies through the instrumentality of the multina-tional corporation. Under such an exclusive framework, realizing the objectives of the new world order will be exceedingly difficult. In light of the failure of the Gilpin models, the multinational has a unique opportu-nity to adopt an innovative approach to international economic interde-pendence and become a legitimate agent of change. Instructively, an MNC–Third World survey of top-level government and corporate leaders provides direction in this regard (Bobo and Tai, 1996). When asked, 'would MNC investment selection be better made if LDCs had more input into the decision making and selection process?' the response was quite surprising. There was a discernible interest in sharing power with the host developing country. This may be interpreted as an early sign of recognition by the multinational that power sharing can reap benefits. Moreover, it may sug-gest that the multinational is beginning to realize that the traditional mode of operation in the Third World, as indicated by the sovereignty-at-bay and dependencia theses, is vastly becoming outdated.

Using a power sharing approach to international economic interde-pendency would create a new image for the multinational, as it would reveal a clear departure from tradition. Through this the multinational has the opportunity to become the change agent necessary to provide required leadership in addressing new world order objectives. But what form should power sharing take? To answer this question, two upper most concerns by both parties must be reconciled. On the one hand, the host government argues that the closed decision making process of the multinational allows it to make exclusive decisions that affect local economic activity over which the government has no control. Hence, despite negotiated business agreements with the multinational, the host government argues that it is largely powerless to control internal development. On the other hand, the multinational is insecure about the longevity of business arrangements with the host country. The basis of this insecurity is the fear of nationalization, local takeover or that the expected return on investment will not be obtained. So closed decision making in part enables confidential strategy on ways to influence local public policy for the purpose of protecting and improving the MNC's position in the local economy. Because fear and suspicion cloud MNC–host country relations, an interactive arrangement that protects the interests of both parties is requisite.

Structuring an interactive arrangement with legitimized power sharing is no simple task. This could conceivably take a number of forms but one in particular would appear to have special promise. An MNC–host government power sharing arrangement might provide for interactive decision making at the highest level of the corporation. Practice wise, this would involve appointment to the corporate board of directors a group of representatives from developing countries who would directly participate in policy making that affects business development in the Third World. Under this arrangement, representatives of host governments would work closely with corporate policy makers on a continuous basis to assure appropriate consideration of relevant issues and concerns from both sides (Bobo and Tai, 1995). Fears of nationalization and takeover and suspicions of wrongdoing would be dispelled since the MNC, through the government representatives, would have a direct line of communication with the host government, and the host country would have a direct and significant voice inside the corporation (Bobo and Tai, 1995).

An arrangement so structured overcomes the shortcomings of the present system in which host country participation in the decision making process is kept at the local level. Invariably localized input is compromised by the filtering process or altogether dismissed by corporate personnel. Direct participation at the corporate level assures open decision making channels and provides opportunity for power sharing between the MNC and the host. Since utility maximization is best accomplished when both parties work in concert, the relationship will benefit from the principle of "the whole is greater than the sum of the parts."

In light of the new world order agenda, the implications of power sharing are numerous. A likely immediate outcome would be the subsidence of disharmony between the MNC and the host country owing to an improved channel of communication. Also, the economic challenge to host country sovereignty through exploitation of natural resources, negative balance-of-trade, negative balance-of-payments, and the like would be mitigated increasingly over time (Mainuddin, 1995). And, participation at the corporate level places the Third World in a position to directly influence and advise the MNC on wealth redistribution opportunities. This would do much to promote the MNC–Third World relationship.

The multinational corporation has yet another unique opportunity to influence the course of the New World Order agenda. Timely reversal of the persistent inequality gap between rich and poor nations and achievement of the wealth redistribution objective will require investigation and consideration of alternative approaches to resolving the problem, however ambitious. No doubt power sharing is ambitious, but because wealth redistribution is decidedly imposing, its achievement will unquestionably require very ambitious attention. In this regard, one problem solving approach may be to consider a fundamental change in the basic philosophy that drives the corporation—the profit motive.

Clearly the quest for profit has produced many positive outcomes not the least of which have been advancements in technology which have in some way benefited all peoples around the world. The motivation to seek profit has served as a great incentive to creativity and innovation. But all isn't well. The pursuit of profit particularly through profit maximization strategies has contributed to a skewed pattern of wealth among peoples and countries (*Hungry for Profit*, 1994). It has facilitated a growing population of "have-nots" while simultaneously placing a larger and larger share of the world's wealth in the hands of a very small group of "haves" (*World Development Report 1994*, 1994).

The prevailing hypothesis in conventional microeconomics regarding the behavior of corporations is that they seek to maximize profits (Friedman, 1953; Alchian, 1950). Profit maximization has its roots in the corporate world of finance where managers and investors alike continuously ponder ways to increase profits—the ultimate objective being to maximize shareholder wealth. After all, this is the cornerstone of business school pedagogy where future corporate managers are inoculated with the academics of running the corporation. All are taught very early in the process that the primary goal of the corporation is to maximize shareholder wealth (Brigham, 1995). But in light of the New World Order doctrine, it is debatable whether the corporation can continue to pursue shareholder wealth maximization and the business school to teach this concept as the firm's primary goal.

The multinational corporation, through its enormous market presence, is in a unique position to influence shareholder wealth maximization ideology. Taking the lead in pursuing a profit strategy that promotes wealth redistribution would give it a forward-looking future in the Third World marketplace. To this end, the multinational may well adopt a *profit satisficing* approach to profit making. As such, corporate profit making behavior would be directed at finding a satisfactory rather than an optimum choice. This suggests that in the interest of facilitating wealth redistribution between rich and poor nations, the corporation would not aim at a maximum but at a satisfactory level of profit (return on investment). More specifically, the corporation would only pursue a reasonable level of profit and when attained, it would feel no need to do anything further. In other words, the corporation becomes a satisfier and does only as well as is necessary (Simon, 1947; Simon 1958; Ayert and March, 1963). This form of behavior would lead to considerable savings to Third World producers (raw material suppliers), business firms and consumers. These savings would do much in the way of wealth redistribution by reducing money outflow from the Third World.

CONCLUSIONS, FUTURE RESEARCH AND POLICY DEVELOPMENT

Much of the current debate on closing the inequality gap between rich and poor nations and the role of the multinational in this process centers around how best to achieve the New World Order doctrine. In this regard, a good deal has been explored here in the interest of developing a serious approach to addressing this matter. While the objectives and opportunities outlined point us in a general direction, detailed assessment of these topics is required to make possible intelligent decision making about specific directions corporate and government policy should take to produce a global uplifting from Third World backwardness to full economic participation. This is more aptly achieved through the setting of research agenda that aggressively investigate the objectives and opportunities and prescribe necessary policy approaches that would facilitate realization of a New World Order.

At least two courses of research are required to assess particularly the opportunities facing the multinational corporation; one that inquires about the plausibility of the power sharing proposal and the *profit satisficing* strategy, and the other, a more prescriptive approach setting forth models of power sharing and *profit satisficing* for business and finance applications. Since we know very little about these topics as proposed, research initiatives must be launched to determine whether the corporation, and the investment community as well, would be willing to entertain the notions of power sharing and *profit satisficing*. Since this would constitute a radical departure from their normal behavior, baseline data must be gathered to inform us about their views on these issues.

Further, would the academic community provide research leadership to assist corporate transition to a profit-satisficing mode? Clear operating frameworks will be needed to assure continued corporate viability. And, should business education adopt *profit satisficing* as the primary goal of the firm? Advancement of wealth redistribution objectives would be considerably enhanced by future corporate leaders who have the appropriate perception of reasonable profit. These and other pertinent questions must be investigated in the process of developing financial models and corporate policy that would support redress of the inequality gap between rich and poor nations.

CHAPTER 8

Internationalization Decision Making and the Global Interdependency Sensitivity Thesis*

The following discourse formalizes the power-sharing approach to inequality remediation proposed in Chapter 7 through a full articulation of its mission and parameters in light of models of business arrangements prevalent in the marketplace. In this context, "Internationalization Decision Making and the Global Interdependency Sensitivity Thesis" revisits the dialogue on models of economic interdependence and MNC–host country relations and extends the discussion to the bargaining framework that characterizes the negotiation of terms and conditions of business arrangements. With this as a backdrop, GIST (Global Interdependency Sensitivity Thesis) is proposed as a means of instituting power sharing in business arrangements between multinationals and host countries in the interest of facilitating resolve of the rich country–poor country dilemma. The interactive arrangement characterized and fully conceptualized in GIST was initially introduced in Chapter 7.

ABSTRACT

In the interdependent relationship between the multinational corporation and the host country, much conflict derives from inequitable business arrangements, foreign control and management of local production, and most significantly external control of the local economy. Robert Gilpin has

*Reprinted with permission. Benjamin F. Bobo, and Lawrence S. Tai, "Internationalization Decision Making and the Global Interdependency Sensitivity Thesis," *Journal of the Third World Spectrum* 4, no. 2 (1997), 23–41.

presented three models of world economic interdependence and MNC–host country interaction, which focus on the ability of rich and poor nations to control their destinies in such an environment. These models attach no significant power or decision-making role to the host developing country nor foresee any ability to successfully act independently in the world economic order. Without such capability the host country will be unable to minimize foreign control of the local economy. Undoubtedly, this will cause even more conflict in the MNC–host country relationship. This paper proposes a power-sharing model that directly addresses this matter with a view towards resolving MNC–host country conflict that stems therefrom.

   Despite the important role that multinational enterprise plays in the transformation of Third World economies, it is by now apparent to observers of the international marketplace that multinationals must be sensitive to the fact that the environment for foreign enterprise especially in developing countries, is dominated by two forces: the powerful emotion of nationalism fueled by patriotic pride and a quest for economic independence; and substantial dependence of rapid economic progress upon the capital and industrial know-how of developed countries.[1]
   History has shown us that these forces are fundamentally and pragmatically in opposition. Thus far, as Fayerweather has warned, the former has been moderated only by the overriding political and economic importance of the latter.[2] It is because of the latter that the host country has tolerated foreign control and management of local production, particularly in strategic resource areas, and further, has tolerated inequitable business arrangements and sharing of gains derived from local production. But frustrations associated with this state of affairs have made the relationship between multinationals and host countries very much a dynamic involvement; the outcome of which, not surprisingly, is leaning heavily in the direction of increased nationalism.
   Harbison and Myers recognized some time ago that:

Eventually the firm is forced to recognize that, in the opinion of the effective political leaders, foreign management and foreign financial control are only temporary instruments for industrial development. In a very real sense, therefore, expatriate managers are expendable, and their power and influence in any rapidly industrializing country will inevitably shrink. Like patrimonial management in the advanced countries, expatriate management too will become an anachronism in modern society. . . . We feel that the wholly owned foreign firm has a limited role to play in the industrializing countries. The future is likely to see an expansion of locally controlled companies which have an affiliation, through licensing, marketing, or consulting arrangements, with large business organizations in the United States, England, and Europe.[3]

Their vision has materialized into varying forms of MNC business arrangements in the Third World. These arrangements display a variety of characteristics and can be generally broken down into the following categories (these categories may be interrelated for certain projects):

a. Technology Transfer Agreements with or without equity participation and with or without turnkey provisions. Formerly these were with detailed licensing agreements; more recently these requirements have been dropped or moderated.

b. Technology transfer in combination with extended turn key and/or management contracts including managerial-technical training on site and in the home country. More recently, these institutional forms include the maximization of linkages via additional training and sub-contracting to develop rapidly local input suppliers. The thrust of these forms is an accelerated "implantation" of a self-sustaining sectoral or sub-sectoral production and, in certain projects, R&D capacity. As regards the latter, the involved MNCs increasingly see themselves as sellers of technological processes rather than products. Sectoral emphasis is primarily natural resource extraction and processing, intermediate input production and capital goods, and certain consumer durables.

c. Tripartite agreements and other forms of joint ventures. These may or may not be part of the above extended technology-transfer arrangements. These joint ventures include a wide spectrum of combinations. Tripartite agreements include the use of, for example, two MNCs—usually from different home countries—with a local participant, either a public enterprise or a local private firm. There are also instances of either single or multiple MNCs, multiple local public and private participation. Multiple MNCs share or are responsible, respectively, for technology, managerial, and marketing functions. The use of public enterprises is growing and is seen as a vehicle for ensuring national absorption of technological and managerial transfers. Public enterprises, in some instances, provide financing while local private participants assume an active managerial and production role. In general, the tripartite form is aimed at acquiring three basic resources of the foreign investment "bundle," i.e., technology, finance capital, and management, from three different sources. An important example of the tripartite arrangement is the use of MNC and local public and/or private participation with financing coming in the form of a long-term capital loan and/or equity position. Another example of the tripartite arrangement, which has important implications for external financial flows to the Third World, is the use of MNC and local private/public participation with long-term capital provided by either private multinational banks or consortia or a combination of private and public multilateral financing. The inclusion of the MNC in the tripartite arrangement eases obtainment of external financing, while local participation insures better fulfillment of development goals, particularly national industrial capacities and, therefore, a more stable and harmonious interaction between foreign investors and host government.

d. Export marketing agreements combined with sub-contracting. Here production is sub-contracted (usually under license) to national firms, while the MNC performs the export marketing. Financing in the form of long-term loan capital may be provided by a mix of public and private, national and multinational sources.[4]

These types of business arrangements in the host country have accomplished satisfactory economic impacts, although there has been little *ex-post* social cost-benefit analysis of ventures implemented under such arrangements. But, most of them throughout the Third World were subjected to extensive social cost-benefit analysis as part of the overall feasibility assessment of these ventures before they were undertaken.[5] To some extent, they have given host governments the opportunity to demonstrate their ability to exercise "countervailing power" over multinationals to some extent comparable to that of the industrialized nations.[6]

These forms of business arrangements have also provided an added dimension to the MNC–host country negotiation and bargaining process. The host country has been faced with "complex constellations of horizontal and vertical integration . . . established by multinational corporations in primary commodity exports, especially in the mining sector, often producing oligopolistic structures in the markets of these commodities."[7] In the absence of such business arrangements, oligopoly situations give multinationals a decidedly overwhelming bargaining advantage in business transactions. But in instances where these forms of business arrangements are utilized, power wielded by multinationals in bargaining and negotiation sessions have been moderated somewhat.

Despite the progress made resulting from advantages offered by these business arrangements, host countries remain far short of achieving a fair sharing of the power exercised by multinational corporations in their joint business activities. The rather subordinate role in which host countries find themselves produces ill feeling among local special interest groups and raises the specter of nationalism. While such arrangements have facilitated the negotiation and bargaining process, they do not reduce the potential for conflict and nationalization to a tolerable or manageable level. That is to say, in environs where the risk of conflict or nationalization is high, as is generally the case in the Third World, these types of business arrangements do not render this risk so inconsequential that major disruption of business operation can be ruled out.

But if the multinational is to maintain a significant presence in the Third World, a mode of interaction must be found that can reasonably assure harmony in the MNC–host country relationship. This will not likely materialize unless the host countries have significant involvement in the decision making and planning processes of all economic activity affecting their internal development. This means that host governments must have at their disposal vehicles that will enable them to influence the course and pace of economic development in their countries. Business arrangements of the type discussed above are such vehicles. But in a world economic order created and controlled by the dominant economic and military powers, do such business arrangements give host countries sufficient participation in corporate decisions that affect the local environment to enable them to take at least reasonable control of internal economic activity?

The literature on MNC–host country relations offers useful perspectives that may help to answer this question. In this respect, Robert Gilpin has presented what he refers to as three models that characterize international economic interdependence and MNC–host country interaction.[8] Gilpin identifies these models as "sovereignty at bay," "dependencia," and "mercantilist."[9] He focuses on world economic interdependency and the ability of rich and poor nations to control their destinies in such an environment.

The sovereignty-at-bay thesis regards the multinational corporation as the embodiment of the liberal ideal of an interdependent world economy. It is credited and admired for having extended the integration of national economies beyond trade and money to the internationalization of production; thus moving the organization of production, marketing, and investment from a national framework to a global scale. In this context, as Gilpin observed:

The sovereignty-at-bay thesis argues that national economies have become enmeshed in a web of economic interdependence from which they cannot easily escape, and from which they derive great economic benefits. Through trade, monetary relations, and foreign investment, the destinies and well being of societies have become too inexorably interwoven for these bonds to be severed. The costs of the ensuing inefficiencies in order to assert national autonomy or some other nationalistic goal would be too high. The citizenry, so this thesis contends, would not tolerate the sacrifices of domestic economic well being that would be entailed if individual nation states sought to hamper unduly the successful operation of the international economy.[10]

Gilpin further noted that:

Underlying this development, the liberal position argues, is a revolution in economic needs and expectations. Domestic economic goals have been elevated to a predominant and other economic welfare goals have become the primary concerns of political leadership. More importantly, these goals can only be achieved, this position argues, through participation in the world economy. No government, for example, would dare shut out the multinational corporations and thereby forgo employment, regional development, or other benefits these corporations bring into countries. In short, the rise of the welfare state and the increasing sensitivity of national governments to the rising economic expectations of their societies have made them dependent upon the benefits provided by a liberal world-economic system.[11]

In the context of the sovereignty-at-bay model, it appears that Third World nations (from their perspective) are caught up in a dilemma that may have no solution. With economic development as a top priority, they sorely need capital and technology; multinational corporations are best equipped to accommodate these needs. But multinationals are international integration minded and are not inclined to pursue the objectives of nation states, as nation states would like. Therefore, the desire to maintain traditional independence and sovereignty while at the same time satisfy the ever expanding economic needs and aspirations of their peoples place them in a compromising position. The disturbing fact, so far as the Third World is concerned, is that a full realization of the sovereignty-at-bay thesis "would be the end of nationality and national governments as we know them."[12] Hence, despite utilization of the various forms of business arrangements in MNC–host country business ventures, if the sovereignty-at-bay thesis is valid the ability of host countries to exercise meaningful power in decision-making that affects local economic development is minimized.

In contrast to the sovereignty-at-bay thesis, the dependencia model outlines a similar vision of the future but with a different twist. The sovereignty-at-bay thesis proposes to upgrade the quality of life for the poor through the transfer of capital, technology and managerial know-how from continually advancing industrialized countries to emerging nations. By so doing global wealth would become decentralized and better distributed among all nations of the world. But the dependencia model sees the flow of wealth and benefits derived from global interaction moving—via the same mechanisms operating in the sovereignty-at-bay thesis—to the centers of industrial financial power and decision making. As such, this is viewed as the development of a hierarchical and exploitative world order by Marxist proponents of the dependencia model. The Marxist view can be explained in terms of the circular and cumulative causation principles.[13] In this context, we would expect benefits derived from the continuous expansion and spread of multinational corporations to accrue largely to those who are already wealthy—the industrialized nations—as opposed to those who are seeking to become wealthy—the developing countries. Gilpin noted that:

In the interdependent world economy of the dependencia model, the multinational corporation also reigns supreme. But the world created by these corporations is held to be far different from that envisaged by the sovereignty-at-bay school of thought. In the dependencia model the political and economic consequences of the multinational corporation are due to what Stephen Hymer has called the two laws of development: the law of increasing firm size, and the law of uneven development. The law of increasing firm size, Hymer argues, is the tendency since the Industrial Revolution for firms to increase in size "from the workshop to the factory to the national corporation to the multidivisional corporation and now to the multinational corporation." The law of uneven development, he continues, is the tendency of the international economy to produce poverty as well as wealth, underdevelopment as well as development. Together, these two economic laws are producing the following consequence:

. . . a regime of North Atlantic Multinational Corporations would tend to produce a hierarchical division of labor within the firm. It would tend to centralize high-level decision making occupations in a few key cities in the advanced countries, surrounded by a number of regional sub-capitals, and confine the rest of the world to lower levels of activity and income, i.e., to the status of towns and villages in a new imperial system. Income, status, authority, and consumption patterns would radiate out from these centers along a declining curve, and the existing pattern of inequality and dependency would be perpetrated. The pattern would be complex, but the basic relationship between different countries would be one of superior and subordinate, head office and branch office.[14]

Within the confines of the sovereignty-at-bay and dependencia models, one clearly notices that no significant power or decision-making role has been attached to developing countries. They effectively have been accorded the position of servants or subordinates of corporate power and ambition. Thus, here again the prospect of employing the various forms of business arrangements to give the host country legitimate decision making power in its dealing with multinational corporations is minimized in the light of the dependencia thesis. In the third model, entitled mercantilist, this apparent injustice presumably would be corrected via an emphasis on national interests, rather than corporate interests, as the primary determinants of the future world economic order. Essentially, national economic and political objectives would be given priority over considerations of global economic efficiency.[15] As Gilpin further noted:

The mercantilist impulse can take many forms in the contemporary world: the desire for a balance-of-payments surplus; the export of unemployment, inflation, or both; the imposition of import and/or export controls; the expansion of world market shares; and the stimulation of advanced technology. In short, each nation will pursue economic policies that reflect domestic economic needs and external political ambitions without much concern for the effects of these policies on other countries or on the international economic system as a whole.[16]

With the history of the world economic order as we know it, it would seem that if the mercantilist thesis were a rational and implementable approach, developing countries would have adopted it already. Certainly there is sufficient justification for it. But in the larger scheme of things, most developing countries simply do not have the necessary resources, nor access to them, to launch such an independent effort.

Although the mercantilist thesis appears to offer the host country the best opportunity to control the local economy, one unavoidable question must be raised. How realistic is it to anticipate a great deal of success from the mercantilist thesis, given the already horrendous inequality gap between rich and poor countries and the difficulty developing countries would encounter in a solo effort to overcome it? Furthermore, since the multinational would likely resist any host country policies that would have a pejorative impact particularly on the home country, presumably utilizing the various business arrangements would not be possible under the mercantilist approach. This would have the consequence of making the host country even more isolated in its pursuit of economic policies that ignore the plight and needs of other countries.

Disturbingly, the Gilpin models foresee no world economic order in which the host developing country has reasonable control of internal economic activity while at the same time engaged in viable business arrangements with multinational corporations. If this is the realistic characterization, business dealings between host developing countries and multinationals are destined for disharmony. But since every conceivable problem has a conceivable solution, perhaps there is an approach to MNC–host country enterprise that would accommodate the interests of the multinational as well as the host country.

THE BARGAINING FRAMEWORK

Presumably, ones contentment with a business arrangement depends upon how well one is able to bargain for desired accommodations and negotiate the terms of the arrangement. Typically, business arrangements among multinational corporations and host countries are complicated by the concern among host governments that through their global network of subsidiaries and associated companies, linked together by an intricate system of common financial, managerial, technological and organizational services, multinational corporations continue to exercise control, directly or indirectly, over the crucial stages of the operational chain of most primary commodity exports; from exploration to production, processing, exportation, transport, marketing, distribution and financing."[17] This, as host governments see it, perpetuates the inequality gap and their inability to control internal economic activity. Developing countries simply cannot overcome the influence that MNCs exert in bargaining situations; this influence strongly affects the outcome of the negotiation of terms and conditions of business arrangements. Without question, the MNC has an overpowering influence on the entire bargaining framework.

Even though the business arrangements discussed earlier have strengthened the host government's bargaining power and facilitated economic growth in developing countries, they have lacked the capacity, more by design than accident, to provide the kind of interaction that would lead host governments to feel that they can assume reasonable control of internal economic activity. In short, they don't appreciably alter the outcomes of the Gilpin models. Though such arrangements as the joint venture have had a generally positive influence on MNC–host government relations, most developing nations still lack sufficient indigenous capital and skill to be able to insist on substantial participation and decision making in ventures involving multinational corporations. After all, without meaningful participation there can be no substantial impact on corporate decisions that affect the local economy. Hence the ability to control internal economic activity is compromised.

Since "sovereignty at bay" and "dependencia" allow virtually no decision making input from host countries, and "mercantilist" proposes a go-it-alone approach, which is largely unimplementable, perhaps a modification of the MNC–host country interaction process can give new direction to the relationship and help to escape the improprieties of the Gilpin models. Procedurally, this task might be accomplished through expansion of the bargaining framework within which terms and conditions of business arrangements are negotiated.

BARGAINING MODELS

A number of bargaining models have been proposed that purport to circumscribe the negotiation process between multinationals and host countries. But none as yet has bridged the gap between Gilpin's assessments of the international economic order and an economic order that would produce sustained harmony in MNC–host country relations. It is, however, useful to briefly review these models for purposes of intellectual insight and Chaitram Singh provides helpful comment on the topic. He explains that bargaining models are of two basic types: static bargaining models which emphasize the initial negotiations between the multinational and the host government, and dynamic models which incorporate change over the life of the business arrangement.[18]

In the context of the static bargaining model, Robert Curry and Donald Rothchild propose a negotiation framework in which "impatience" and "reciprocal demand intensity" are the primary variables used to explain MNC–host government interactions. They argue that the host government's impatience to conclude business arrangements with the MNC works to its disbenefit, suggesting that the consequence of impatience is a contract that is unfavorable to the government. The model would appear to be flawed in this regard since impatience may be disadvantageous for the MNC as well. Curry and Rothchild's second variable, "reciprocal demand intensity," identifies how intensely the government desires what the multinational has to offer and vice versa. Typically, as they suggest, the government exhibits the greater demand intensity because of the absence of alternative firms with which to negotiate or strike a deal.[19]

The principal deficiency of the Curry-Rothchild model, as Singh points out, is that it largely ignores time in the business arrangement. Since the business arrangement is usually for an extended period of time, there exists the potential for renegotiation of the original agreement. Ignoring the issue of renegotiation does not allow consideration of the impact of the host country's domestic politics on the bargaining process. On this shortcoming of the Curry-Rothchild model, Singh suggests that an interactive bargaining model is needed to better understand the many facets of renegotiation.[20]

One such interactive model has been proposed by Raymond Mikesell who argues that the multinational initially has the upper hand in the bargaining process because of its enormous resources. In Mikesell's view, after the initial business arrangement is concluded, which reflects the advantages that the MNC offers and the initial level of risk incurred, the relationship becomes strained. As the production process is established and profits realized, the government usually argues that it was too generous in the concessions made in the initial arrangement and pressures the firm to renegotiate or update the terms of the agreement.[21]

Though the Mikesell model takes into consideration the time factor; it does not accurately reflect, as Singh suggests, the impact of domestic politics on the bargaining process. Often, multinationals encounter charges of economic exploitation by domestic political opposition groups who generate enormous pressure to restructure business arrangements in favor of the host country. MNC–host country interaction models that fail to recognize the influence of such sociopolitical behavior in the negotiation of business arrangements are unlikely to achieve full representation of the bargaining process.[22]

Theodore Moran has proposed the balance-of-power model that purports to make up for the shortcomings of its competitors. To capture the dynamics of MNC–host country relations, Moran employs two explanatory variables: uncertainty about whether the investment can be made a success, and a host country learning curve. As the uncertainty variable implies, no one knows the real potential of the business and thus the MNC assumes the majority of the initial risk since it, as is typical, supplies the capital, technology and management needed for the undertaking. If the venture succeeds, uncertainty is reduced and the opportunity for renegotiation and power shifting appears. The bargaining process at this point is essentially as described by Mikesell and others.[23]

Once the venture is operating in a successful mode, Moran argues that the host country has incentive to develop its skills and expertise because of increased benefit to the country by doing so. It enables the country to move up the "learning curve" and promote a shift in the balance of power in its favor. At some point in time, the host country is able to replicate the functions of the multinational, i.e., achieve complete technology transfer, thus making national ownership a possibility.[24]

Importantly, the issues involving renegotiation of the business arrangement and host country "learning curve" are especially relevant to the design of MNC-host government interaction frameworks that promote harmony and generally reduce nationalistic fervor.[25] But Moran's model, like the others, falls short of addressing a major weakness in MNC–host country interaction theses. How are business arrangements monitored and changing needs of operating ventures accommodated after renegotiations are concluded and during the "leaning curve" stage so as to (a) convey a clear impression of integrity in multinational decision making, (b) ease the difficulty inherent in revising plans and procedures to resolve unexpected problems occurring in the production process, and (c) abate fears about, for example, transfer pricing practices?

Uncertainty about what takes place in MNC decision-making channels stirs nationalistic fervor and leads to MNC–host country conflict. Nationalist behavior is not simply a result of imprudent or unethical practices on the part of the MNC but is also a consequence of the illusion of impropriety. To many, illusion is reality; what is perceived is what is believed. Perception can be a strong motivator particularly when it leads to suspicion and distrust. There are instances in which this may be justified. For example, when the negotiation and renegotiation processes are done, the multinational is very likely to retain management control. This allows the corporation to protect the decision making process and, if so desired, manipulate economic variables such as production rates, prices, reinvestment and disinvestment. A number of accounting and financing techniques can be used to accomplish these tasks despite the terms of the business arrangement. One such technique, transfer pricing, persists as a major source of conflict between multinationals and host countries. On this point, the host country is uncomfortable with the profit calculations of the MNC and constantly doubts whether company decision makers outside of the country might not be employing a variety of mechanisms to maximize income.[26]

Further, since moving up the "leaning curve" sufficiently to produce a shift in the balance of power can take many years, how are the integrity and perception issues addressed in the interim? Perceptibly, these are the major factors that lead to distrust and conflict in MNC–host country relations. Franklin Tugwell, an insightful contributor to the literature on MNCs, argues that the main source of instability of, for example, concession agreements, is the mistrust and uncertainty that are built into the concessionary system.[27] MNC–host country interaction models ignore resolution of these issues. Failure to resolve the questions of integrity and perception signals a major weakness in interaction models that purport to explain and improve the MNC–host country bargaining and negotiation process.

GLOBAL INTERDEPENDENCY SENSITIVITY THESIS

With the foregoing models of international economic interdependence and MNC–host country interactive bargaining as backdrop, the Global Interdependency Sensitivity Thesis (GIST) is proposed. A power sharing model of MNC–host government interaction, GIST specifically addresses the integrity and perception issues. This is not done simply from the perspective of the host country but from the perspective of the MNC as well.

As already discussed, previous models either give the bargaining advantage to the multinational through the "impatience" and "reciprocal demand intensity" arguments or ultimately to the host country by way of the renegotiation, uncertainty and "learning curve" propositions. The balance of power is initially in favor of the corporation but later shifts to the host country. In the meanwhile a power struggle ensues that is driven by suspicion and distrust from both sides.

Typically, the host government targets the closed decision making process of the multinational where, allegedly, decisions are made that affect local economic activity over which it (host government) has no control. As a consequence, it is further alleged, their ability to control internal development is impeded despite favorable terms negotiated in business arrangements.

Multinationals are insecure about the longevity of business arrangements with the host country. They fear nationalization, local takeover, or that the expected return on investment will not be realized. So they maintain closed decision making in part to enable confidential strategy on ways to influence local public policy by manipulating prices and investment, by playing host countries off against each other, and even by intervening directly in the local political process.[28]

Fear and suspicion cloud MNC–host country interaction and lay fertile ground for conflict and disharmony. With a view toward ameliorating the pejorative aspects of the Gilpin models and building on the interactive bargaining framework, GIST conceives an interactive arrangement that will greatly reduce, if not eliminate, cause for suspicion and fear between the MNC and the host country.

The objective of GIST is to incorporate the interactive bargaining framework into the decision making process at the highest level of the corporation, the home based headquarters establishment. As such, reciprocal demand intensity, negotiation, renegotiation, investment success uncertainty, learning curve and domestic politics are integrated and incorporated as important attributes of the MNC–host country business development process, and recognized as sensitive factors that require proper nurturing. In practice, implementing this objective would involve appointment to the corporate board of directors a contingent of government representatives from host countries who would participate in the conception of corporate policies and practices that affect the conduct of business in host developing nations and govern management decision-making at the subsidiary level in those countries. This would considerably strengthen the MNC–host country interactive bargaining process as representatives of hosting governments work closely with corporate policy makers on an ongoing basis to assure appropriate consideration of sensitive issues and concerns from both sides.

Under this arrangement, suspicions of wrongdoing and fears of nationalization and takeover would be mitigated since the host country has a significant voice inside the corporation and the multinational has a direct line of communication with the host government as provided via the government representatives. Resistance by local opposition parties would be quelled since their concerns about exploitation and closed decision making channels would be addressed by GIST. The need to engage in improprieties by MNC management would be dissipated since host governments and local opposition parties would be placated by the GIST arrangement.

In the GIST framework, the principle of 'the whole is greater then sum of the parts' would prevail. The MNC and the host government working together in harmony would realize greater benefit from the combined power of their sources than otherwise would be the case. Under nationalization, the individual parties would be separated from the advantages that each has to offer and thus would realize a lower gain from deployment of their resources. In a takeover situation, the host country becomes owner and manager of the enterprise but is without the marketing and distribution capability of the multinational. This would be a formidable obstacle especially for developing countries since they tend not to be hooked into worldwide marketing and distribution channels. Without such access, maximizing sales and revenue would be virtually impossible. In some cases, even continuation of the enterprise would be problematic. Likewise, a takeover ceases operation of the enterprise by the multinational. Without access to the local resources that made the investment possible, the revenue stream enjoyed by the multinational would disappear.

The GIST proposition receives some measure of support from the multinational corporate sector as revealed in an MNC–Third World survey of top-level government and corporate leaders.[29] When asked, "would MNC investment selection be better made if LDCs had more input into the decision making and selection process?" the response from MNCs showed signs of interest in the idea. This may be rather surprising particularly since the traditional mode of operation in the Third World has not been consistent with GIST. There are those who feel that host country input should be limited to the MNC subsidiary level and that this provides sufficient input on policy matters concerning business conduct and practices of the local entity. But with the parent organization pursuing global profit maximizing strategies, the subsidiary is simply an instrument of the parent to accomplish its overall objectives.

On the matter of local representation, Clive Thomas has observed that:

Much state activity . . . has been directed towards publicizing and pressuring multinational companies into allowing nationals to participate in the higher levels of management. This strategy, it is argued . . . would . . . serve to nationalize these companies in their operations and decision-making, through the participation of nationals in the crucial management areas . . .

There are two basic weaknesses to this strategy. First, it underestimates the social power of these institutions and the degree of their "totality" in the control of individuals. Local persons move into particular institutional structures, with their own ethos, values, life styles, and ways of doing things—all of which are derived from the imperative of exploiting local resources for the benefit of metropolitan capital. These nationals therefore work in a situation where there are strong built-in pressures to conform to the values and behavioral patterns of the enterprise. This pressure continues unless the individual leaves. But as this socialization process takes place, instead of the company becoming more and more national, it is in fact the nationals who are likely to become more and more an extension of the . . . multinational corporation.

The second weakness of this strategy is the phenomenon of organizational substitution, which has been made easy through the technological possibilities of virtually instant communications. This process permits the companies to let nationals fill managerial positions nominally, and at the same time empty these managerial positions of any decision-making significance, by simply referring back to Head Office decisions which would normally and routinely have been made locally if they had uncontrolled rights to appoint management.[30]

These observations underscore and affirm the need for GIST. Under the current MNC system, host country participation in the corporate decision making process is kept at the local level. The more localized the input, the more likely it is to be compromised. GIST avoids this pitfall by allowing host country input at the very highest level of the organization and outside of the employed personnel framework. With access at the apex of the decision making structure, no lower level decision would escape oversight. Further, since the corporation would not employ government representatives, pressure to conform to corporate norms and values would be neutralized.

GIST is not simply another conceptual configuration proposed as refinement of the interactive bargaining framework. It is the capstone of the numerous propositions that together serve as a prescription for harmonizing MNC–host country relations. GIST could virtually transform any one of the Gilpin models into a palatable arrangement for rich and poor countries alike with far more tolerable consequences. It has the desirable quality of being able to produce Pareto optimality. That is, roughly speaking, a policy measure can be considered "desirable" if it results in either everyone being made better off, or someone being made better off without anyone being made worse off.[31]

CONCLUSION

GIST views the world as a conglomeration of nation systems which either by historical accident or grand design have become interdependent and characterized by an inequitable distribution of gains derived from the relationship. A continuation of this inequity portends a world economic order beset by increasing economic disparity between rich and poor countries. Can the multinational corporation continue to play a strategic role in the developing world in light of such adversity? Can harmony exist between MNCs and host countries under the present system of international business?

It is inconceivable that the eternal destiny of the developing world holds no significant alteration in the MNC–host country business relationship. Under current arrangements, the multinational may very well suffer demise in the not too distant future. Nationalism and corporate takeover may become a regular occurrence as poorer nations experience increasing declining standards of living or no measurable gains.

The extent of future involvement of MNCs in the developing world will likely depend on how astutely they address the causes of nationalism and reverse the adversarial relationship so persistent between them and host countries. At the same time, host countries must play a role in the harmonizing process. Efforts by multinationals to improve conditions must be recognized and supported. After all, corporate takeover is no foolproof way of taking charge of their destiny and, if ill conceived, may inflict even greater hardship upon the local population.

GIST offers the necessary prescription for curing the ailing MNC–host country relationship. The missing link in the "sovereignty at bay," "dependencia" and "mercantilist" models of the future is the lack of legitimate decision-making input from host countries. Even the bargaining models are deficient in this regard. It is quite apparent that any interdependent economic order or mode of doing business that excludes host developing countries from participation in decision making that affects local internal development will not encourage harmonious relations; an atmosphere of distrust and conflict will likely prevail. GIST provides the framework for opening corporate decision making channels and does so in a way that accommodates the interests of the multinationals and the host country.

NOTES

1. John Fayerweather (1964). LRP for International Operations. In John S. Ewing and Frank Meissner (eds.). *International Business Management Readings and Cases*. Belmont, California: Wadsworth Publishing Company, 31.

2. Ibid.

3. Frederick Harbison and Charles A. Myers (1959). *Management in the Industrial World*. New York: McGraw-Hill Book Company, 391. See also John Fayerweather, ibid., 131–132.

4. See Ronald E. Muller and David H. Moore (undated). *Inter-American Relations and Latin American Investment by U.S. Multinational Corporations: Exploration of an Emerging New Harmony*. Prepared for U.S. Department of State, 25–27.

5. Ibid.

6. Muller and Moore appear to regard this as one of the major products of the new forms mode of interaction. See Muller and Moore, ibid., 28.

7. Benny Widyono (1978). Transnational Corporations and Export-Oriented Primary Commodities. *Cepal Review*, 138.

8. Robert Gilpin (1975). Three Models of the Future. In C. Fred Bergsten and Lawrence B. Krause (eds.), *International Organization*, 29(1), 37–47.

9. The titles of course are not new. Sovereignty at bay is taken from Raymond Vernon's book (1971) on the multinational corporation. *Sovereignty at Bay*. New York: Basic Books. The literature on dependencia is extensive. A good statement of this thesis is Osvaldo Sunkel, Big Business and 'Dependencia': A Latin American View. *Foreign Affairs, 50*, April 1972, 517–531. For a critical view of the dependencia thesis, see Benjamin J. Cohen (1973). *The Question of Imperialism: The Political Economy of Dominance and Dependence*, New York: Basic Books, Chapter 6. By Mercantilism, Gilpin refers to the priority of national economic and political objectives over considerations of global economic efficiency. This use of the term is broader than its eighteenth-century association with a trade and balance-of-payments surplus.

10. Robert Gilpin, ibid., 40.

11. Ibid.

12. John Diebold (1993). Multinational Corporations: Why be Scared of Them? *Foreign Policy, 12*, 87.

13. Historically, regional arrangements have tended to pit the developed world against the developing world. The problem posed by such an arrangement can best be explained by the principles of circular and cumulative causation. We observe that difference in economic competitiveness between rich and poor nations has produced striking regional per capita income disparities. Poor nations have attempted to close the inequality gap between themselves and industrialized countries by soliciting and engaging the assistance of industrialized countries' machinery to exploit their mineral resources, and by encouraging freer trade between rich and poor nations. But contrary to what the equilibrium theory of international trade would seem to suggest, the play of the market forces does not work towards equality in the remunerations to factors of production and, consequently, in incomes. If left to take its own course, economic development is a process of circular and cumulative causation, which tends to award its favors to those who are already well endowed and even to thwart the efforts of those who happen to live in regions that are lagging behind. The back setting effects of economic expansion in other regions dominate the more powerful, the poorer a country is. (Gerald M. Meier (1989). *Leading Issues in Economic Development*. New York: Oxford University Press, 385.) Putting this in another way, normally market forces tend to increase, rather than to decrease, the inequalities between regions. This can be easily illustrated by grouping nations into two regions: rich and poor. Within the rich region, economic integration or cooperation has already taken place, and has produced sustained economic development within the units comprising the region. As the level of economic development advances, expansionary momentum tends to make the units even stronger, thus increasing the aggregate strength of the region. The process of circular and cumulative causation tends to reward the progressive and well-endowed region and even to thwart the efforts of the lagging region. Therefore, what we come to realize here in the rich region–poor

region scenario is that market forces lead to the clustering of increasing returns activities in certain areas of the global economy. These areas become centers of agglomeration and accrue increasing internal and external economies regardless of the initial location advantage, e.g., mineral resources, a transport facility, etc. The limited advantages of cheap labor, common among Third World nations, are insufficient to offset agglomeration advantages. What this means then is that in a free trade economy such as a system of regions, as trade between industrializing and economically less developed regions is opened up, neither the principles of comparative advantage nor classical mechanisms of adjustment apply. Instead, because of increasing returns to scale, rich regions gain a virtual monopoly of industrial production. Monopoly power enhances economic development in rich regions and inhibits the poor. Further, because competition in industry is imperfect while it is nearly perfect in agriculture, movements in terms of trade favor the rich regions, which are of course comprised of industrialized nations. Trade by itself does not lead to economic development. This has to be brought about by pol icy interferences. (Gerald M. Meier, ibid., 385–386, and Harry W. Richardson (1993). *Regional Growth Theory*. London: The Macmillan Co., 29–30.)

14. Robert Gilpin, ibid., 43–44; and The Multinational Corporation and the Law of Uneven Development (1972). In Jagdish Bhagwati (ed.), *Economics and World Order: From the 1970s to the 1990s*. New York: The Macmillan Co., 113–114.

15. Ibid.

16. Ibid.

17. Benny Widyono, ibid., 138.

18. Chaitram Singh (1989). *Multinationals, The State, and The Management of Economic Nationalism: The Case of Trinidad*. New York: Praeger, 1–8.

19. Ibid., 5 and 6; Robert L. Curry, Jr. and Donald Rothschild (1974). On Economic Bargaining between African Governments and Multinational Companies. *The Journal of Modern African Studies*, 12, 2, 173–189.

20. Ibid., 5 and 6.

21. Ibid., 6 and 7; and Raymond E. Mikesell (1971). Conflict in Foreign Investor–Host Country Relations: A Preliminary Analysis. In Raymond E. Mikesell (ed.). *Foreign Investment in the Petroleum and Mineral Industries: Case Studies in Investor–Host Country Relation*. Baltimore: The John Hopkins Press, 38.

22. Ibid., 38.

23. Ibid., and Theodore H. Moran (1994). *Multinational Corporations and the Politics of Dependence: Copper in Chile*. Princeton: Princeton University Press, 159–160.

24. Ibid., 7 and 8.

25. Some contributors to the literature on MNCs argue that nationalism, in some instances, may be increased by successful ventures and the ability to take over and operate technically advanced ventures. Yet others alert us to the possibility that nationalism could interfere with the host government's development goals. See Chaitram Singh, ibid., 9.

26. See Chaitram Singh, ibid., 8. Some argue that such practices stem from the MNC's insecurity about the longevity of business agreements with the host country.

27. See Chaitram Singh, ibid., 8; and Franklin Tugwell (1995). *The Politics of Oil in Venezuela*, Stanford: Stanford University Press, 145–175.

28. Singh, ibid., and Tugwell, ibid.

29. Benjamin F. Bobo (1981). *Corporate and Third World Involvement: A Reciprocal Relationship.* Riverside, California: University of California; and Benjamin F. Bobo and Lawrence S. Tai (1996). Multinationals in the Third World: Reciprocity, Conflict Resolution and Economic Policy Formulation, *Journal of the Third World Spectrum*, 3(1).

30. Clive Y. Thomas (1975). Industrialization and the Transformation of Africa: An Alternative Strategy to MNC Expansion. In Carl Widstrand (ed.). *Multinational Firms in Africa.* Uppsala: Scandinavian Institute of African Studies, 337–338.

31. Amartya Sen (ed.) (1970). *Growth Economics.* Baltimore: Penguin Books, 33 and 49–50.

CHAPTER 9

Multinationals and the Caribbean: A Post-Colonial Perspective*

The Caribbean region poses a development dilemma that may be well served through an expanded business arrangement with the multinational corporation. Economic success in the region would advance new world order objectives and promote diminution of Third World inequality. However, providing a greater role for the multinational corporation meets with apprehension by some observers of the Caribbean situation who fear corporate dominance of the region's economic activity. A power-sharing interactive business arrangement model is provided in Chapter 8 that offers a means of moderating the tendency for corporate dominance. This chapter proposes an expanded role for the multinational corporation in Caribbean economic development under the assumption that the power-sharing model could be employed as a facilitating mechanism to allay fears of corporate dominance. With this in mind, the following presentation identifies opportunities to promote economic growth in the Caribbean that will benefit both the region and the corporation.

If the Caribbean is ever to achieve its full economic and market potential, the region's postcolonial objectives might well prescribe a greater role for the multinational corporation. Integration of the island states into a system driven by the laws of comparative advantage and organized

*Reprinted with permission. Benjamin F. Bobo, "Multinationals and the Caribbean: A Post-Colonial Perspective," *Journal of the Third World Spectrum* 6, no. 1 (Spring 1999), 96–97.

around production geared primarily toward supplying the internal regional market is seen as essential to achieving full economic prosperity. In this context, it is useful to recognize the shortcomings of colonial regimes in their management of Caribbean economics. Clearly, colonial regimes not only in the Caribbean but also throughout the Third World failed to install systems that promoted wealth sharing and sustained economic vitality. As disconcerting is the realization that postcolonial efforts in large part have produced no better results.

The multinational can play a potentially significant role in the integration process. Some observers of the Caribbean situation may perhaps find it problematic to expand the multinational's role in development objectives arguing that this would subject national states and governments to secondary roles as determinants of economic activity. But as BaNikongo asserts, what is observed in the Caribbean today is not a usurpation of efforts by the corporation but a cessation of initiative by governments.[1]

As the Caribbean region is an integral part of the Third World spectrum, economic success in the region would facilitate well new world order objectives which, as is widely perceived, must be accomplished before any sustained development can take place in the developing countries. This has become the predicament of the postcolonial regime.

With a view toward developing more effective postcolonial approaches to sustained growth in the Caribbean, this paper will assess the opportunities available to the multinational corporation to assist that process. Further, the paper will propose corporate *profit satisficing* as an alternative to profit maximization and an effective means of creating wealth sharing, a feat that postcolonial efforts have yet to realize.

POSTCOLONIAL OPPORTUNITIES

Participation of the multinational corporation (MNC) in Caribbean postcolonial development offers several opportunities to promote economic growth and wealth sharing that were unavailable to colonial regimes or certainly not pursued effectively by them. The MNC can further the growth process through assisting the:

- Integration of Caribbean islands,
- Creation of economy of scale,
- Development of an economic system governed by Ricardian comparative advantage
- Ladder and queue progression.

Before weighing the advantages of multinational participation in Caribbean development, it is important to clear the air on several sources of criticism of the MNC. While there is clear and supportable evidence that the capital, technology, management and marketing expertise of the MNC has been utilized to promote host country development objectives, there is also constant fear that the MNC may dominate development priorities. While critics may not accept neoclassical trade theory as a means of seeing the positive characteristics of the MNC, there are perhaps other means of reconciling the disparate views taken of the MNC. Meier has offered helpful comments in this regard. He deliberates that while an MNC is likely to project the power of an oligopoly; so too may indigenous independent companies or "simple" international enterprises. Further, an MNC may be involved in the costly process of import substitution; but so too may a domestic firm or a simple international corporation. An MNC may be depleting too quickly a wasting asset; but such behavior may be observed among indigenous enterprises. An MNC may be a vertically integrated operation that uses transfer prices to carry out the business of intrafirm trade; but this procedure may be also used by "simple" foreign investment from source country to a host country.[2]

Best, a Caribbean nationalist, has criticized the fact that the Caribbean policy has remained "passively responsive to metropolitan demand and metropolitan investment" and has suggested that important industry, e.g., manufacturing, tourism, bauxite extraction, has involved heavy dependence on multinational enterprise. The troubling feature is that invited enterprise produced little technology transfer hence did little to enhance local technical skills. Lewis had hoped that multinational firms would share the "tricks of the trade" with indigenous workers, but, unlike Best, recognized that nothing in the Caribbean development strategy had encouraged nor required a process of full and complete technology transfer.[3] In assessing the behavior and contributions of multinational firms, care should be taken to clearly identify whether undesirable outcomes (from the host's viewpoint) are a direct result of MNC wrongdoing or insensitivity, or the host's abdication of responsibility. If as BaNikongo suggests, the host government takes the necessary initiative to properly mesh local development objectives with those of the foreign corporation, the MNC-host relationship can be a truly beneficial one.[4] A recent study of factors germane to improving the MNC–Third World relationship by Bobo and Tai found that both host country policy makers and corporate leaders felt that a reciprocal business relationship in which objectives of host and MNC were duly addressed offered the greatest potential for a harmonious and profitable engagement.[5]

INTEGRATION OF CARIBBEAN ISLANDS

Integration of the Caribbean economies will be no simple feat. Comprising thirteen countries covering some 272,000 sq. km. with a population of about six million, the Caribbean countries though splintered in terms of border contiguity have an important characteristic that bodes well for integration policy. These countries, Antigua & Barbuda, Bahamas, Barbados, Belize, Dominica, Grenada, Guyana, Jamaica, Montserrat, St. Kitts &Nevis, St. Lucia, St. Vincent, Trinidad and Tobago have remarkably similar culture largely due to a common heritage and historical development. Caribbean integration can be well served by this feature especially in developing a common economic policy.

Caribbean economic integration may be likened to corporate merger. The combined entities can produce results that were not possible as stand alone units. In short, the whole (the merged or integrated units) is greater than the sum of the parts. Advocates of economic integration believe that its formation will accelerate the development of the member countries by (1) stimulating a more rational establishment and expansion of manufacturing industries, (2) enhancing trade and increasing gains therefrom, and (3) providing greater benefits from intensified competition. These outcomes will, it is expected, result in more efficiently productive member countries as a unified body.[6]

CREATION OF ECONOMY OF SCALE

Establishing and expanding manufacturing industries on a more rational basis is well couched in the creation of economies of scale. Economies of scale are production advantages deriving from expanded firm and market size. A large corporation, such as a multinational firm, can select more efficient production techniques than can a small-scale firm. A large manufacturer of clothing products, for example, can use elaborate assembly lines with robotics and computerization, but smaller firms must rely on less advanced technologies.[7] Employing an integration strategy in the Caribbean so endowed would mean encouraging foreign investment, particularly of the multinational kind, that would lead to increased market scope and firm size over time. Proper investment incentives could produce "spillovers" that would result in local producers, existing and newly formed, taking up positions in the market to support and supply ancillary needs of the multinational. This would avoid what Wonnacott referred to as the "hub and spokes trap" whereby the multinational as the hub and as an instrumentality of a developed country links the developed country to all the Caribbean countries, the spokes, which are not integrally related among themselves.[8] Moreover, as time passes, local producers would become more efficient and cost-effective through the competitive process. As local firms become more and more efficient, they cannot only supply to the multinationals more cost-effective support products, but can also become primary suppliers to the Caribbean market. The importance of this was recognized by a former Prime Minister of Trinidad and Tobago who noted that "in the Caribbean we produce what we do not consume and consume what we do not produce."[9] Clearly it is important to produce what you do not consume because of the value of export earnings. But it is as important to produce what you do consume because it promotes import substitution and relieves pressure on export earnings. In total the integration strategy will produce an overall more inclusive structure of market participation, while at the same time promoting the use of more efficient production methods, hence increasing labor productivity and economic growth in the Caribbean.

RICARDIAN COMPARATIVE ADVANTAGE

A country has a comparative advantage in a product when it can produce that product at a lower cost than that product can be produced by another country. This principle, advanced by David Ricardo in 1817, determines the commodities and services that a country will export or import. Caribbean integration, to produce the greatest benefits, must engage this principle. Indeed the very success of economic integration among the island nations will depend on how well this principle is employed in determining what each member country will specialize in producing and offer for trade. Specialization and trade increase the productivity of a country's resources and allow for larger total output than otherwise would be possible, hence greater income.

The task for an integrated Caribbean is to put the concept of comparative advantage into practice. This could be quite challenging given that the basic determinant of a nation's comparative advantage is relative factor endowment, that is, the quantities of labor, capital, and natural resources available from within. These are inputs that are necessary for production and each country is endowed with different quantities of them. If, for example, labor is the relatively abundant factor in a country, then the production process will be relatively labor-intensive, wages relatively low, and prices of commodities produced also relatively low. In this scenario, the country will have a comparative advantage in labor-intensive products.[10]

This is a likely scenario for Caribbean integration. Caribbean nations have limited relative factor supplies of natural resources and capital. Thus based on their own means, the integrated nations must emphasize their relative factor supply of labor. But this is where the integration process will be challenged. Successful exploitation of the labor advantage will require some minimum technological proficiency even in a labor-intensive mode. Girvan has reported that the Caribbean has developed virtually no capabilities in this regard, and Chernick has observed that while technical education is expanding through academic emphasis, by and large, the Caribbean work force lacks industrial skills and attitudes.[11]

Though vocational training through the formal education process can quite ably produce the required level of technical proficiency to support establishment of comparative advantage in the Caribbean, post-independence educational reform has fallen far short of this achievement. But perhaps despair is not warranted here. Technical competency can be obtained through the multinational corporation. On-the-job and specialized training programs are regular features of the corporation and may be utilized to supplement formal schooling and even as a stand-in where the formal process is absent.

Further, the Caribbean can enhance its power of comparative advantage through accessing an external factor supply of capital. The multinational corporation offers this factor resource. It is heavily endowed with capital supplying capability, which can be utilized to support Caribbean economic integration.

LADDER AND QUEUE

Caribbean integration will be subjected to the normal 'ladder and queue' structure of development and world trade. The pace of progression in the ladder and queue process will depend on integration development strategy. Exhibit 9.1 illustrates what can be expected in progressing up the ladder and moving through the queue.

Typically countries enter world markets through natural resource–intensive exports. Caribbean countries to some extent have reached this rung through exporting bauxite, sugar, oil, etc. If countries are fortunate, their workforce acquires at least basic technical skills at this level through employment in export industry. These skills are necessary to help

Exhibit 9.1
Ladder of Comparative Advantage

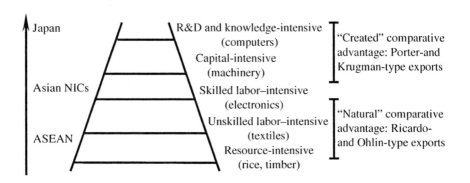

Source: Gerald M. Meier (1995). *Leading Issues in Economic Development*, New York: Oxford University Press, 458. © 1995 by Oxford University Press, Inc. Used by permission of Oxford University Press, Inc.

countries further develop export capability (and import substitution capability as well) which, over time, pushes them to higher rungs on the ladder of comparative advantage. In this regard, Caribbean nations have not done well. Unlike the Caribbean, comparative advantage achievement is in full swing in Asia. Japan's accomplishments are well known. Its progression up the ladder has been followed by Korea which initially exported primary products in the late 1950s, moved upscale to textiles and plywood in the 1960s, and followed in the 1970s with iron and steel products and electrical machinery. Asian NICs, e.g., Hong Kong, Taiwan, South Korea, and Singapore, are following Japan up the ladder. These countries are more and more encouraging the substitution of machines for labor and moving toward high technology production. Countries behind the Asian NICs in the queue, e.g., Indonesia, Malaysia, Thailand, and the Philippines are gaining a foothold on the ladder and seeking opportunities through comparative advantage that will push them to the next rung and beyond.[12]

The ladder and queue process offers a formidable challenge to Caribbean integration. Moving from natural resource–intensive exports to simple manufactures and then to more complex and high tech manufactures will require relative factor endowment that is well beyond the Caribbean's current capacity. Labor is relatively plentiful but unskilled; natural resources are available but limited; and capital is lacking in degree and sophistication. How then can Caribbean integration move forward with any realistic hope of success? The multinational corporation may be the key ingredient needed in the integration scheme. The multinational has the capacity to provide sufficient capital to support industrial development, turn unskilled laborers into skilled technicians, and convert natural and imported resources into import substitutes. A well thought out integration strategy with the MNC as essentially a relative factor endowment could spell success for Caribbean integration.

MNC: THE INTEGRATING FORCE

The multinational corporation has been spoken of as essentially a change agent having the capacity to spur Caribbean integration and development principally because it is a unit of integration in the world economy.[13] What is needed in the Caribbean case is a physical stimulus that can assist in a substantial way to thrust economic integration in a forward direction. With its ability to transmit factors (capital, skills, technological know-how, management expertise) and its economies of scale in R&D and marketing, the MNC is the prime mechanism available to the Caribbean as an integrating force. Integration of the thirteen nations is inhibited by national barriers to commodity trade and impediments to international factor movements. By its multinational operations and intrafirm transactions, the MNC transcends these obstacles. As a planning and implementation unit that makes resource allocation decisions, the MNC becomes the mechanism for making effective the Caribbean's potential comparative advantage. The MNC makes available the complementary resources of capital, technology, management, and market outlets that may be necessary to effectuate a comparative advantage to the labor surplus factor endowment prevalent in Caribbean countries.[14] The labor endowment is the Caribbean's unrealized wealth. The MNC through its ability to train labor and put it to its highest and best use can make this wealth a reality.

PROFIT SATISFICING: SHARING THE REWARDS OF INTEGRATION

There is yet another opportunity for the multinational corporation to assist Caribbean integration. Benefits to be derived from Caribbean integration are potentially enormous. The net benefit (net money flows) to member countries will in large measure determine the real success of Caribbean integration and MNC participation. The MNC's share of benefits derived from international operations is typically quite large. This is due primarily to profit maximization strategies pursued by the corporation.

A prevailing hypothesis in conventional microeconomics is that corporations seek to maximize profits.[15] Profit maximization is rooted in the corporate world of finance where managers and investors continuously explore ways to maximize shareholder wealth. Shareholder wealth maximization is a rather imposing practice—one that has contributed to a skewed pattern of wealth among peoples and countries.[16] It is regarded as facilitating a growing population of "have-nots" while simultaneously placing a larger and larger share of the world's wealth in the hands of a very small group of "haves."[17]

The multinational corporation is in a unique position, through its enormous market presence, to moderate the practice of shareholder wealth maximization. To this end, the corporation may well adopt a *profit satisficing* approach to profit making. In this vein, corporate profit making strategy would be directed at a satisfactory rather than an optimum choice. Thus, in the interest of facilitating wealth sharing between rich and poor, the corporation would not pursue a maximum level of profit but a satisfactory or reasonable level (return on investment). When attained, it would feel no further need to pursue higher profit. Essentially, the corporation becomes a satisficer doing only as well as is necessary.[18] This form of profit making would lead to considerable increased net benefit to the Caribbean integration process by reducing money (profit) outflows.[19]

CONCLUSIONS AND FUTURE RESEARCH

Integration of the Caribbean nations is likely to prove a difficult process. Not only are there thirteen administrative powers to unite, the relative factor endowment in the Caribbean is far less than desirable. But successful economic integration is not out of the realm of possibility and the multinational corporation can conceivably offer significant help in this regard. This paper has explored ways that the integration process might be enhanced through participation of the MNC but more research is needed.

At least four courses of research are required to assess how best to pursue the opportunities available to the multinational corporation in assisting Caribbean economic integration; one that addresses how sovereignty and national autonomy of the thirteen separate governments can be successfully incorporated in the integration effort; one that examines potential integration schemes relative to Caribbean integration objectives; one that inquires about the products, technology and marketing strategy that would offer the greatest opportunity to bestow an effective comparative advantage to the Caribbean's labor surplus factor endowment; and finally one that inquires about the plausibility of *profit satisficing* and how it might be implemented in a Caribbean integration scheme. This should yield the necessary inputs to allow formulation and design of a workable integration scheme.

NOTES

1. BaNikongo, BaNikongo (1995). The Splintered Caribbean in an Integrated World: Planning for the 21st Century. *Journal of Third World Studies*, XII(2), 106.

2. Gerald M. Meier (1995). *Leading Issues in Economic Development*. New York: Oxford University Press, 256.

3. Jay R. Mandle (1996). *Persistent Underdevelopment*. The Netherlands: Gordon and Breach Science Publishers SA, 80.

4. BaNikongo, ibid.

5. Benjamin F. Bobo and Lawrence S. Tai (1996). Multinationals in the Third World: Reciprocity, Conflict Resolution and Economic Policy Formulation. *Journal of the Third World Spectrum*, 3(1).

6. Meier, ibid., 507.

7. Campbell R. McConnell and Stanley L. Brue (1996). *Economics*. New York: McGraw-Hill, Inc., 387.

8. See BaNikongo, ibid., 113.

9. Ibid., 110.

10. Meier, ibid., 455.

11. See Mandle, ibid., 81.

12. Meier, ibid., 457.

13. Ibid., 257.

14. Ibid.

15. Milton Friedman (1953). *Essays in Positive Economics*, University of Chicago Press; and Armen Aichian (1950), Uncertainty, Evolution and Economic Theory. *Journal of Political Economy*.

16. *Hungry for Profit* (video). New York: Richter Productions, 1994.

17. *World Development Report* (1994), New York: Oxford University Press.

18. Herbert A. Simon (1947). *Administrative Behavior*. New York: Free Press; and Simon (1958). *Organizations*. New York: Wiley; and Richard Cyert and James March (1963). *A Behavior Theory of the Firm*. Englewood Cliffs, NJ: Prentice Hall.

19. Benjamin Bobo (1996). Multinationals, the North and the New World Order: Objectives and Opportunities. *Proceedings of the Fifth World Business Congress*. International Management Development Association. Hamilton, Bermuda, 112–113.

CHAPTER 10

Third World Investment Strategy: The African Predicament

Africa is even more in need of development assistance than the Caribbean, and again an expanded role for the multinational corporation is proposed. In large measure, Africa is the underperformer among poor regions of the world. The continent's economic predicament is no less than alarming; it is characterized by heavy debt, low per capita income, and a host of other ills. African governments are assessing their situation and seeking sustained means of stimulating economic development. This chapter highlights the challenges to African economic development and, in wrapping up the discussion, proposes MNC involvement. As in the case of the Caribbean, an underlying assumption here is that Africa would be well served by a greater meshing of MNC and African objectives, particularly in the power-sharing interactive business arrangement context proposed in the GIST presentation. Solving the African predicament or even reasonably approaching a resolve would be one of the great successes in the battle against inequality, and in redress of the rich country–poor country dilemma.

The World Bank identifies 42 heavily indebted countries, 34 of which are in Africa. This is particularly alarming since it means that more than 60 percent of some 55 nations in Africa are mired in debt. Moreover, their per capita incomes are largely at the bottom of the world economic ladder. No other continent comes close to such disturbing distinction. One observer reports,

Africa is the great exception to the defining and otherwise global economic trend of recent decades: steady improvement in people's lives. In absolute terms, the head count of global poverty has fallen by 400 million. Some places (China, India) have seen steeper drops than others. Region by region, though, poverty has dropped everywhere, except in Africa. There, it continues to rise. Africa is making progress here and there, but far more slowly than are other poor regions. On virtually every measure, it is the outlier, the under performer. Africa is the great development failure.[1]

Further, as another observer notes, "In sub-Saharan Africa 40% of people exist on less than $1 a day, and average per capita income is lower now than in the 1960s. One African in five lives in a country severely disputed by war."[2] It is difficult to resist asking what went wrong. But in reality, the appropriate question may be—what never went right? Numerous terms ably describe the character of the continent, but none seems to quite capture the full essence as does *predicament*. The continent is indeed in a predicament, overcome by an impaction of social, political, and economic forces that raise doubt of any hope of resolve. How did Africa arrive at this port of despair and how can it depart?

   Robert S. Browne has written a thought-provoking paper entitled *How Africa Can Prosper*, in which he offers very enlightening comment on the African predicament.[3] The paper is particularly noteworthy in that Browne in numerous ways underscores Andre Gunder Frank's proposition concerning the "development of underdevelopment" referenced in this volume. Browne asserts that regional trading blocs more and more favored by Europe and the United States erode the economic bargaining power of African states.[4] This view essentially parallels Frank's premise that developed countries have usurped the economic potential of Third World countries to support their own economic objectives.[5] Both points of view offer valuable insight into how Africa has developed its unenviable condition. To be sure, regional trading blocs pose formidable competition for African states, and developed countries have unjustly availed themselves of African natural resources without fair and due compensation. But other factors create overwhelming challenges to African economic development and help to further explain the African predicament. Browne calls attention to a number of these factors.

ARRIVAL AT THE PORT OF DESPAIR

   In initializing his argument, Browne asserts that free trade policy so staunchly supported by Europe and the United States is clearly contradicted by the European Union and NAFTA (North American Free Trade Agreement).[6] These organizations create formidable barriers to free trade and cast a dim light upon the notion of comparative advantage—the guiding principle for free trade. When country A can produce a good or service more cheaply than country B, it is said that country A has a comparative advantage. When country B can produce a good or service more cheaply than country A, then country B has a comparative advantage. The important principle derived from this is that a country should specialize in the production of goods and services in which it has a comparative advantage because such behavior results in the most efficient production and optimum general economic welfare.[7] In terms of international trade, optimum general economic welfare refers to the general betterment of all nations—including African nations.

However, if an African nation held a comparative advantage, it would be rendered ineffective by regional trading blocs such as the European Union and NAFTA, which restrict the free flow of commerce among nations. Worse yet is the restrictive power of the G8, the largest industrial nations in the world. Even with a comparative advantage, how does an African nation achieve entry into this brotherhood of nations? All advocate free trade, but none supports it as Adam Smith proposed—that is, only completely unfettered trade will give free rein to the principle of comparative advantage.[8] Paul R. Krugman writes, "If there were an Economist's Creed, it would surely contain the affirmations 'I understand the Principle of Comparative Advantage' and 'I advocate Free Trade.'"[9] An African nation may well write, "If there were an Economist's Creed, it would surely contain the affirmations 'I understand the Principle of Comparative Advantage' and 'I advocate Free Trade'—as soon as I achieve it." The problematic nature of free trade links to other impediments to Africa's economic development. Browne underscores the matter of mini-states and economic irrationalism.[10] Africa is for the most part a compilation of very small nations; the largest are comparatively small relative to the United States, Japan, or the European Union. Domestic markets of mini-states are generally too small to accommodate enterprise of any efficient scale, thus making it exceedingly difficult to sustain development initiatives. Smallness often has the unique problem of critical mass—too few resources, people, skills, and innovators, and too little capital. Hence, there is no engine of growth to spawn economic independence, and certainly not comparative advantage. An economic unit created as a mini-state of government and too small to achieve critical mass or an efficient scale of production is an irrational undertaking. The critical mass problem is exacerbated by trade barriers. With limited avenues to international markets and limited capacity to compete, particularly with the G8, African countries simply are unable to take advantage of lucrative trade opportunities to any significant degree.

Amplifying the problem of critical mass is that African countries are in the difficult position of being price-takers rather than price-makers. Browne argues that this is in part because they rely primarily on export of natural resources and import of manufactured products.[11] Natural resource exports tend to provide very limited comparative advantage, and primary dependence on imports points to a serious weakness in the ability to achieve "created" comparative advantage (see the discussion in Chapter 9). As such, African countries don't wield pricing power associated with comparative advantage. Further, because their economies are small, they exercise less influence over the prices of their exports and imports than might otherwise be the case if they had critical mass.

Communications between African countries and the outside world are often less problematic than direct communications among African countries themselves, which further hampers development efforts. Absence of an African telecommunications superhighway, long within the capacity of communications technology, has prevented development of an intra-continental system of linkages that would promote easier business relationships among African countries.[12] That this remains a problem for the continent perhaps points to the persistence of the effects of colonialism and the desire of outside interests to maintain a system of linkages that primarily encourage trade between Africa and Europe (and generally the G8) rather than among African countries. This is perhaps consistent with Andre Gunder Frank's argument that "contemporary underdevelopment is in large part the historical product of past and continuing economic and other relations between the satellite underdeveloped and the now developed metropolitan countries."[13] No doubt, poor communications linkages among African countries will persist for some time and continue to obviate networking opportunities so important to business development, hence economic growth.

A further obstacle to African economic development, according to Browne, is the lack of economic complementarity among African countries, particularly neighboring ones. Most of them produce mineral or agricultural commodities that are exported overseas; these products are rarely used in the unprocessed form, and few African countries have the capacity to convert them into finished or consumer goods on a significant scale.[14] The demand for consumer goods provides very attractive trade opportunities among nations. The limited capacity to produce consumer goods impedes opportunities for comparative advantage and thereby thwarts intra-African trade. Because they are unable to supply mutual needs or to counterbalance mutual deficiencies—capacities necessary for economic complementarity—African countries lose the power of development that these capacities facilitate.

The lack of an international currency, Browne contends, also contributes to the challenges facing African economic development. This is a rather serious problem among Third World countries on the whole, and certainly is an impediment to intra-African trade. This is no less a problem for trade between Africa and the outside world. With no mutually acceptable transaction currency and the nonconvertibility of most African currencies, intra-African trade as well as international trade must be conducted in hard currency. Because Africa has limited means to generate hard currency, that is, to produce goods and services that can be sold for dollars, francs, or pounds, not only is trade impeded, but imports of commodities that support economic development activities are restricted as well.[15] This places African countries in a veritable catch-22. Their development is constrained because they lack sufficient hard currency, and they lack sufficient hard currency because their development is constrained.

Another matter according to Browne that has drawn rather significant attention regarding Africa's economic development predicament is the notion of collective self-reliance. Alarmed by their inability to reverse the persistently declining economics of the continent, in the late 1970s and early 1980s, African countries adopted a sort of export-substitution strategy. As such, Africa was to pursue more direct production of goods it needed rather than producing goods for export and using the proceeds of the sales to purchase imports. This was seen as giving Africa a sense of self-reliance. Further, recognizing the critical mass problem, African governments were called upon to create regional markets in a move toward regional economic integration, thus making the development initiative one of collective self-reliance. The Economic Community of West African States (ECOWAS) and the Preferential Trade Area of Eastern and Southern Africa (PTA) are essentially prototypes of this initiative but have had little success.[16]

The collective self-reliance initiative raised the ire of the donor community and particularly the World Bank. As the export-substitution strategy was effectively an import-substitution program, Browne contends that the World Bank rejected it because of its departure from the Bank's export-led development philosophy. Further, according to Browne, the World Bank in concert with the wishes of developed countries "find it in their interests to keep the African countries as mainly exporters of raw materials and importers of manufactured items rather than to assist them in becoming tenacious industrial competitors, as the newly industrialized countries of East Asia have become."[17]

That Africa stands as a symbol of development failure doesn't simply speak to the ineffectiveness of African initiatives, but also to the insidious nature of outside interests. While one may elect to debate Browne's commentary on the African predicament, it is clear that Africa's arrival at the port of despair was not all its own doing; there were many hands at work, and not all in the best interest of Africa. And, while Browne provides important insight into Africa's disappointing progress, a very fundamental matter looms large within the scope of development failure. Perhaps South Africa's president, Thabo Mbeki, identifies the matter best when he conveys that "good governance on our continent, comprehensively understood, is of fundamental interest to the peoples of Africa."[18]

President Mbeki further directs that Africa must ensure "that measures for good governance are put in place through which our governments are accountable to their peoples; that best practices are agreed upon and put in place for economic and political governance."[19] He also notes that "many African countries are embracing globalization. Their leaders speak of the need for good governance. Equally important, African leaders— and their foreign friends—are now emphasizing the importance of honest government and respect for human rights. As Amartya Sen, the Nobel laureate, has eloquently explained, development requires—and, indeed, is inseparable from—greater freedom."[20]

Generally, governance is problematic throughout Africa and the Third World. Without a radical change in governance on the African continent, no amount of development initiatives will have a significant chance of succeeding. Poor governance is perhaps as much to blame for Africa's arrival at the port of despair as any other factor. Despite the insidiousness of outside interests, Africans have sufficient independence to adopt and embrace a fundamental precept in the pursuit of good governance—the rule of law. Clearly, good governance encompasses more than the rule of law and how it's practiced. However, there is some notion that good governance is difficult to define. Hilton L. Root, in his book *Small Countries, Big Lessons: Governance and the Rise of East Asia*, confides that:

good governance, a much sought after precious commodity . . . evades definition. It arouses the sharpest disagreements and inspires the greatest introspection. Social welfare depends upon it, yet no one agrees on its definition. Some nations believe it to be too subjective to be discussed with outsiders. Other governments believe it to be too volatile a topic to be discussed even among citizens. Some governments are willing to discuss governance, providing the word is not mentioned in the discussion. Some assume their own experience provides the universal thread, while others believe their case is unique, its evolution impenetrable from the outside. Yet today it is obvious that beliefs and assumptions must be put aside and a dialogue opened, as progress toward world development clearly hinges on progress in good governance.[21]

While defining good governance may be a difficult task, prescribing what gives rise to good governance may be well within our capacity. Logical and rational thought, based upon experiential observations, judgment, wisdom, and the like, would seem to support the notion that good governance largely evolves from an institutional mapping that prescribes and implements an organization of governmental decision-making units complete with a government philosophy or set of guiding principles (a constitution), procedures for implementing these principles, and rules of law to assure that they are observed and practiced. The degree to which this mapping affords an efficient and effective outcome depends largely upon the nature of the principles, procedures, and rules of law, and how these elements are operationalized. The following presentation offers a prescription for good governance and, furthermore, suggests that the elements of the prescription are either poorly represented or poorly delivered in the African case.

In this prescription, usage of "good" is a quality measure that implies implementation and operationalization of principles and procedures without chaos, that is, such that resulting outcomes are efficient and effective and that affected constituencies are in general agreement. With "good" setting the tenor of performance, the institutional mapping would encompass the interplay of five essential elements: good rules/constitution, good policy apparatus, good institutions, good political feasibility, and good government capacity. Thus, good governance derives from the design, implementation, and delivery of these elements. More than any other, the key task here surrounds the ability of a government to deliver what it promises,[22] and to provide its citizenry opportunities to actualize their expectations.

A legitimate government form, it seems, would have a constitution that sets forth foundational philosophy and rules that prescribe a system of fundamental principles and laws that delineate the structure, nature, functions, and limits of government. At the very core of this prescript is how much power to allow the central government, how the citizenry will be represented, the number of representatives, and how the representatives will be elected. The constitution stands at the forefront of the institutional mapping and provides the core justification for the governance process.

Essential to good governance is the character of the policy apparatus. A policymaking process that supports formulation of public policies appropriate for the general welfare of the citizenry is vital to ensuring fair representation to all. Policies should accommodate the social, economic, and political dimensions of the citizenry's needs. Because these policies imply promises to the citizenry, it is important to the policymaking process that the government is capable of implementation and delivery. The interplay of the elements in the institutional mapping depends heavily upon government to carry out what has been proposed.[23]

Good governance further requires good institutions and institutional capacity. Bodies of government and systems of society designed and operating to efficiently and effectively facilitate the policy apparatus serve the general welfare. Daron Acemoglu, in his paper *Root Causes: A Historical Approach to Assessing the Role of Institutions in Economic Development*, argues that

good institutions have three key characteristics: enforcement of property rights for a broad cross section of society, so that a variety of individuals have incentives to invest and take part in economic life; constraints on the actions of elites, politicians, and other powerful groups, so that these people cannot expropriate the incomes and investments of others or create a highly uneven playing field; and some degree of equal opportunity for broad segments of society, so that individuals can make investments, especially in human capital, and participate in productive economic activities. These good institutions contrast with conditions in many societies of the world, throughout history and today, where the rule of law is applied selectively; property rights are nonexistent for the vast majority of the population; the elites have unlimited political and economic power; and only a small fraction of citizens have access to education, credit, and production opportunities.[24]

Good institutions and institutional capacity can directly assist government in promoting and coordinating policy objectives as they provide frameworks and mechanisms to facilitate desired outcomes.[25]

Good governance also depends upon good political feasibility. The ability to gain public support through free speech and broad participation in the political process is crucial to achieving good governance. Consensus building and broad coalitional support for government limits favoritism and special interest group protection that renders government ineffective in delivering policies that benefit the entire citizenry. Practices such as observance of the one-person–one-vote rule and institutionalized dialogue instill confidence in the public policy decision-making process. Outcomes such as income equality; wealth distribution across the masses; and inclusionary social, economic, and political participation promote political feasibility.[26]

The presence of government capacity works in concert with the other elements of good governance. The administrative capability to enforce policy decisions in a fair and consistent manner is necessary to achieve effective and efficient outcomes as prescribed by public policy. Good government capacity requires that bureaucracies have autonomy from special interest groups, that agencies have oversight, and that judicial systems have autonomy from political power. Government cannot effectively carry out nor achieve policy objectives where public administrative capacity is weak.[27]

All things said, good governance derives from not one but several interdependent or mutually supporting elements of government structure. Good rules/constitution, good policy apparatus, good institutions, good political feasibility, and good government capacity all work in concert to ensure an accountable, predictable, and transparent policy environment. Absent these elements, achieving successful economic development outcomes will be in a practical sense impossible. This is particularly relevant in the African case, where economic activity is impeded by flawed processes occasioned by nontransparent and discretionary decision making; weak institutional capacity, particularly in the areas of regulation, service delivery, and social spending; and the incapacity to achieve the balance between private and social costs and benefits. Critical to stimulating robust economics is ensuring that the regulatory environment is supportive of economic activity.[28] This has been a daunting challenge for Africa as some or all of the elements of good governance are in distress, and moreover, an effective and efficient interplay of the elements has not been achieved.

DEPARTING THE PORT OF DESPAIR

So what then is Africa to do? Clearly, there are numerous problems to tackle. The continent is turning its attention to the New Partnership for Africa's Development (NEPAD), the socioeconomic development program of the African Union, and an initiative of the Organization of African Unity. Conceived as a partnership between African leaders and G8 countries, Africa has high hopes that NEPAD will provide the direction and impetus for successful economic development so long sought.[29] Africa's optimism is premised on the view that

the NEPAD program sets out a critical set of actions to speed up African economic development through integration of trade, finance, labor, and infrastructure between individual African economies. Deeper integration gives rise to a number of direct and indirect benefits, including, but not limited to, lower transaction costs (tariffs and exchange rates); increased flows of goods, services, capital, and people; expansion of economic opportunities; increased public revenues and greater means for social development; broader transfers of knowledge and technology; greater regional political stability; and fewer asymmetric exogenous and endogenous shocks and, hence, fewer negative spillovers.[30]

Success of NEPAD rests heavily upon G8 countries to recognize Africa as a partner in world trade and thereby to fully open their markets to African exports, facilitate G8 investment in Africa, expand debt relief, and provide significantly higher levels of aid.[31] As such, there is reason for pessimism. G8 members stress that their support of NEPAD is not a Marshall Plan for Africa. Their support is more of a political commitment, thereby requiring demonstrated action by African countries to foster good governance and the rule of law, human investment, poverty reduction, and economic growth policies. This expectation on the part of the G8 may not be realized, as African governments in the past have tended to underfund or ignore commitments. In addition, promises made by G8 members are rather suspect, as they have hedged on delivery of pledged support for previous plans for African economic development.[32]

With the potential of NEPAD to lift Africa from the port of despair yet to be determined, other approaches to development may be considered. One approach that is receiving a good measure of attention is that employed by nongovernmental organizations (NGOs). These are nonmembership support organizations engaged in relief, rehabilitation, or community development initiatives particularly in Third World countries. NGOs, it is argued, utilize development strategies that fall between market-led and state-led strategies. These strategies emphasize grassroots development and therefore are viewed as fostering a "third or middle sector" enabling the development of marginalized populations. NGOs provide goods and services where markets are inaccessible to the poor or where governments lack capacity to address their needs. In NGO strategies, people are organized and trained to solve their own problems and are active participants in their own development.[33]

This people-centered approach to development is gaining support from the international donor community as many of these donors are channeling an increasing share of their development funds through NGOs. Reportedly, in 1980, donor funds made up less than 10 percent of NGO budgets; by the 1990s, donor funds accounted for 35 percent. World Bank support is particularly noteworthy. "From 1973 to 1988, NGOs were involved in about 15 World Bank projects a year. By 1990 that number had jumped to 89, or 40 percent of all new projects approved."[34] "And in 1997, approved World Bank projects in Third World countries involving NGOs were: 84 percent in South Asia, 61 percent in Africa, and 60 percent in Latin America and the Caribbean."[35] Notwithstanding donor interest in NGOs, critics argue that funds from such powerful donors as the World Bank may compromise their independence and effectiveness.[36] While NGOs offer definitive assistance to addressing the massive development problem facing Africa, NEPAD is conceived to address the whole of the problem though not yet implemented. Despite the upside capabilities of these sources of help, there are some downside risks. Both require government or government-sponsored aid to carry out program activities. Traditionally, such support comes with strings attached and is complicated by government red tape. Demands made upon recipients by donors can compromise development initiatives and obscure lines of autonomy between them. Further, bureaucratic inefficiency can slow or disrupt the implementation of development plans, as required government approvals are subject to administrative procedure and political influence. For these reasons, African economic development may not be well facilitated solely by NEPAD and NGOs. So what are Africa's options at this point?

Africa's residency at the port of despair is unquestionably a very serious predicament. Marshalling all possible resources in an effort to resolve the matter would appear requisite. Clearly, NEPAD and NGOs offer alternative approaches to African economic development and no doubt will achieve useful outcomes. However, with NEPAD relying on G8 assistance (essentially a government-to-government model), and NGOs relying on World Bank funding (essentially a government-to-corporation model), there is a third approach to development, and importantly, one that escapes the downside risk of these models. This alternative is the corporation-to-government model, which calls for the involvement of the multinational corporation in African economic development. This model does not fall prey to bureaucratic red tape, nor is it openly susceptible to or delivered with strings attached—certainly not to the extent of politically motivated government aid. To be sure, G8 assistance has a component of the corporation-to-government model based on the G8 members' commitment to encourage direct foreign investment in African countries, but this calls for external government action. The MNC model avoids this potentially politically compromising approach altogether in that there is a very direct relationship established between the corporation and African governments from the outset, and importantly, no external government input is required. Although external government policies may encourage foreign direct investment by multinationals, multinationals can and do act quite independently of such influence as opportunities and situations dictate.

The efficiency of the multinational corporation is without parallel. Examples of the multinational's capacity are numerous, even though there is much debate as to the kinds of effects it generates. "Economic liberals see them as forces for positive change, spreading good things like technology and efficiency around the world. Economic nationalists see them as threatening the sovereignty of nation-states. Marxists and structuralists worry that they are creating a world marked by inequality and dependency."[37] As the theme of this book associates the multinational as a force for positive change in the Third World, but not overlooking the dangers of its power, the discourse that follows in Chapters 11 and 12 sets forth a specific framework within which the MNC can advance the interests of the corporation as well as the host country in a constructive and gainful manner. Hence, the multinational is viewed as a change agent with the expertise and, given the appropriate operating framework, the capacity to "reasonably" level the playing field between rich and poor countries. In the process, poor countries would develop some measure of comparative advantage. At that point, it seems pragmatic that these countries would be in a position to further develop comparative advantage under their own powers and capacities.

NOTES

1. Clive Crook, "When Economic Development Just Isn't Enough," *National Journal* 34, nos. 33–35 (2002), 2436.

2. Greg Mills and Jonathan Oppenheimer, "Partners, Not Beggars," *Time Europe* 160, no. 2 (2002), 35.

3. Robert S. Browne, "How Africa Can Prosper," in David N. Balaam and Michael Veseth, eds., *Readings in International Political Economy* (Upper Saddle River, NJ: Prentice-Hall, Inc., 1996), 280–293.

4. Ibid., 280.

5. Andre Gunder Frank, "The Development of Underdevelopment," in David N. Balaam and Michael Veseth, eds., *Readings in International Political Economy* (Upper Saddle River, NJ: Prentice-Hall, Inc., 1996), 64–73.

6. See Browne, ibid., 280.

7. The general reader will find very concise statements on comparative advantage and free trade in Christine Ammer and Dean S. Ammer, *Dictionary of Business and Economics* (New York: The Free Press, 1977), 8, 168.

8. Ammer and Ammer, ibid., 168.

9. See Paul R. Krugman, "Is Free Trade Passé?" in Linda S. Goldberg and Michael W. Klein, eds., *Current Issues in the International Economy* (New York: HarperCollins College Publishers, 1992), 3.

10. Browne, ibid., 280.

11. Ibid., 280–281.

12. Ibid., 281.

13. Frank, ibid., 65.

14. Browne, ibid., 281–282.

15. Ibid., 282.

16. Ibid., 283, 286.

17. Ibid., 283.

18. Thabo Mbeki, "Mbeki: African Union Is the Mother, NEPAD Is Her Baby," *New African* 415, no. 44 (2003).

19. Thabo Mbeki, "New Partnerships for Africa's Development," *Presidents & Prime Ministers* 10, no. 6 (2001), 30–32.

20. Philippe Legrain, "Africa's Challenge," *World Link* 15, no. 3 (2002), 3.

21. Hilton L. Root, *Small Countries, Big Lessons: Governance and the Rise of East Asia* (New York: Oxford University Press, 1996), 145.

22. Ibid., 147.

23. Ibid., 147.

24. Daron Acemoglu, "Root Causes: A Historical Approach to Assessing the Role of Institutions in Economic Development," *Finance and Development* (The International Monetary Fund) 40, no. 2 (2003), 27.

25. Root, ibid., 150.

26. Ibid., 151–155.

27. Ibid., 151–155.

28. Trevor A. Manuel, "Africa and the Washington Consensus: Finding the Right Path," *Finance & Development* (The International Monetary Fund) 40, no. 3 (2003), 19–20.

29. Richard Cornwell, "A New Partnership for Africa's Development?" *African Security Review* 11, no. 1 (2002), 91–96; Thabo Mbeki, "Mbeki: African Union Is the Mother, NEPAD Is Her Baby, ibid., 44; and Thabo Mbeki, "New Partnerships for Africa's Development," ibid., 30–32.

30. Manuel, ibid., 20.

31. S.K.B. Asante, "A Partnership of Unequal Partners," *New African* 419 (2003), 14–17.

32. Ibid.

33. J. Wagona Makoba, "Nongovernmental Organizations (NGOs) and Third World Development: An Alternative Approach to Development," *Journal of Third World Studies* XIX, no. 1 (2002), 53–55.

34. Ibid., 55–56; and Marguerite Michaels, "Retreat from Africa," *Foreign Affairs* 72, no. 1 (1993), 103.

35. Makoba, ibid., 56.

36. Ibid., 56–57; Marguerite Michaels, ibid.; and Nicolas Van de Walle, "Aids Crisis of Legitimacy: Current Proposals and Future Prospects," *African Affairs* 98 (1999), 346.

37. Leon Grunberg, "The IPE of Multinational Corporations," in David N. Balaam and Michael Veseth, eds., *Introduction to International Political Economy* (Upper Saddle River, NJ: Prentice-Hall, Inc., 1996), 338–359.

CHAPTER 11

Whose Wealth to Maximize: The Third World as Stakeholder*

Resolving inequality is no doubt a monumental task. The literature is pronounced with suggestions and propositions, and the foregoing dialogue joins these efforts in assessing the problem of inequality and in fact proposing an approach to redress. This initiative sees the multinational corporation as the central figure in tackling the inequality problem and indeed as the change agent with the motivation and tools necessary to bring the problem under control. The primary motivation of the multinational corporation is shareholder wealth maximization, largely driven by the profit motive, specifically profit maximization. The effort to maximize profits leads to efficient resource allocation, which is asserted to be in the best interest of society. Parenthetically, the profit motive is a key factor in the economic progress of G8 countries. Casting the multinational corporation as change agent in tackling the inequality problem invariably promotes the profit motive as the tool of change. While embracing the profit motive in Third World economic development may be the key to promoting sustained growth, pursuing it in terms of profit maximization can have rather harsh consequences in some environments, so that the potential ill effects must be reconciled. *Profit satisficing* is proposed as a means of reconciliation. "Whose Wealth to Maximize: The Third World as Stakeholder" discusses this matter and undertakes an analytical recitation to demonstrate that *profit satisficing* does not violate the profit maxim.

*Reprinted with permission. Benjamin F. Bobo, "Whose Wealth to Maximize: The Third World as Stakeholder," *International Third World Journal and Review* 11 (2000), 19–26.

S. J. Chang's paper entitled "Whose Wealth to Maximize" published in the *Journal of Financial Education* raises important questions about the firm's objective to maximize shareholder wealth that are particularly pertinent in today's global economy.[1] In a nutshell, Chang poses what well may be the ultimate question—"Should shareholder wealth maximization or the resultant stock price maximization (SWM) be the *only* relevant goal for the firm to pursue?" The import of shareholder wealth maximization extends back to the teachings of Adam Smith who, as Chang deliberates, never foresaw his contributions to the behavioral theory of the firm making possible the multinational corporations of today. Moreover, would Smith ever have imagined that these global mega-firms would serve as instruments of home country government policy[2] and, as Andre Gunder Frank asserts, would essentially arrange the uninitiated hosts, particularly Third World, into a system of satellites from which resources are extracted for the good of home society,[3] in large part for the sake of shareholder wealth maximization?

CORPORATE GOOD VS. GREATER GOOD

In view of the workings of shareholder wealth maximization, one wonders whether Smith's and others' contributions have not simply explained the firm's behavior but defined it as well.[4] There is virtually a push-pull effect operating on firm behavior. As managers read the posits of theorists, they are in some ways pushed along by arguments of what has happened and pulled along by assertions of what should or could happen. This is not to suggest that theorists predetermine the firm's behavior, but the influence is rather apparent. This goes to the very foundation of *whose wealth to maximize*. Arguments for and against SWM, as pointed out by Chang, themselves challenge each other as to whether the corporate good (shareholder's interest) or the greater good (customer's and society's interest) should be the target of management's primary toils. That the challenge is public and that management is exposed to it indirectly prepares management to accept or reject SWM. Hence, management's future behavior is somehow predicated upon and indeed influenced by debate on the matter.

The literature well reveals the debate to which management is subjected.[5] Most apparent is the general acceptance of shareholder wealth maximization as an accurate description of a firm's goal. There are, however, some dissenting views as pointed out in Chang's paper that are particularly noteworthy. Cyert and March very early on devised a behavioral theory of the firm that cast doubt on the validity of SWM as an accurate portrayal of management's primary aim.[6] They as well as others to follow argue that the greater good, such as customer satisfaction and the welfare of the community-at-large, is not being adequately reflected in daily market valuations. From this point of view, the traditional SWM-driven corporate governance may make the basic principles of financial economics insufficient to meet the challenges of today's corporate management.[7] Coase supports this argument in suggesting that corporate behavior should be examined not only from the shareholder's perspective, but also the customer's and society's. Coase regards these as stakeholders in the larger scheme of shareholder wealth maximization, and therefore, deserve to be reflected in daily market valuations.[8]

Although the full implications and consequences of the opposing viewpoints are not yet known, shareholder wealth maximization as presently construed may suffer a delimiting character by virtue of its designers. Eiteman and Stonehill strongly assert that modern finance is based on assumptions about market behavior and investor preferences found primarily in the U.S. and U.K., and that these assumptions are not easily transferable to other countries.[9] Balling supports this view by noting that "most finance textbooks with a global circulation are written by authors from the Anglo-Saxon world."[10] Chang's impression of SWM is that "the applicability of such uniquely defined paradigm is limited on foreign soils."[11] These views suggest that consideration of the customer and society-at-large in shareholder wealth maximization seems particularly pertinent, especially in light of the Andre Gunder Frank argument.

If Frank's impression is at all relevant, it may be particularly so within the context of demands being made by host Third World nations who are taking issue with their satellite status and are demanding a closing of the inequality gap between the developed and the developing world through a doctrine of wealth redistribution.[12] In one scenario, they see the multinational corporation with its enormous resources as a change agent with the capacity to make a real difference in this regard.[13] Indeed, the multinational has at its disposal several options that give it the ability to single handedly impact the inequality gap perhaps far beyond any benefit currently provided to the host country through external sources, e.g., foreign aid.[14]

PROFIT SATISFICING

One option with such potential magnitude would require a serious address of Chang's statement in which he questions whether shareholder wealth maximization should be given supreme priority in the firm's pursuit of financial returns. Importantly, the multinational corporation must necessarily embrace the idea that the customer and society are stakeholders, that they are affected by corporate activity, and that their interests are no less important than those of shareholders, if not more, in the corporate investment equation.[15] With this stakeholder premise as operating protocol, the option alluded to above becomes far less likely to be rejected outright and far more likely to be included in discussions of alternative views to the traditional concept of shareholder wealth maximization.[16]

What then is this option that could potentially give the power to significantly impact the wealth gap between rich and poor countries? Instructively, shareholder wealth maximization invariably leads the corporation to pursue profit maximization strategy, since it is integral to (but not fully reflective of) SWM. It is clear that shareholder wealth maximization requires a more direct consideration of risk and return than does profit maximization,[17] but profit maximization makes a major contribution to the determination of owner's wealth. Herein lies the power source. Profit maximization wields a big stick in that it fosters a practice of charging whatever price the market will bear. Milton Friedman has asserted that the responsibility of the corporate manager is to conduct business in accordance with the shareholder's desire, which is to make as much money as possible.[18] On the upside, this could be relatively enormous. It places an overwhelming burden on especially Third World consumers who already face severe budget constraints. Under the stakeholder premise outlined above, the multinational has the option of releasing some of the power of profit maximization. This may be approached through an alternative profit motive scheme—*profit satisficing*.[19] This pricing behavior would be directed at finding a satisfactory rather than an optimum choice. Hence, in the interest of facilitating wealth redistribution between rich and poor nations, the corporation would not aim at a maximum but rather at a satisfactory level of profit. As such, the corporation would only pursue a reasonable level of profit and when attained, it would feel no need to do anything more. Essentially, the corporation becomes a satisficer and does only as well as necessary.[20] The *profit satisficing* option may be considerably beneficial to Third World stakeholders in the way of wealth redistribution by increasing their share of the benefits realized from resource exploitation.

THE NOTION OF NON-MAXIMIZING

Many students of corporate behavior including economists such as Michael Porter, Richard Nelson, and Sidney Winter argue that firms in reality exhibit a *profit satisficing* character.[21] They assert that firms are simply incapable of assessing all possible market conditions, calculating probable outcomes, and selecting those that maximize expected profits. Alternatively, as they suggest, firms pursue existing operating routines as long as they successfully produce satisfactory profits, and not until profits become unreasonably low or fall low enough to threaten their survival do firms investigate new ways of operating or seek new lines of activity.[22]

Those opposing the notion that firms display non-maximizing behavior argue that efficient resource allocation is best achieved under profit maximizing strategy and that indeed firms as well as investors are strongly motivated by the pursuit of profits. Charging whatever price the market will bear is perhaps the cornerstone of profit maximizing behavior, and is directly promoted under shareholder wealth maximization. Proponents of profit maximization assert that the level of profits is a function of competitive ability not the incapacity of the firm to manage in a maximizing mode. This view is consistent with the dominant hypothesis in economics, which characterizes firm behavior as profit maximizing. Alchian and Friedman assert that a firm that does not maximize profits is destined for failure.[23]

If the firm behaves as if it is profit maximizing be it through efforts to maximize expected discounted cash flows or through some other means, and does so by producing only that output which results in the highest possible profit, then it fits the true character of a profit maximizer. Classical economic theory depicts this type of firm behavior as most prevalent and most likely to succeed. This typical firm then is the target of the *profit satisficing* argument discussed herein in that it has the option to remain a profit maximizer or to convert to a profit satisficer. The former exacts maximum profits from stakeholders while the latter takes only what is satisfactory and no more.

Does *profit satisficing* mean that a firm is less likely to succeed? This is a pertinent and yet rather sticky question. Exhibit 11.1 offers a starting point in addressing this matter. Although the profit-maximizing firm produces only that output which results in the highest possible profit, the "best"

Exhibit 11.1
Output of the Firm Under Profit Maximizing and Profit Satisficing

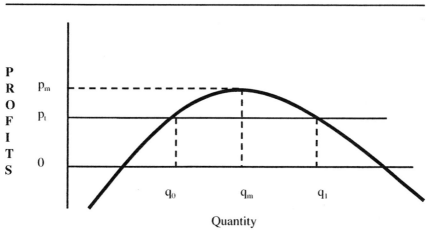

See Lipsey, R.G., Courant, P.N., Purvis D.D. & Steiner, P.L. (1993). *Economics* 10th ed. New York: HarperCollins College Publishers.

level of output depends on the motivation of the firm and its views on shareholder wealth maximization.[24] The exhibit depicts output of the firm under profit maximizing and *profit satisficing*; the curve shows the level of profits associated with output levels. A profit-maximizing firm produces output q_m and earns profit p_m. A *profit satisficing* firm with a target level of profits, p_t is willing to produce any level of output between q_0 and q_1. Therefore *profit satisficing* permits a range of outputs on either side of the profit maximizing level. This flexibility may be a more practical way to approach profit making since the target level of profit is attainable through various output levels, thus perhaps, allowing greater opportunity for the firm to succeed.

There are other factors that bear consideration in assessing the firm's likelihood of success particularly in the Third World arena. Andre Gunder Frank's argument that Third World countries have been exploited largely for the benefit of the First World cannot be ignored.[25] It is in this context that the firm, the multinational corporation, is regarded as an instrument of First World efforts to sustain economic systems in developed countries. An outright rejection of the multinational by Third World hosts could seriously curtail corporate revenues, thereby bringing into question the continued viability of the firm. Further, the call for a redistribution of wealth between the First World and Third World is of particular importance. The inequality gap between developed and developing countries persists, and the recent global economic turmoil has exacerbated the situation. The multinational has perhaps a unique opportunity, through *profit satisficing*, to show leadership in addressing the inequality issue. Millions of Third World consumers, stakeholders to be sure, are pejoratively affected by the wealth gap. Their happiness or lack thereof, could play a significant role in determining just how successful the firm will be in the future.

EFFICIENCY WITH EQUITY

Shareholder wealth maximization as currently practiced depends on an unrelenting devotion to efficiency subscribing fully to maximum exploitation of society's resources and their allocation to highest and best use, with the most able stakeholders accruing the greatest benefit therefrom. Most textbooks take the theoretical direction in providing that SWM leads to the greatest efficiency in allocating resources and to the greatest economic good for the greatest number.[26] Is there tolerance for equity in this approach? Primeaux and Stieber argue in the affirmative from the perspective of neoclassical economic theory. Addressing the matter from the profit maximization side of SWM, they begin with the basic interpretation of profit maximization as that set of conditions where the marginal revenue of the firm is equal to its marginal cost. At that point, the firm will be operating at an output level that provides society the maximum amount of goods and services that can be produced with available resources. This asserts Primeaux and Stieber, is the most efficient allocation of society's resources.[27] But is it the most equitable allocation of resources?

Downplayed in profit maximization, hence SWM, is the notion of fair-sharing the benefits of resource exploitation among society's members. In the context of this discussion, fair-sharing would mean taking only a reasonable profit thus affording Third World stakeholders greater sharing of resources by virtue of less profit. On the face of it, this may give the appearance of requiring lower prices on goods and services. But such is not necessarily the case, since a price reduction may not lead to the highest and best use of society's resources. There may be more practical approaches to achieving this objective. For example, fair sharing could mean undertaking a policy of *stakeholder givebacks* in that the corporation commits a portion of its profits to needed Third World projects, such as infrastructure, schools, parks and recreation, housing, health care, agriculture, etc. These initiatives would be outside those activities that normally would be undertaken to support corporate objectives. Hence, a *profit satisficing* policy doesn't necessarily, as one may fear, call for abandoning the profit maximization model or including *profit satisficing* parameters in the model.

Admittedly, *stakeholder givebacks* may raise concern about the profit-maxim rule: mr = mc. That is, does *profit satisficing* disturb the precept that each factor of production is paid according to its worth and that the marginal productivity of each factor approximates to its price. This matter can be best addressed through empirical research. But, obviously, data would be hard to come by since the concept has yet to be applied. However, there is perhaps a means of purporting no disturbance to the profit maxim rule, hence, early validation of the notion of *stakeholder givebacks*. In the context of this discussion, *stakeholder givebacks* receive treatment much as does profit sharing, a well-accepted medium of stakeholder (the employee) recognition. It is generally observed that profit sharing preserves the profit maxim.[28] Although there are only a few studies available on the relationship between profit sharing and profitability, empirical results support use of profit sharing. FitzRoy and Kraft, using 1979 data on German metalworking firms, found positive effects of profit sharing on profitability.[29] Using 1979–89 data on British firms, Bhargava also found a positive relationship between profit sharing and profitability.[30] These findings were supported by Mitchell et al. using 1986 data on U.S. firms. Their results showed that profit sharing increases firm profits.[31]

As asserted here, *profit satisficing* through *stakeholder givebacks* would be no less profit maxim preserving than profit sharing. The object of profit sharing is to induce a special degree of effort, efficiency, cooperation, and other desirable results not readily occasioned by other means.[32] These inducements affect profits in a positive way, leading to an enhancement of firm value. In a like manner, *profit satisficing* is viewed as having the capacity to improve firm value in the sense that national sentiment toward the firm in the Third World responds to a caring image.[33] *Stakeholder givebacks* would signal that the firm has the country's broader interest in mind. Well known are the traditional contributions made through the provision of products people are willing and able to buy, including tax revenues, foreign currency earnings, employment, and technology transfer. These benefits to welfare clearly produce positive marks on the firm's image. But more can be done to maximize the firm's contribution to welfare and thereby maximize a positive image. *Stakeholder givebacks* have the power to take the firm beyond traditional contributions to welfare and image building. When appropriately targeted, *givebacks* could boost internal capacity in the Third World and stimulate economic growth.

Rostow has postulated that investment in capacity building prompts the emergence of "leading sectors," the growth of which is thought to be instrumental in propelling the economy forward.[34] Support for important matters as infrastructure development, educational facilities, small business enterprise, and the like, would lead to capacity building. Clearly, these are long run initiatives with equally long run outcomes. But once the forces of *profit satisficing* are set in motion and ultimately take hold the impact on the well being of the firm may be even more profound than in the case of profit sharing. *Profit satisficing* is quite simply an investment in image building. Numerous benefits to the firm are conceivable. Entry options strategy, negotiated agreements and concessions, employee relations, public relations, name identity, product demand, and a host of attendant factors may benefit quite significantly. The perceived risk associated with the nature and level of investment upon entry into Third World markets may be lessened over time as host governments and populations develop greater appreciation of the foreign investor. An improved image would do much to offset the risk of asset nationalization, rejection of foreign presence, acts of aggression against personnel and facilities, uncooperative government agencies and officials, and so on. The ability of the firm to negotiate more favorable terms and conditions of business arrangements, i.e., with regards to taxation, profits repatriation, import restrictions, wage rates, ownership structure, etc., would be heightened by an improved image. The image of the firm is crucial to eliciting employee loyalty and public respect. Efficiency and productivity are well served when workers have high regard for the firm. And, efforts to promote product awareness in the marketplace are made less onerous by a receptive public. Further, a good image facilitates name identity, an important factor in establishing market presence. Ultimately, greater name identity leads to more robust product demand.

The host of benefits the firm stands to realize as a result of investment in image building through *stakeholder givebacks* invariably places the firm in an enhanced profit mode. Over the long run, the prospect of increasing profits through *stakeholder givebacks* would promote competition and efficiency in Third World markets. In the usual case, opportunity to profit maximize is vigorously pursued by the firm. *Stakeholder givebacks* offer such an opportunity. Long term, the *stakeholder givebacks* game could push profitability significantly beyond traditional profit making approaches.

As firms find their place in *stakeholder givebacks* schema, a primary concern is the potential free-rider problem: firms may not be as forthcoming with *stakeholder givebacks* as expected since an individual corporation receives only 1/n of the benefit generated by its philanthropy. This too is a concern for profit sharing.[35] However, proponents of profit sharing assert that the free-rider problem can be mitigated and indeed solved as the profit sharing games are repeated over time. They argue that laborers would learn to work collectively, thereby benefiting from the advantages of cooperative behavior and group coalescence over the inferior equilibrium of free riding. Peer monitoring, they further contend, is another means of overcoming the free-rider problem. Workers can monitor each other, and apply sanctions in certain situations.[36] The view taken regarding the free-rider problem and *stakeholder givebacks* essentially tracks that taken by proponents of profit sharing.

Essentially, free riding in the *stakeholder givebacks* game also would be solved through repetition over time. Firms would learn that the cumulative effect of cooperative effort in *profit satisficing* over the long run would produce benefits that are superior to those achieved through free riding. Further, the market leader effect would play an important role in assisting *profit satisficing* to overcome the free rider problem. Free rider inclined firms would be encouraged by the need to keep pace with the competition as early participants in the *stakeholder givebacks* game move forward with *profit satisficing* policy. The threat of exposure as a free rider is an overriding motivation to cooperate.[37]

The effectiveness of *profit satisficing* depends on *stakeholder givebacks* implementation strategy. What should be the *profit satisficing* level (p_t)? How much is too much? How little is too little? Is there an optimum level of participation? Should *profit satisficing* vary across industries or sectors based on risk? How can firms carry out *profit satisficing*? These are questions for future research and analysis as they are outside the scope of this discussion.[38] However, experience with profit sharing taught us that time and trial and error ultimately will identify the appropriate level of p_t. As for operationalizing a *profit satisficing* policy, it is perhaps too early in the discussion of this issue to suggest with any degree of certainty what form this might take. But, important devices that may be helpful exist internal and external to the firm. Internally, the philanthropy mechanism may be engaged. As it is typically an operating unit within many firms, cost should not increase significantly.[39] Externally, a low-cost option could involve the not-for-profit sector. The capacity of this device is well known and an accepted means of actualizing philanthropic activities.[40]

THE ETHICS ISSUE AND THE PRINCIPAL-AGENT PROBLEM

Corporate managers adopting a *profit satisficing* policy may find themselves in an ethical dilemma, or what appears to be so. The ethics of profit making in the context of this discussion is essentially bimodal. On the one hand, a corporate manager has an ethical responsibility to maximize shareholder wealth as governed by the principal-agent relationship between shareholder and manager.[41] The shareholder, the "principal," and the manager, the "agent" of the principal, have essentially a contractual relationship. As such, the principal fully expects her/his agent to pursue shareholder wealth maximization as a primary goal since this behavior is consistent with her/his primary motivation for investing in the firm. Adopting a *profit satisficing* policy on the part of the agent may be viewed as abandoning shareholder wealth maximization by the principal no matter how plausible and socially responsible the notion *of stakeholder givebacks* may seem.

The flip side of the manager's responsibility to the shareholder is the troubling recognition of a responsibility to the firm's broader arena of stakeholders. The manager, particularly multinational manager, is confronted with the ever persistent income gap between First World and Third World consumers, and the impact of profit maximizing behavior on further exacerbating the problem. To be sure, there is no agency relationship between the manager and Third World consumers. But if the notion that "the customer is always right" has any validity, then the expectations of Third World consumers may well be as important as those of the shareholders. Moreover, if Third World consumers are in fact stakeholders, wealth maximization strategy should include their interests as well as those of shareholders. Third World consumers want to close the inequality gap and the call for wealth redistribution between rich and poor nations is a clear signal of their expectations. *Profit satisficing* may be an important step in legitimately addressing such expectations.

This view of the principal-agent relationship having been considered, another perspective of the matter deserves comment. *Profit satisficing* may in actuality improve the principal-agent relationship. The corporate manager is essentially compelled to pursue available opportunity to maximize shareholder wealth, to be sure within risk-return parameters. *Stakeholder givebacks* offer the opportunity to pursue this objective with a range of potential long run benefits to the firm; benefits that potentially lead to profit maximization beyond traditional means. Profit maximization furthers the shareholder wealth maximization agenda. *Profit satisficing* makes imminently good sense even if the firm is focused on the short run.

Though profit policy may be short run in nature, the firm exists over the long run. An investment in future benefits, as the notion of *stakeholder givebacks* proposes, would eventually inure the firm. Over time, returns to shareholders would be impacted in a positive way as *profit satisficing* takes hold. In this light, the principal-agent relationship is well served.

WISDOM OF *PROFIT SATISFICING*

Whether *profit satisficing* can, or should, become an operational alternative to profit maximization remains to be seen. It would no doubt require a modification of shareholder wealth maximization objectives. But as Chang suggests, as corporate management is becoming more diverse, multi-national, and cross-cultural, alternative approaches to maximizing shareholder wealth merit further discussion in the finance community.[42] Certainly ignoring the cries of the Third World for greater equality among rich and poor nations is unwise. Emerging Third World markets will be the source of lucrative future business opportunities, the successful cultivation of which will depend on the multinational corporation's image in Third World countries.[43] Protecting that often fragile image will likely mean that multinationals must treat Third World people as bonafide stakeholders rather than mere spectators. Chang notes that for example, when multinationals open new facilities in Third World countries, SWM does not fully recognize the impact of pecuniary costs on the welfare of stakeholders or the social and cultural implications of such projects. Barnet and Muller also raise concerns in this regard, noting the negative effect on local economies of accounting practice indiscretions on the part of the firm—underpricing exports, overpricing imports, and overvaluation of technology.[44] Stakeholders can suffer untold injury from corporate activity and in a like manner corporations can suffer deep trauma to their image by ignoring stakeholder welfare.

Arguably, no matter how pertinent the concern for stakeholders, conventional wisdom well may lead us to conclude that the shareholder wealth maximization model handles the complexities of corporate decision-making and market dynamics as well as can be expected. Those who believe firmly in shareholder wealth maximization in promoting efficient markets would reject alternatives to SWM, fearing less efficient outcomes. This fear of the unknown, however, may not be sufficient rationale to ignore the possibilities. When Adam Smith first ventured into the free market arena, a journey that later gave birth to the notion of profit maximization, he surely was beset with grave concerns about the potential pitfalls and dangers of the unknown. But time and scholastic thought have smoothed the bumpy road that lay ahead of him.

Many may view efforts to address the interests of Third World stakeholders through *profit satisficing* as a step back to the Middle Ages when the theory of *a just price* was the centerpiece of economic doctrine and the fundamental ideal that no one should take advantage of another was the operating rule.[45] Some may even view it as a challenge to capitalism.[46] On the contrary, the interest in *profit satisficing* seeks neither to elevate medieval thought nor to give credence to Marxian principles. The failure of these to produce any appreciable advances in socioeconomic development is well documented.[47] Rather the objective is simply to make capitalism, using a currently popular expression, more user friendly. The stakeholder surely has as credible a position in the corporate objective as the shareholder; one supplies the capital, the other consumes the product of the capital. Can the corporation exist without the interplay of both parties? Hence, should the welfare of one be subordinated to the other? If the conventional corporate objective is to give adequate recognition to this relationship, further scholarly inquiry is requisite. In Chang's closing statement the task is clear: "our evaluation of corporate objective should by no means be static or immutable."

FINAL COMMENTS

An inclusionary approach to shareholder wealth maximization whereby the full scope of parties served by as well as affected by the corporation's pursuit of profit invariably makes good sense. In the global scheme, everyone has a stake in how the world's resources are used. As stakeholders, those who have benefited less from the exploitation of those resources can reasonably present a fair-sharing case. While neoclassical theory and capitalist philosophy have argued well for highest and best use of our resources, the distribution of the benefits therefrom has been less than equitable. The many examples of poverty and degradation around the globe sufficiently attest.

Corporate objective can be a powerful tool in addressing poverty and the inequality gap between rich and poor nations. Through its vast resources and enormous capacity, the multinational corporation has the ability to raise the stakeholder to a higher level of importance in shareholder wealth maximization ideology. The *profit satisficing* proposal is one means of doing so, and the Third World context offers a platform that is perhaps unrivaled on the globe. Certainly, poverty there is in need of serious redress.

Profit satisficing, to be sure, would be a radical departure from traditional profit maximizing strategy. Can it stand the test of efficient resource allocation and highest and best use principles? Can it produce a more equitable distribution of the benefits of resource exploitation without unduly compromising efficiency? Since little is known about *profit satisficing* as a corporate objective, research initiatives are needed to further evaluate its potential. At the very least, clear operating frameworks will be needed to assure continued corporate viability.

NOTES

1. Chang's discussion of shareholder wealth maximization is quite insightful. See S.J. Chang (1997). Whose Wealth to Maximize. *Journal of Financial Education* 23, 1–13.

2. These issues are discussed in John Fayerweather (1972). The Internationalization of Business. *Journal of the American Academy of Political and Social Science*, 403. See also R. Gilpin (1975). *U.S. Power and the Multinational Corporation*. New York: Basic Books, Inc.; and P. Jalee (1968). *The Pillage of the Third World*. New York: Monthly Review Press.

3. See Andre G. Frank (1966). The Development of Under-development, *Monthly Review* (September).

4. A thorough presentation of contributions to economic analysis underlying shareholder wealth maximization is presented in W.F. Kuhn (1970). *The Evolution of Economic Thought*. Chicago: South-Western Publishing Co.

5. Chang quite ably discusses the various viewpoints as presented in the literature.

6. See R.M. Cyert and J.G. March (1963). *A Behavioral Theory of the Firm*. New Jersey: Prentice Hall.

7. See A. Bhide (1994). Efficient Markets, Deficient Governance. *Harvard Business Review* 72, 128–39; and C.K. Prahalad (1994). Corporate Governance or Corporate Value Added?: Rethinking the Primacy of Shareholder Value. *Journal of Applied Corporate Finance*, 4(6), 40–50.

8. See R.H. Coase (1937). The Nature of the Firm. *Economica*, 386–485. For additional insight, see M.C. Findlay III, and G.A. Whitmor (1974). Beyond Shareholder Wealth Maximization. *Financial Management* 3.

9. See David K. Eiteman and A.I. Stonehill (1986). *Multinational Business Finance* 4th ed. Reading, MA: Addison-Wesley. Additionally, McGoun and Kester discuss the problem of implanting the Western corporate virtues in Asian countries (noted in Chang, Whose Wealth to Maximize).

10. See Chang, Whose Wealth to Maximize, 2.

11. Ibid.

12. For an extensive discussion of Third World demands, see Benjamin F. Bobo (1996). Multinationals, the North and the New World Order: Objectives and Opportunities. *Proceedings of the International Management Development Association*, 107–114.

13. See R.D. Steade (1978). Multinational Corporations and the Changing World Economic Order, *California Management Review 21*, 6; and Benjamin F. Bobo and Lawrence Tai (1994). Topicos Sobre Las Relaciones Norte-Sur y El Nuevo Ordern Mundial [Issues in North-South Relations and the New World Order] *Contabilidad Y Auditoria*, 95–118.

14. Ibid.

15. See S.J. Grossman and J.E. Stiglitz (1977). On Value Maximization and Alternative Objectives of the Firm. *Journal of Finance* 32, 387–415; Chang, 5–7; and B. Cornell and A.C. Shapiro (1987). Corporate Stakeholders and Corporate Finance. *Financial Management 16*, 5–14.

16. See Chang, 1–9.

17. See R.H. Anthony (1960). The Trouble with Profit Maximization. *Harvard Business Review 38*, 126–134; and R.B. Coffman (1983). Is Profit Maximization vs. Value Maximation also Economics vs. Finance? *Journal of Financial Education, 12*, 37–40.

18. See P. Primeaux and J. Stieber (1994). Profit Maximization: The Ethical Mandate of Business. *Journal of Business Ethics, 13,* 287–94.

19. For an earlier discussion of *profit satisficing* see Bobo (1996). Multinationals, the North and the New World Order: Objectives and Opportunities. *Proceedings of the International Management Development Association,* 107–114.

20. Ibid. Simon raised the satisficing issue in his work on administrative behavior. See H.A. Simon (1947). *Administrative Behavior.* New York: Free Press, and *Organizations* (1958). New York: Wiley.

21. See M. Porter (1987). From Competitive Advantage to Corporate Strategy. *Harvard Business Review 65,* 43–59; and R. Nelson and S.G. Winter (1982). *An Evolutionary Theory of Economic Change.* Cambridge, Mass: Belknap Press.

22. Ibid. See also, Anthony (1960). The Trouble with Profit Maximization. *Harvard Business Review,* 38.

23. Profit maximizing behavior is characterized in A. Alchian (1950). Uncertainty, Evolution and Economic Theory. *Journal of Political Economy 21,* 39–53; and Milton Friedman (1953). *Essays in Positive Economics,* Chicago: University of Chicago Press.

24. R.G. Lipsey, P.N. Courant, et al. (1993). *Economics,* 10th ed. New York: HarperCollins College Publishers.

25. Frank presents a compelling case on First World exploitation of Third World countries largely to the benefit of First World countries. See Frank, The Development of Underdevelopment.

26. This is quite apparent as characterized in B. Stewart (1993). Continental Bank Roundtable on Global Competition in the 90s. *Journal of Applied Corporate Finance, 6,* 51–55; A.M. Okun (1975). *Equality and Efficiency: The Big Tradeoff.* Washington, DC: The Brookings Institute; N.G. Mankiw (1998). *Principles of Microeconomics.* New York: The Dryden Press; and E.W. Nafziger (1990). *The Economics of Developing Countries,* 2nd ed. Upper Saddle River, NJ: Prentice Hall.

27. Primeaux and Stieber offer an informative presentation using the profit maxim approach to discussing shareholder wealth maximization. See Primeaux and Stieber (1994). Profit Maximization: The Ethical Mandate of Business. See also G. Poitras (1994). Shareholder Wealth Maximization, Business Ethics and Social Responsibility. *Journal of Business Ethics, 13,* 125–34.

28. Kim sheds further light on the relationship of profit sharing to profitability. See Seongsu Kim (1998). Does Profit Sharing Increase Firm's Profits? *Journal of Labor Research, 19*(2), 351.

29. See Felix FitzRoy and Kornelius Kraft (1986). Profitability and Profit Sharing. *Journal of Industrial Economics, 35,* 113–30.

30. See Sandeep Bhargava (1994). Profit Sharing and the Financial Performance of Companies: Evidence from U.K. Panel Data. *Economic Journal, 104,* 1044–56.

31. Daniel J.B. Mitchell, David Lewin, and Edward E. Lawler, III (1990). Alternative Pay Systems, Firm Performance and Productivity. In Alan S. Blinder, ed. *Paying for Productivity: A Look at the Evidence.* Washington, DC: The Brookings Institute, 15–95.

32. See Kim (1998). Does Profit Sharing Increase Firm's Profits? 352.

33. This *profit satisficing* perspective is discussed in Benjamin F. Bobo (1999). Multinationals and the Caribbean: A Post-Colonial Perspective. *Journal of the Third World Spectrum, 6*(1), 96–97.

34. The central thesis in Rostow's argument is that the growth of leading sectors can foster economic take-off, a process in which the scale of economic activity

reaches a critical level and produces progressive and continuous positive structural transformation. See W.W. Rostow (1959). The Stages of Economic Growth. *Economic History Review*, 63–40.

35. Kim discusses this problem in the context of profit sharing. See Kim (1998). Does Profit Sharing Increase Firm's Profits? 352.

36. Ibid.

37. Ibid.

38. Future research on this topic could have potentially high payoffs since the concept advanced here suggests that *profit satisficing* may make a strong contribution to the understanding and resolution of issues surrounding the welfare of the Third World as well as the firm, particularly regarding the ability of the multinational corporation to serve as a change agent in the Third World development process.

39. This matter is discussed in Leland Campbell and Charles S. Gulas (1999). Corporate Giving Behavior and Decision-maker Social Consciousness. *Journal of Business Ethics*, 19(4).

40. See Jennifer Mullen (1997). Performance-Based Corporate Philanthropy: How Giving Smart Can Further Corporate Goals. *Public Relations Quarterly*, 42(2), 42; and Charles T. Clotfelter and Thomas Ehrlich (1999). Philanthropy & the Nonprofit Sector in a Changing America, *Wilson Quarterly* 23(3), 125.

41. See Lipsey, Courant, Purvis, and Steiner, *Economics*.

42. See Chang (1997). Whose Wealth to Maximize, 1–13.

43. See Bobo (1996). Multinationals, 107–114.

44. See R.J. Barnet and R.E. Muller (1974). *Global Reach*. New York: Simon and Schuster.

45. See Albino Barrera (1997). Exchange-value Determinization: Scholastic Just Price, Economic Theory and Modern Catholic Social Thought. *History of Political Economy*, 29(1).

46. Kornai discusses socialist and capitalist ideologies in Janos Kornai (2000). What the Change of System from Socialism to Capitalism Does and Does Not Mean. *Journal of Economic Perspectives*, 14(1).

47. Ibid.

CHAPTER 12

GIST and Profit Satisficing: Toward More User-Friendly Shareholder Wealth Maximization

Viewing the multinational corporation as change agent, GIST and *profit satisficing* are proposed in the interest of giving the corporate motive broader appeal and application. This initiative moves the corporation to a new and more progressive mind-set whereby the corporate manager thinks in terms of enhancing the wealth of both stakeholder and shareholder. A mind-set transition is requisite to developing and advancing a new corporate decision-making process necessary to facilitate inequality diminution. Since the prevailing corporate decision-making apparatus does not focus on the inequality issue, new decision-making processes are needed for this purpose, particularly if the multinational corporation is to become the proposed change agent. This chapter articulates a new corporate decision-making apparatus that provides a framework and structure for transitioning the corporation from an exclusively shareholder wealth maximization mind-set to one of stakeholder wealth enhancement. This section of the book is perhaps the single most important entry in the entire undertaking because it lays out a step-by-step decision-making procedure to enable corporate management to understand and adopt the new apparatus that is critical to addressing the inequality issue.

Making shareholder wealth maximization (SWM) more user-friendly presupposes that it is of kindred character. To be sure, SWM is not simply a concept and certainly not one without portfolio. It powers the largest economy in the world, enables the most robust production and distribution system known to mankind, and in so doing embodies the

mind and spirit of the most innovative people in the world. Is SWM therefore congenially representative of a people's mind-set, and perhaps more
importantly, can it equitably serve the will and interest of all peoples?
Does it have the capacity to resolve the rich country–poor country
dilemma? No doubt these place a heavy and formidable burden on SWM,
but its essential strength may be gleaned through the broader treatise of
capitalism. SWM, in a manner of speaking, operationalizes capitalism.
Recall that capitalism's greatest detractors, Karl Marx and Friedrich
Engels, appreciated capitalism for its exuberance,[1] although at the same
time they assumed that it would be transcended by socialism through the
natural order of social development. That capitalism has sustained itself
over time is testament to its robust character.

Marx and Engels, in their *Manifesto of the Communist Party* (1848),
acknowledged capitalism's triumph over feudalism. Fully enthused that
this was merely a replacement of one society by another, they acclaimed
that the "bourgeoisie" created greater forces of production than all preceding generations combined. The innovative and entrepreneurial efforts of
the bourgeoisie, as Marx and Engels reveled, revolutionized the production
and distribution of goods and services, built infrastructure, and constructed
machinery to produce yet more machinery. But such laudatory comments
were merely a means of casting a wide net over capitalism that would ultimately, as Marx and Engels perceived, produce its own downfall. They
envisioned that the enormous increase in products emanating from the systemic advances of the bourgeoisie would require continually expanding
markets to absorb them. This need, they declared, would force the bourgeoisie into a global hunt and settlement pattern out of necessity to recreate
the world into its own image; such would push capitalism beyond sustainability. Moreover, Marx and Engels viewed capitalism as a historical stage
of social development, and that it would be replaced by a more advanced
form of society—socialism. Under this construct, workers would be the ruling class, the means of production would be collectively owned, and production and distribution would be guided by economic planning.[2]

It is clear that Marx and Engels underestimated the power of capitalism. The transcendental process has not manifested, and socialism is not
the order of the day. To be sure, capitalism shows imperfections; many
argue that unemployment, inflation, challenges to authority, social unrest,
crime and violence, and infrastructure decay are signs of weakness in the
capitalist structure.[3] As apparent as these ills are in today's capitalist society, are they not in many ways far more amplified in noncapitalist society?
Importantly, opposition to capitalism has made profit making around the
world more difficult and riskier,[4] and thereby has made shareholder
wealth maximization in ways problematic. But the quest for profits and
the pursuit of shareholder wealth maximization are quite formidable
forces that drive capitalism, that stimulate economic growth, that

empower the production and distribution of goods and services, and that ultimately engender an allocation of resources with such efficiency (if not equity) as to generally provide maximum long-run benefit to society. Shareholder interest and the profit motive are at least partly responsible, perhaps largely so, for the failure of socialism to transcend capitalism as Marx and Engels expected. The capacity to override the forces of opposition, as these pursuits have achieved, inspires one to examine the source of their strengths.

Clearly, no system is a panacea for all. Capitalism's emphasis on efficiency rewards its supporters with a massive endowment but leaves in doubt its equitable distribution. Socialism espouses a more equitable distribution of economic rewards, but its lax pursuit of efficiency generates little endowment to distribute. The substantiality of the endowment is a very formidable matter. What is it about capitalism's shareholder wealth maximizing–profit making character that produces G8 results? How might such accomplishment translate to other nations, particularly poor ones? Contextually, it is useful here to review more thoroughly the various aspects of shareholder wealth maximization; instructively, an understanding of SWM might well begin with an understanding of profit maximization, a matter given some degree of attention in Chapter 11. Microeconomics pedagogy often presents profit maximization as the goal of the firm, while finance sets shareholder wealth maximization as the goal.[5] To some extent the difference is a matter of semantics, but in large measure, the two concepts vary significantly. Understanding the scope of the differences while at the same time grasping the individualities will help to address the objective of making SWM more user-friendly later on.

Profit maximization focuses on capital resources utilization efficiency, but does not specify the time element pertinent to the measurement of profits. Are profits to be maximized in the short run or the long run; in the current year or, say, over a five-year period? Elimination of routine maintenance, research and development, executive perquisites, and employee education expenditures could quite readily increase current profits in the short run. This would satisfy the profit maximization goal, but would not be in the best long-run interest of the firm. Profit maximization also does not precisely stress uncertainty and timing. The relative degree of risk between and among investment alternatives and the differences in risk characteristics across alternatives could weigh heavily in the investment selection decision. The timing of investment returns (cash flows) is also of major concern in profit maximization. Short-run profits ignore long-run potentialities; one year's profits don't allow consideration of the impact of out-year profits on net present value decisions. This could lead to inappropriate investment decisions.[6] In the applied world of finance, profit maximization falls short of the robustness required to address the complexities faced by financial managers in investment selection decision making.

Maximizing shareholder wealth, the goal of financial managers, provides for a more vigorous operation of the firm. Under this responsibility, the full effects and precise measure of risk and complete range and timing of investment returns are recognized, leading to a more rational and accurate investment decision. Hence, maximization of shareholder wealth is more so in the best interest of the shareholder than maximization of profits.[7] But shareholder wealth maximization itself has a decidedly significant limitation. The rather exclusionary focus on shareholders as management objective overshadows the utility that can be derived from more user-friendly shareholder wealth maximization. That is, in the broader context of this management objective, emphasis may be placed on the stakeholder as discussed in Chapter 11. Understandably, management may be unable to conceptualize how stakeholders can be incorporated into the process of maximizing the benefits of corporate enterprise, and how this can be in the best interest of the firm in the long run. Outline of a clear path from shareholder wealth concerns to consideration of the larger matter of stakeholder interest can assist management in this regard.

THE SWM PATH TO SWE: MOVING FROM SHAREHOLDER TO STAKEHOLDER

Placing the interest of the shareholder in the larger context of the stakeholder is quite simply an exercise in inclusion. It has the capacity to address the equity shortcoming of capitalism. Moreover, successful recognition of the stakeholder in financial decision making could essentially shut off any potential challenge of socialism to the capitalist model. This being said, a necessary caviat is important here. Clearly, as change agent, the multinational in ways will create competition as host countries develop know-how and economic capacity, which serve to move them up the "ladder of comparative advantage" (see Chapter 9).

Indeed, the multinationals may be concerned about the competition that derives from their efforts. In reality and quite frankly, this brings the multinationals to a crossroad of sorts: they are faced with a trade-off between having the lion's share of the economic pie in an unstable environment (the existing situation), and sharing the economic pie in a more congenial environment (the proposed situation). The decision is theirs to make.

Modeling the Process of Inclusion: *The Case for Third World Stakeholders*

The Third World is perhaps the most notable example of the failure of economic and financial objectives to create a reasonable standard of living for all of mankind. The capitalist model has not done it, and the socialist model cannot do it. One may ask, what good is efficiency if its rewards are not shared equitably? Another may ask, what good is equity if there is nothing to share? Clearly, the challenge is to create maximum efficiency with maximum equity. There is no doubt a trade-off, but it need not be such that the Third World model is sustained. There is a path to equity enhancement without compromising efficiency, hence to explicit inclusion of Third World stakeholders in multinational corporation financial decision making. The following discussion sets forth that path utilizing important concepts presented elsewhere in this volume.

Beginning with the basic business model as designed to pursue shareholder wealth maximization, the discussion employs a number of illustrations that depict a stepwise progression of MNC financial decision making with a view toward promoting Third World stakeholder inclusion. The elements or decision points conveyed by these illustrations are by no means an exhaustive representation of the numerous factors that may be considered in financial decision making.

A simple model of shareholder wealth maximization may appear as shown in Exhibit 12.1. In the basic business model, the firm, represented here by the MNC, is enabled by investors—the shareholders or owners of the firm—who provide the financial resources or equity capital required to induce growth. They have voting rights that permit them to elect a board of directors, approve corporate charter amendments, authorize issuance of new common stock, adopt bylaws, approve merger proposals, and to act on other key matters involving the firm.[8] A board of directors responsible for general policymaking and corporate affairs guides the MNC. The board is supported by a management team responsible for managing day-to-day operations and executing the policies instituted by the board. The management team plans the MNC's activities, sets its goals, and prepares a strategy for achieving them. This process focuses on corporate growth opportunities and is oriented to the goal of maximizing the wealth of the owners. Accomplishing the goal involves allocating resources available to the MNC to achieve greatest efficiency. Important to this management responsibility are acquiring needed resources and selecting capital projects, and utilizing these in a highest and best-use manner.[9]

Efficient allocation of the MNC's resources enables a dynamic production process. The appropriate inputs from resource allocation lead to robust outputs in the form of cost-effective and price-competitive products. The success of the production process allows the marketing of the products in such a manner as to meet and, in the best-case scenario, overcome the challenges of the corporation's competition. As such, the corporation is able to maintain its market share and perhaps even expand market penetration. Price-competitive products coupled with an aggressive marketing strategy facilitate product sales as the corporation targets its supply to meet demand. From time to time, production, marketing, and sales lead each other or take place simultaneously.

Exhibit 12.1
Shareholder Wealth Maximization

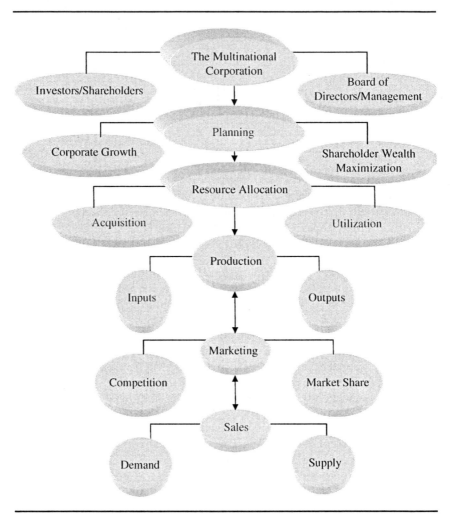

The overall corporate structure, and the management and implementation of the firm's policies and growth activities set the stage for shareholder wealth maximization. How well the policies and activities are
carried out, and the degree of efficiency achieved in the process determine
the magnitude of SWM accomplished. Magnitude of success notwithstanding, the managers of the multinational corporation adopt the goal of
shareholder wealth maximization and pursue it with vigor. This assures
the providers of equity capital to the firm that their expectations and
interests are of primary concern.

The next step along the path to Third World stakeholder inclusion focuses on the derivation of the multinational corporation, and its decision-making structure. In other words, why does a firm become multinational, and how does it manage and control its operations, particularly since it must oversee not only domestic facilities but foreign subsidiaries as well?

While the MNC follows the basic business model of the firm, it has some rather unique characteristics. With production facilities at home and abroad, the expanse of the multinational's sphere of operation gives rise to a wide-reaching decision-making apparatus in pursuit of shareholder wealth maximization. The multinational business form derives from certain advantages that accrue to the firm as a result of establishing production facilities in foreign countries. There are firm-specific competitive advantages that allow the MNC to compete more effectively with foreign corporations as they conduct operations in foreign territory. These advantages principally include size, technology and marketing superiority, and brand name. Producing in various countries creates bigness and market power. These attributes allow the firm to obtain financing relatively easily and to pursue shareholder wealth maximization in ways that otherwise may be impossible or impractical. The firm may possess advanced technological skills and marketing know-how that support production efficiency and product marketing in ways superior to competitors. And a brand name can give the firm tremendous marketing power along with market penetration, as name recognition is a powerful means of attracting consumer interest.[10]

Many firms prefer complete ownership and control of their firm-specific advantages, or certainly to the largest extent possible. This preference exists for two primary reasons. First, the firm captures all of the benefits produced by the advantage when its control remains within the MNC. Since technology and marketing superiority enable the firm to realize higher rates of return, there is a financial incentive to maintain control. Second, less than complete ownership raises uncertainty about quality control and supply, particularly when production of an item requires many steps. The uncertainty may be of sufficient magnitude that full control of the operation is warranted. Thus, internalization of the firm-specific advantages, as the process is commonly called, makes good financial sense because it is more profitable to produce a product that requires many operations, or several locations, within the same firm rather than between different firms.[11]

There are also location-specific advantages to producing at the foreign location that give rise to the multinational business form. Raw materials used in the production process that are of foreign origin are more available and more cost-effectively obtained at the foreign site. Transport costs are minimized and labor costs are the same as those enjoyed by foreign competitors. Trade barriers and other disincentives to exports imposed by foreign governments to protect indigenous producers can be avoided or

minimized by producing in the foreign market. Factors such as these
influence the development of the firm into a multinational organization.[12]

To actualize and accommodate firm-specific and location-specific
advantages, the firm takes on a multinational character and employs a
decision-making structure that provides for management control of the
international operation. Exhibit 12.2 outlines the general structure that
enables the MNC to function as a domestic and foreign organization, and
that expands the opportunity to pursue shareholder wealth maximization.
Consistent with the basic business model, the multinational is headed by a
board of directors, whose members typically have a domestic as well as an

Exhibit 12.2
Shareholder Wealth Maximization
The MNC Decision-Making Structure

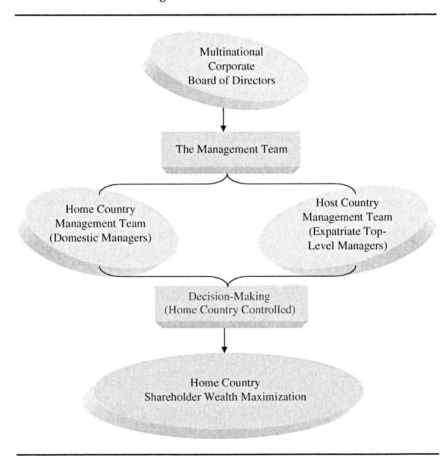

international business perspective. The board operates through the MNC's headquarters located in the home country, and provides overall direction and policy for the entire organization.

A corporate management team domiciled at the headquarters office is responsible for executing corporate policy, coordinating production activities, and overseeing management of the various domestic and foreign production facilities. The corporate team assures that strategy and objectives common among the domestic and foreign facilities are carried out in a consistent manner. Further, all management objectives and strategy employed by the various facilities are subject to review and approval by the corporate management team.

Each production facility has its own management team. In the home country, the team is comprised of domestic managers fully competent in the art of accomplishing tasks through the deployment and supervision of company personnel. They are responsible for carrying out the day-to-day activities of the corporation. The foreign or host country management team may be differently arranged. Often, expatriate senior managers head the team with indigenous personnel serving as middle- and lower-level managers. This is particularly apparent in the Third World setting, as indigenous management skills are not considered sufficiently honed to assume the more advanced management decision-making responsibility.

The host country management team is given a certain measure of latitude in making decisions related to activities of the foreign facility. But the multinational typically maintains home country control of decision making, particularly involving major foreign issues. The desire is to assure that corporate policy is fully reflected in important decisions that determine the success of the foreign facility. Moreover, since the foreign operation is viewed as providing an opportunity to further the interest of equity investors, successful foreign enterprise supports the goal of shareholder wealth maximization.

In recent years, corporations have begun to broaden their focus on shareholder wealth maximization to emphasize the interests of stakeholders as well as equity investors. Stakeholders in this context are parties having a direct economic link to the firm. While investors are themselves stakeholders and indeed the principal parties in the business endeavors of the firm, other parties receiving attention include employees, customers, creditors, and suppliers. The stakeholder focus does not compromise the goal of shareholder wealth maximization, as management seeks not to maximize stakeholder well-being outside of the equity investor, but simply to preserve it. Preserving stakeholder well-being is often considered part of the corporation's "social responsibility." Thus, the equity investor remains the primary focus of management objective, but concern for other stakeholders is expected to provide long-run benefit to the firm through fostering cooperation rather than conflict with them.[13]

Shareholder wealth maximization with stakeholder emphasis is depicted in Exhibit 12.3. Corporate philosophy enables the decision-making process passing from the multinational's board of directors to the management team. The management team conducts the business of the corporation with the preservation of stakeholder well-being as its modus operandi. Maximizing the wealth of the owners remains the focus of management's efforts, but maintaining positive stakeholder relationships holds an important position in corporate growth decisions. Under this mind-set, employment of resource allocation models that effectuate

Exhibit 12.3
Shareholder Wealth Maximization with Stakeholder Emphasis

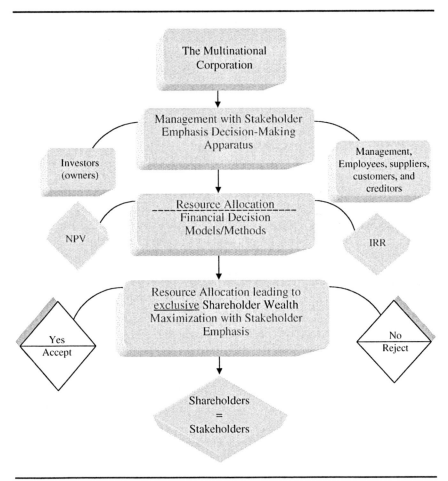

financial decisions qualitatively, if not quantitatively, reflect the stakeholder emphasis. While there remains a rather exclusive focus on shareholder wealth maximization, the resource allocation process employs accept-reject criteria that are not only driven by decision rules such as net present value (NPV) and internal rate of return (IRR), but also by management philosophy that embraces the notion of corporate "social responsibility." In the final analysis, the interests of the shareholders as well as the stakeholders are well served.

Since the destruction of the Twin Towers in New York City on September 11, 2001, corporate dialogue may well focus on an even broader set of interests—society's poor people and very poor countries. Such initiative is requisite not simply for the purpose of recognizing the importance of a broader constituency, but rather recognizing the importance of a broader constituency with a purpose. The need for an expanded focus is particularly underscored by comments such as, "What we discovered on Sept. 11 is that chaos in poor, weak countries halfway around the globe matters very much to us"[14] and "The terrorists weren't poor, yet the kinds of poverty we see today provide breeding grounds for tremendous animosity to the United States."[15]

The broader focus has not just now become necessary, but has been needed for a long time. It is one thing to simply sympathize with the plight of the poor and to indirectly engage in activities that address their needs. It is yet another to become directly involved in ways that assure redress of the conditions that create their needs. Analogously, a wealthy country providing foreign aid to a poor nation helps to address poverty with the hope that the recipient *can* get along, but a wealthy country providing the means by which a recipient can ultimately provide for itself assures that the recipient *will* get along. The latter is not only in the best interest of the receiving nation, but makes imminently good sense particularly in light of the September 11 tragedy. The attack on the World Trade Center put people in touch with the whole world in ways never before apparent. There is now growing recognition that poverty is a fertile breeding ground for adversity, and adversity seeks its own level. Demise of the Twin Towers is painful testament. It is indeed unfortunate that long-needed focus on the plight of poor people comes at such expense. Continuous neglect of the problem only emboldens those who would profit from tragedy.

Redress of poverty and the plight of poor nations as a practical matter can be in large measure achieved through the shareholder-stakeholder paradigm. A supporting argument for shareholder wealth maximization is that it is in the best interest of not only the shareholder but also its various stakeholders, and society as a whole. As stated elsewhere in this volume, maximizing shareholder wealth comes about as a result of efficiently allocating the corporation's resources to producing the greatest output with the least input. This not only maximizes shareholder wealth, but also provides benefits to stakeholders in the form of income to employees, goods and services to customers, revenue to vendors, and taxes for governance and social programs to serve society at-large. While the corporation does indeed provide a noble service and benefit to society, the issue remains that it can, and since September 11 should, more directly address the persistent and growing problem of poverty. Making goods and services available to society does not in and of itself assure that society can take advantage of those goods and services, which are unaffordable to many, despite how cost-effectively they may be produced and supplied. In short, many in society are ill-prepared for consumerism.

A basic principle of economics is that the consumer is one who is *ready*, *willing*, and *able* to buy goods and services, else there will be no consumer. Perhaps the most critical element here is "able." Arguably, every person in need of at least the basic necessities of life is "ready" and "willing" to buy those necessities, but a very large segment of society is not "able." Perhaps most prominent among those unable to afford the basic necessities are the millions of poor people in the world's abundance of poor countries. They are simply unable to take advantage of the SWM benefits. This very fact places rich countries—the principal beneficiaries of shareholder wealth maximization—in conflict with poor countries, the inhabitants of which form the corporation's broader stakeholder constituency. No doubt, the corporation's goal of shareholder wealth maximization can be better pursued through good relations with rather than in conflict with this stakeholder group.

Present corporate objective to preserve stakeholder well-being may be appropriate regarding groups having a direct economic link to the corporation, but may be rather shortsighted when the stakeholder sphere includes the Third World, especially constituents having no direct economic link. Third World constituents on the whole are poor and in many instances desperately so. Preserving their state of well-being is simply preserving a condition of poverty. Clearly, this business philosophy offers little hope to victims of intergenerational poverty, as Third World people generally are, and certainly no solution to the breeding ground for adversity. The resolve here may lie in a philosophical modification of the corporate objective. In that an exclusive focus on shareholder wealth maximization with stakeholder well-being preservation appears to lack the fortitude to encompass the interest of Third World stakeholders, a more inclusive approach to well-being may offer opportunity for serious redress of the poverty problem.

Exhibit 12.4 suggests an approach that calls for shareholder wealth maximization with inclusive stakeholder emphasis. Under this philosophy, the notion of inclusion enables the decision-making process, passing from the multinational's board of directors to the corporate management team. The corporate management team now comprises both home and

Exhibit 12.4
Shareholder Wealth Maximization with Inclusive Stakeholder Emphasis

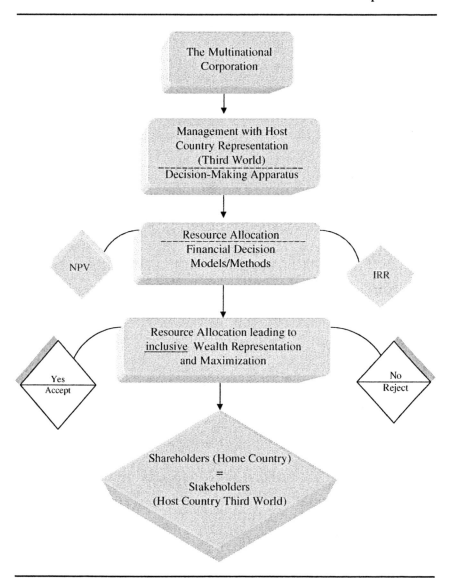

host country representation, hence enabling direct inputs to the decision-making process from not only home country management personnel, as is traditionally the case, but also Third World management personnel. Maximization of owners' wealth continues to be the overriding initiative, but the interest of the Third World stakeholder is given a higher level of importance. As such, the resource allocation process guided by Net Present Value (NPV) and Internal Rate of Return (IRR) objectives is now undertaken with a view toward direct consideration of Third World stakeholder needs. Accept-reject criteria reflect the modified philosophy of greater inclusion of Third World stakeholder interest. The idea here is that the philosophy that drives the multinational is critical to making capitalism more user-friendly. Efficiency maximization is seen as being compatible with equity enhancement, though these may not be achieved at the same level. The approach to resource allocation undertaken by the multinational will determine in the long run the magnitude of the wealth factor for the world at-large, not just the home country.

Operating the corporation with a long-run perspective and a more worldly view of the wealth factor offers wider opportunity for stakeholder inclusion. Concern for stakeholder interest in the context of corporate social responsibility is already part of the corporate management mind-set. Expanding the management team to include host country personnel sends a signal to the world at-large that the multinational's concern is not lip service, as is the common perception of Third World hosts, but rather is bona fide management objective. Working with the Third World to seriously address the poverty situation moves to the corporation's short list of top priorities. Corporate social responsibility transitions from mere corporate concern to corporate action. Stakeholder well-being transitions from preserve to pursue. A new mind-set is manifested, as is represented by Exhibit 12.5. Shareholder wealth maximization becomes shareholder wealth maximization–stakeholder wealth enhancement, giving a new meaning to corporate social responsibility. Though stakeholder wealth enhancement may imply a different measure of resource allocation than shareholder wealth maximization, the fact that corporate objective adopts this approach formally sets the stage for moving stakeholder well-being to a new wealth dimension. Short of this, it is unlikely that Third World poverty will experience any appreciable decline, particularly if left to its own devices.

At this stage, as advanced in Exhibit 12.5, the multinational formally articulates shareholder-stakeholder wealth emphasis objectives in operating policy. Importantly, the agency relationship—the principal-agent issue discussed in Chapter 11—undergoes a philosophical adjustment of sorts, as the contract between shareholder and manager now recognizes the expanded focus of the corporate objective. It is absolutely crucial that the shareholder embraces the new philosophy, as it has no validity otherwise. The notion that stakeholder wealth can be enhanced is no doubt a venturesome proposition, particularly given profit-maxim concerns (discussed in Chapter 11). But society demands redress of the poverty problem and the multinational can be a formidable change agent in this regard.

Exhibit 12.5
Shareholder Wealth Maximization-Stakeholder Wealth Enhancement:
Corporate Social Responsibility

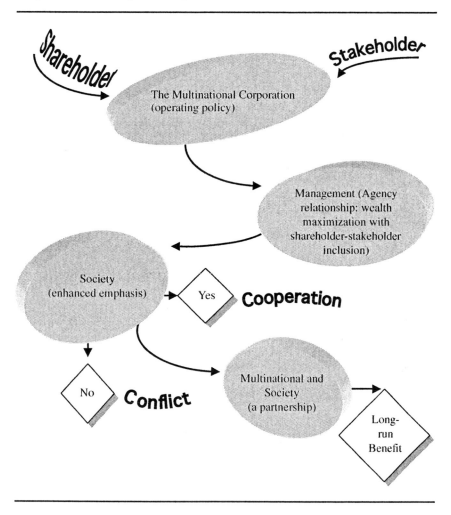

Enhanced emphasis on the needs of society places the multinational in a leadership role, one that it can well sustain. Recognizing society's interest beyond the traditional efficient production of goods and services expands the opportunity for greater cooperation among society's various constituencies. Success by the multinational in bringing about a diminution of poverty in the Third World clearly diminishes breeding places for adversity. In this role, the multinational effectively partners with society.

Perceptibly, the long-run benefit to both the multinational and society resulting from cooperation rather than conflict is potentially enormous. The economic upheaval and social alarm associated with adversity is certainly not in either party's best interest.

Adversity becomes the Achilles' heel. Left to its own devices, Third World poverty will no doubt give rise to social discord, thereby potentially compromising shareholder wealth maximization objectives. A disgruntled and unstable community that serves as a resource supplier and consumer of the multinational's goods and services can undoubtedly create a vexing problem.

Partnering with society beyond the production function is a noble venture, but more than this it is a problem-solving initiative. The approach taken by the multinational at this stage effectively solidifies its intentions regarding redress of the rich country–poor country "haves" and "have-nots" dilemma. Exhibit 12.6 outlines the course of travel for the multinational and prescribes an approach that can enable the process. Here the corporation places wealth inequality on the front burner, so to speak, and thereby addresses the problems of individual incapacity—the "able" factor—and the poor country dilemma on the global scale. The initial focus is on the most impoverished of the world, with a progressive move toward including the array of economically disadvantaged countries.

Multinational management takes a very formal as well as formidable step in addressing the inequality problem through utilization of GIST (presented in Chapter 8). Restructuring the corporate policymaking and management teams to include indigenous representation from the host country among top-level managers internationalizes the decision-making apparatus. Poor country redress is facilitated immeasurably by host country representation at the corporate level. The decision-making process utilizing the GIST framework stimulates and promotes corporate growth and expansion designed to problem solve inequality. GIST produces a partnership arrangement that gives the corporation the capacity to effectively address equity.

As problem solving takes place, management will need to think "outside the box" to avoid the theoretical trapping of profit maximization. Recall the argument that profit maximization leads to the most efficient allocation and utilization of scarce resources, thus providing the greatest benefit to society. Thinking "outside the box" allows management to focus on the concern that profit maximization has a discriminating character. It is kindest to those who are most able to compete for goods and services supplied by the corporation, hence the "able" factor. How does management overcome the "able" factor? One way is to adopt profit satisficing (presented in detail in Chapter 11) as the profit motivation of the corporation. This method of profit making provides a means of addressing a broader range of issues, such as wealth inequality, again the "able"

Exhibit 12.6
Shareholder-Stakeholder Partnership: The Multinational, GIST, and Profit Satisficing

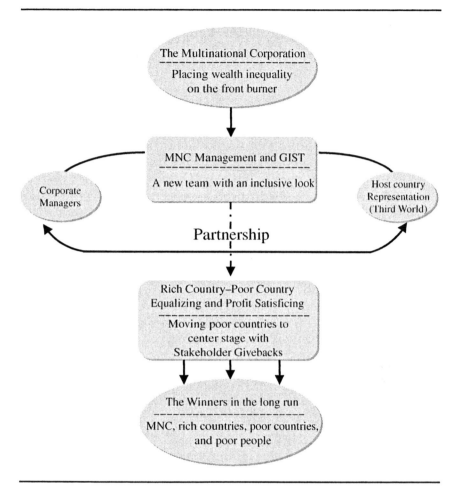

factor, and the rich country–poor country dichotomy without compromising the profit-maxim rule: (mr = mc). Profit satisficing expedites the principal-agent issue in that it sends a signal to the world at-large that the multinational has firmly adjusted its profit-making philosophy to accommodate its expanded corporate objective.

Profit satisficing can be undertaken through *stakeholder givebacks* (presented in Chapter 11), which offer a very constructive means of providing various technology and infrastructure so necessary to support economic development. Operating under a profit satisficing philosophy facilitates the movement of poor countries to center stage. Although this is a long-run strategy, once achieved, the sharing of center stage with rich countries provides expanded opportunities for poor countries to move up the ladder of comparative advantage and to achieve more advanced stages of development (presented in Chapters 1 and 9). The end result is a larger world economy with more inclusive participation and greater economic benefit to all. Clearly, everybody wins—multinational corporations, rich countries, poor countries, and especially poor people in poor countries. And perhaps above all, the breeding place for adversity becomes a breeding place for diversity.

Stakeholder givebacks can facilitate the factors of production. Productive factors, the resources required to produce goods and services, offer a very useful context in which to further advance the *stakeholder givebacks* concept. The resources are usually arranged into three components—land, labor, and capital. Generally speaking, land involves natural resources in fixed supply, which cannot be depleted; labor involves employment of physical and mental skills in the production of goods and services; and capital involves goods produced for the purpose of producing other goods and services.[16] Usually, the multinational corporation transmits factors to Third World hosts. This process to some extent has been successful in stimulating development, but has fallen far short of closing the wealth gap between rich and poor nations. *Stakeholder givebacks* may potentially complement the process, and may induce greater efficiency in foreign direct investment. As envisioned, this may have the effect of moderating the wealth gap between rich and poor countries. Further envisioned is maximizing shareholder wealth, the essential goal of foreign investment, while at the same time enhancing stakeholder equity, the essential goal of *stakeholder givebacks*. How might this complementarity and efficiency inducing process take place? This is perhaps the crucial question posed by the *stakeholder givebacks* concept, which instills corporate objective outside the traditional corporate decision-making apparatus, thereby giving rise to the profit-maxim concern (which has been previously addressed), and to the matter of process.

As for process, Exhibit 12.7 imagines a scenario in which the multinational adopts the notion of *stakeholder givebacks* occasioning it to focus strategically on the labor factor. In this scenario, labor consists of the human resources that are unemployed or underemployed for lack of cooperating factors previously supplied by the multinational[17] and/or resulting from the incapacity of the general economy in the host country. Unemployment or underemployment also results from ineffective public policy, particularly in the area of compulsory education. In this context, host governments engage strategic choices and make political and social decisions about the allocation of resources in terms beyond the usual market processes.[18]

Exhibit 12.7
Stakeholder Givebacks

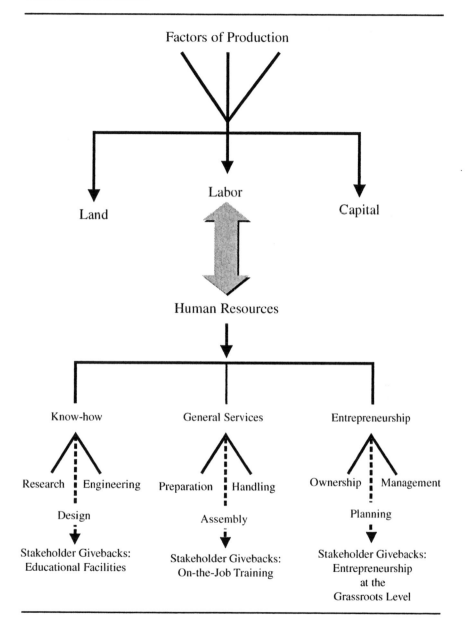

Factors of Production

Land

Labor

Capital

Human Resources

Know-how

General Services

Entrepreneurship

Research   Engineering

Design

Preparation   Handling

Assembly

Ownership   Management

Planning

Stakeholder Givebacks:
Educational Facilities

Stakeholder Givebacks:
On-the-Job Training

Stakeholder Givebacks:
Entrepreneurship
at the
Grassroots Level

Addressing the heretofore ineffectiveness of factor inputs, the scenario at hand views human resources as comprising three categories—know-how, general services, and entrepreneurship. Know-how involves development of the full range of intellectual capacity from basic to advanced skills and technological knowledge in research, design, and engineering. These skills are typically provided through formal educational institutions. As Third World countries are deficient in this regard, the multinational can offer helpful assistance in the way of *stakeholder givebacks*. In so doing, educational facilities are contributed by multinationals that augment host country efforts. Through such means, human resource development receives more intensive resource allocation, setting the course for a more competitive productive factor.

The second category of human resources, general services, involves development of human capacity in the direct production of goods, particularly in the areas of preparation, assembly, and handling. Here, the multinational assists the host country through development of specialized on-the-job training programs including vocational training facilities; special emphasis on this training assists development of practical skills necessary to support economic growth activity. These skills are essential to successful movement up the ladder of comparative advantage.

The third category, entrepreneurship, involves development of human capacity as owners, planners, and managers of business enterprise. Entrepreneurial or managerial ability is also considered a fourth factor of production.[19] Entrepreneurs are viewed as innovators, and coordinators of productive factors. Schumpeter connects innovation to the entrepreneur, arguing that successful innovation produces economic growth through introduction of new products and more efficient production processes, expansion of existing markets and development of new markets, development and exploitation of new sources of materials and capital, and industrial reorganization.[20] In this instance, the multinational uses its vast talents to create entrepreneurship at the grassroots level. Through *stakeholder givebacks*, the multinational develops mentoring programs exposing host country individuals to business innovators and corporate leaders. This effort establishes role models with whom the hosts come to identify. Over time, the entrepreneurial spirit is inculcated and eventually adopted.

Clearly, the multinational can be an effective change agent in ways not constrained by the traditional shareholder wealth maximization decision-making process. *Stakeholder givebacks* provide resource allocation opportunities that assist the host country in developing more efficient factors of production without compromising the profit motive. Developing an environment that is more conducive to business enterprise makes good sense. Developing the whole environment in which productive factors are maximized is even more sensible. This is consistent with the theory of growth and, in particular, unhooking our view of growth from the concept of an aggregate production function. Theoretically, the concept of the aggregate production function contains factors other than simply physical capital. According to the marginal productivity of any factor, an increment to a factor causes an increment to product. Put another way, increment to input produces increment to output. When factor earnings (returns per unit of capital, etc.) are used as measures of the contributions of productive factors to the process of economic growth, a substantial amount of growth—the residual—is unaccounted for or unexplained. The residual is a composite of the effects of many different forces including improvement in the quality of labor or human resources through education, experiential learning, and on-the-job training. Therefore, economic growth is not just defined by the aggregate production function, but other matter as well.[21] Use of the concept of *stakeholder givebacks* places the multinational in the position of recognizing the need to act "outside the box," that is, outside the concept of the aggregate production function. In so doing, the multinational transmits factors in a way that augments the traditional process. As such, economic growth is further spawned, potentially giving rise to a closing of the rich country–poor country wealth gap.

Acting "outside the box" clearly calls upon the multinational to assume essentially a new role in facilitating Third World enrichment. Whether or not to assume this role may be a matter of ethics. What is the right thing to do? Should the concept of "ready, willing, and able" apply only to those who happen to be so? As is commonly the case, doing the right thing is far and away secondary to doing what is most expedient or financially rewarding. If the multinational is to get the job done, as it well can, ultimately it may have to question its ethical character. Which corporate actions exude good ethics and which do not? Exhibit 12.8 offers a framework in which the multinational's decision-making process can be scrutinized. The traditional factors that drive this process, placing exclusive emphasis on shareholder wealth maximization and home country wealth accumulation, are paired up with factors that broaden the traditional corporate emphasis with a view toward acting "outside the box." The decision to act outside the box, or not, may in fact point to the multinational's ethics. Though what constitutes good ethics may be arguable, the need to exercise good ethics may not. To be sure, the multinational's decision-making process is subject to question. In the rich country–poor country context, the questioning may appear as follows.

Does the multinational's traditional recognition of the "corporate good" constitute good ethics? By comparison, would the multinational's recognition of the "greater good" constitute more ethical behavior? Which should be the multinational's modus operandi? Acting steadfastly for the good of the corporation may translate into maximizing its stock price, but ignoring the greater good—that is, the good of society at-large—may

Exhibit 12.8
Shareholder-Stakeholder/Rich Country–Poor Country: Ethics and "Ready, Willing, and Able"

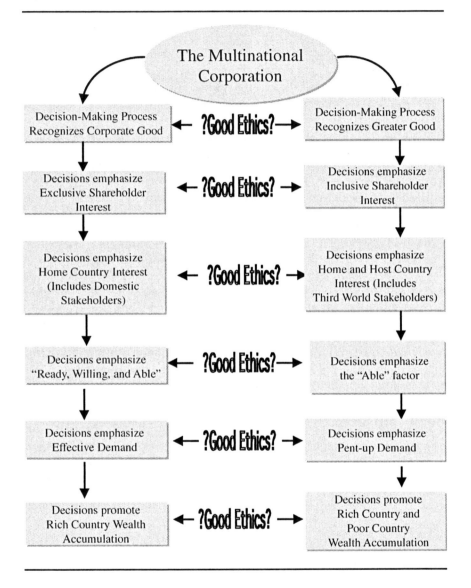

translate into life choice constraints for the individual, and may compromise the welfare of the communities in which the multinationals operate. Understandably, if some multinationals act in a socially responsible manner and others do not, the socially responsible multinationals may be operating at a disadvantage. Hence, if good ethics require social responsibility, there is need for multinationals to act collectively. This matter has been addressed in the free-rider discussion in Chapter 11.

Does the multinational's exclusive emphasis on shareholder interest constitute good ethics, or does a more inclusive approach to maximizing wealth offer more ethical corporate character? Acting in the interest of the shareholder certainly satisfies the agency obligation (see Chapter 11), but what about the stakeholder, and indeed the larger community of stakeholders? Is there an obligation to attend to their interest? Should there be?

For the multinational, is it ethical to place strict emphasis on home country welfare or, since the multinational in effect carries multiple nationalities, would it be more ethically responsible to emphasize home as well as host country interests in the corporate objective? Wouldn't it be ethically prudent to focus not just on shareholders but stakeholders as well, and in this context, stakeholders in the host community where the multinational does business? Setting corporate objective to reach beyond domestic stakeholders to include particularly those in the Third World may well add a new dimension to corporate ethics. A fair sharing of the rewards of business enterprise would make corporate objective particularly noteworthy. Isn't fair sharing good ethics?

As the multinational conducts business enterprise, is it ethical to assume that all potential customers are ready, willing, and able to participate in the marketplace? Wouldn't it be more appropriate ethical behavior to recognize that many are simply not able to compete for goods and services in a reasonable manner? Multinationals' profit making is associated with market-clearing transactions. Those who are able to participate in market activity—that is, are ready, willing, and able to purchase goods and services—satisfy wants and needs. When these participants have voiced and realized their desires in the marketplace, then so far as the corporation is concerned, all is well. Why so? To understand the corporation's mind-set, consider the following. In a market-clearing event, the market itself is said to be in equilibrium and the satisfaction of buyers and sellers is maximized. In other words, the equilibrium of demand and supply in market transactions maximizes the total benefits consumers and producers receive. In the state of market equilibrium, the quantity of a good that consumers are willing and able to buy exactly balances the quantity that producers are willing and able to sell.[22] Thus, it is said, everyone wins.

But how do less-fortunate individuals really fare in this total benefits maximization schema? Clearly, not everyone participating in the market receives the same level of benefit. This may be unreasonable to expect, since desire and ability to pay may differ from individual to individual. However, should those who are unable to achieve a reasonable level of benefit, say to afford basic necessities, be ignored? Many individuals, particularly in the Third World, are in such a position. Hence, would the multinational's market behavior be more ethical if it were to emphasize the "able" factor in its transactions?

Continuing with this line of thought, the matter of ability to pay points to the broader topic of demand. The multinational focuses its attention on the demand for its goods and services; shareholder wealth maximization hinges on it. But it is not just demand that captures the multinational's attention, rather it is effective demand. That is, the multinational is not only interested in an individual's willingness or desire to purchase the corporation's goods and services, but perhaps even more so in the individual's ability to pay. In the Third World context, just how ethical is the emphasis on effective demand? With such a large body of its inhabitants unable to afford basic necessities, is it good ethics to ignore their desires, even though they can't be expressed in terms of purchasing power? Put another way, is it sound ethics to ignore or downplay pent-up demand—individual desires, wants, or needs, absent the means (ability, money, opportunity, etc.) to satisfy them?[23] Kindleberger and Herrick write, "the market system can be 'efficient' only in terms of how well it meets the effective demand of those with income."[24] Alchian and Allen confide, "we know of no more common denial of the law of demand than the repeated talk about 'vital needs.' At best, such talk is the result of ignorance that goods are scarce."[25] Basic necessities are indeed vital needs. The inability to afford basic necessities certainly places them outside the realm of effective demand. So then, what does this suggest: that it is ethical to emphasize effective demand in the corporate objective, or to emphasize pent-up demand instead?

Placing emphasis on effective demand surely stands squarely with the promotion of efficiency in the marketplace. The multinational's behavior in this regard will promote shareholder wealth maximization and in so doing facilitate wealth accumulation in the home country. But does the promotion of efficiency rule out attention to the "able" factor, which provides an opportunity for stakeholder wealth enhancement, and in so doing, facilitate wealth accumulation not just in the home country but in the host country as well. Isn't corporate objective served by the latter and perhaps more so, if development of a broader consumer base has any merit? Which approach suggests more profound ethics? Which approach would more formidably address the rich country–poor country dilemma?

The ethics of corporate objective provide much opportunity to query the goal and motives of shareholder wealth maximization. Such exercise is useful in identifying new approaches to addressing the rich country–poor country dilemma. When thinking within the strict confines of neoclassical economics, it is perhaps difficult to conceive of an approach to business enterprise that maximizes shareholder wealth and also enhances stakeholder equity as proposed herein within the same corporate objective. What becomes apparent is that corporate objective may need to simply deploy "outside the box." This approach may hold tremendous prospects for bringing into balance the vast wealth difference between rich and poor countries, and thus creating a more able consumer, so important to the multinational.

Hence, as we chart a path to Third World stakeholder inclusion in the multinational decision-making process, our challenge is to create enhanced equity without compromising efficiency. The aforementioned steps along the path articulate the many factors and issues germane to modeling the process of inclusion. In making the case for Third World stakeholders, a win-win scenario is essentially derived in which it is clearly recognized that the multinational as the agent of change faces a task of balancing efficiency and equity. It must assure its capital suppliers that it is realizing the greatest output from the scarce resources utilized in the production of goods and services. Concomitantly, as the change agent, it must fairly distribute the benefits of the resources among its stakeholders. Exhibit 12.9 presents essentially a summation of the model of Third World stakeholder inclusion. Both shareholder and stakeholder interests are given high priority in which everybody wins in a very significant way. Two important ingredients are key to creating a win-win scenario. The global interdependency sensitivity thesis places Third World decision-making representation at the highest level of the multinational's policy-making apparatus, where sensitivity for Third World concerns can be encouraged, promoted, and monitored. Profit satisficing governs the motive for profit making, which provides for a more equitable distribution of the multinational's gains from business operations. The two ingredients are merged into the multinational's corporate objective to create greater equity without compromising efficiency. In other words, the multinational retains the wherewithal to maximize its economic pie, while at the same time more equitably dividing the pie among its stakeholders. The win-win scenario sets forth a path to stakeholder inclusion that minimizes conflict between efficiency and equity.

Creating greater equity for the stakeholders, hence greater wealth in the long run, prepares the host environment to become a more formidable location for business enterprise and further, creates more consumer-able host populations. This is made possible by expanding corporate objective to emphasize profit satisficing–stakeholder equity enhancement. In so doing, the multinational takes advantage of the opportunity to employ the *stakeholder givebacks* scheme, which provides for development of the whole environment leading to more robust economic growth. Recall that economic growth is not just defined by the aggregate production function, as previously discussed. Improvement in the quality of human resources through education, experiential learning, and on-the-job training, all of which can be facilitated through *stakeholder givebacks*, also contribute substantially to economic growth. Further, *stakeholder givebacks* can provide infrastructure,

Exhibit 12.9
Rich Country–Poor Country
A Win-Win Scenario

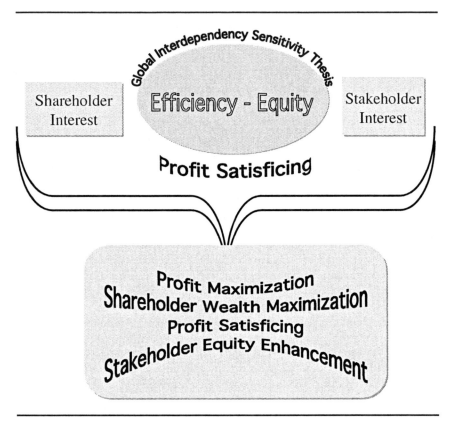

medical facilities, and the like, which also facilitate economic growth. In a growth environment, the multinational can more aggressively focus on wealth and equity. A larger pie means larger shares; everybody wins.

NOTES

1. John G. Gurley, *Challengers to Capitalism* (New York: W.W. Norton & Company, 1979, 8).
2. Ibid.
3. Ibid., 3.
4. Ibid.
5. Parenthetically, the firm is the business organization under which capitalism and its operators, that is, shareholder wealth maximizers, profit maximizers, and the like, create products and services.

6. David F. Scott, Jr., et al., *Basic Financial Management* (Upper Saddle River, NJ: Prentice Hall, Inc., 1999), 2–3.

7. Ibid.

8. Jeff Madura and E. Theodore Veit, *Introduction to Financial Management* (New York: West Publishing Company, 1988), 458.

9. See chapter 13 for comment on highest and best use.

10. For a discussion of this matter, see Leon Grunberg, "The IPE of Multinational Corporations," in David N. Balaam and Michael Veseth, eds., *Introduction to International Political Economy* (Upper Saddle River, NJ: Prentice-Hall, Inc., 1996), 343–345; and Paul R. Krugman and Maurice Obstfeld, *International Economics* (New York: HarperCollins College Publishers, 1994), 159–161.

11. Ibid., 343–344.

12. Ibid., 344–345.

13. Lawrence J. Gitman, *Principles of Managerial Finance* (New York: Addison-Wesley, 2003), 17.

14. Comment by Joseph Nye, dean of Harvard's Kennedy School of Government, in Martin Wolk, *Rich Country, Changing Role*, MSNBC, 4 September 2002.

15. Comment by Stephen Kobrin, Wharton School of Business, in Martin Wolk, *Rich Country, Changing Role*, MSNBC, 2002.

16. Christine Ammer and Dean S. Ammer, *Dictionary of Business and Economics* (New York: The Free Press, 1977), 147.

17. Gerald M. Meier, *Leading Issues in Economic Development* (New York: Oxford University Press, 1995), 258.

18. Ibid., 69.

19. Ammer and Ammer, ibid., 147.

20. Joseph A. Schumpeter, *The Theory of Economic Development* (Cambridge, MA: Harvard University Press, 1961). See also E. Wayne Nafziger, *The Economics of Developing Countries* (Englewood Cliffs, NJ: Prentice Hall, Inc., 1990), 284.

21. Meier, ibid., 91–92.

22. N. Gregory Mankiw, *Principles of Microeconomics* (New York: The Dryden Press, 1998), 76, 134.

23. Ammer and Ammer, ibid., 446.

24. Charles P. Kindleberger and Bruce Herrick, *Economic Development* (New York: McGraw-Hill, Inc., 1977), 22.

25. Armen A. Alchian and William R. Allen, *Exchange and Production, Theory in Use* (Belmont, CA: Wadsworth Publishing Company, Inc., 1969), 76.

CHAPTER 13

User-Friendly Shareholder Wealth Maximization and B-School Pedagogy

Addressing the inequality issue will undoubtedly involve a long-term initiative. The multinational corporation with GIST and *profit satisficing* ingrained is viewed as central to that undertaking, and indeed critical to developing wealth maximizing strategy with a view toward redress of the rich country–poor country dilemma. But in the long term, the initiative may be facilitated by a new pedagogical approach to wealth maximization. The corporate manager will be called upon to provide implementation leadership that will be fashioned by wealth maximization precepts learned in the business school. Broadening wealth maximization pedagogy to encompass *profit satisficing* has the benefit of bringing dual forces to bear on inequality. Hence, the business school and the multinational corporation are essential features of the perceived initiative against inequality. This chapter addresses the pedagogy matter and offers grounds for development of a new pedagogical approach to wealth maximization.

The literature is replete with arguments that capital flows from rich to poor nations accomplish little more than sustaining the wealth of the rich and the poverty of the poor. In fact, as the views hold, the rich are becoming increasingly better off while the poor are moving in the opposite direction. Recalling Andre Gunder Frank's assertion, capital flows from rich to poor nations, globalization in current jargon, have resulted in the development of underdevelopment. One observer writes,

As we anticipate the ongoing challenges of the new millennium, we bear witness to the unabated mercilessness of global capitalism and the impassable fissure between capital and labor. Today, millions of workers are being exploited by a relatively small yet cunningly powerful global ruling class driven by an unslakable desire for accumulation of profit. Little opposition exists as capitalism runs amok, unhampered and undisturbed by the tectonic upheaval that is occurring in the geopolitical landscape. . . . Mutagenic forms of greed and social relations that permit such greed to flourish have produced severance packages for corporate bosses that exceed the combined salaries of an army of factory workers.[1]

Suggesting that the globalization of capitalism has minimized the importance of education regarding the effects of globalization, the observer calls for "revolutionary pedagogy . . . to encourage the development of critical consciousness among students and teachers in the interests of building working-class solidarity and opposition to global capitalism."[2]

While a rethinking of the pedagogy may be in order, rejecting global capitalism as a platform for a new pedagogy is highly impractical. The case supporting the globalization of capital has been articulated in the foregoing discourse. Consistent with this discourse, a new pedagogy may be useful in improving the benefits derived from global capital for all stakeholders. In this context, a more user-friendly shareholder wealth maximization pedagogy may be requisite. Pragmatism would suggest that the institution most directly responsible for teaching shareholder wealth maximization, the business school, serve as the focal point of such deliberation.

Current business school pedagogy emphasizes the maximization of shareholder wealth, and concomitantly, the maximization of profit. Greed produces the motivation for individuals to become shareholders prompted by the expectation that invested capital will create larger capital. This expectation leads to a desire for capital accumulation, which in turn leads to wealth accumulation. There is the presumption that shareholder wealth maximization leads to the most efficient allocation of scarce resources, hence the allocation of resources to their highest and best use, which is in the best interest of society. This is where the difficulty and indeed the criticism of capitalism arise. That three-quarters of the world's population live on about \$2 a day[3] leads many to espouse the failings of capitalism. To be sure, the criticism tends to ignore, for example, systemic social and political problems of national economies that stand apart from any that may be associated with globalization. Some attention has been given to this matter in previous discourse.

But there is the problem not so much of "greed," but of "greedy." How much gain is enough? When is wealth maximized? How much profit is necessary? Does the profit maxim mr = mc tell the full story? What is the benefit to society of efficiently allocating scarce resources to the production of goods and services that many cannot afford? Why do so few have so much and so many have so little? These questions raise the specter of abuse of society's trust. In short, has "greed" become "greedy," prompting an attitude of "the more–the better" and "take whatever the market can bear"? The literature addresses these matters from various perspectives and certainly there have been statements made on the topics herein. Capitalism is not perfect and global capitalism will not come without faults. But capitalism has the power to empower the whole of the stakeholder population; it simply needs to be made more user-friendly. Although the multinational is called upon to use its formidable powers to undertake a more user-friendly capitalism, it is clear that an institutional transition from the now-favored profit maximization to the proposed *profit satisficing* may be necessary at the pedagogical level. Corporate managers practice what they are taught. For the most part, they receive their education about maximization of corporate profits and shareholder wealth in the business school, which therefore becomes the focal point of a new pedagogy.

The business school curriculum requires the study of economics and finance. As discussed in Chapter 12, microeconomics pedagogy prescribes profit maximization as the goal of the firm, while finance sets shareholder wealth maximization as the goal. Suffice it to say that these complement each other, that is, finance theory requires that the information from the microeconomic model be known for all future periods.[4] The microeconomic model is driven by the profit maxim mr = mc. Profit is a central issue in business circles and indeed a prominent factor in business school pedagogy. The emphasis on profit making serves to highlight greed as an acceptable motivation for investing. Essentially, business students are taught that greed is good. Yet the profit maxim appears incongruent with the desire for wealth distribution equity, and the closing of the rich country–poor country gap. This appearance exists even though mr = mc leads the corporation to the most efficient allocation of resources in the production of goods and services for society. This, it is argued, is in society's best interest. It is this peculiarity, so to speak, that may be addressed in the pedagogy. How can the profit motive accommodate greed while at the same time ameliorate pejorative distributional effects? How, then, does the current pedagogy respond to this challenge?

The notion of *profit satisficing* has been introduced in this dialogue and extensively explored in Chapters 11 and 12. Adopting *profit satisficing* in business school pedagogy not so much to replace profit maximization but rather to enhance it can conceivably produce numerous beneficial distributional effects for stakeholders. The rich country–poor country dilemma is not a problem that can be redressed simply by marginal economics. The sheer magnitude of the problem suggests the need for an expansion of economic thought to reflect more directly the interest of the stakeholder, not just that of the shareholder. Past relations between rich and poor countries reveal much about the inadequacies of the traditional economics, and the new globalization may amplify the inadequacies even more, certainly if a necessary course correction is not undertaken.

As the multinational leads the new globalization, its interests may be better served in recognizing that the human development paradigm in poor countries is in serious distress. How the multinational conducts the new globalization and its success in winning the appreciation of affected countries will depend much on what corporate managers perceive to be their role in redressing the paradigm, and on their understanding that a new way of thinking about how they conduct business may be requisite. The new globalization will build on capital flows and trade relationships of the past, in which free trade has been the rallying cry of rich countries. The rich country–poor country makeup of the world does not necessarily speak well of past relations. Should the past way of thinking simply continue in the future? Paul R. Krugman's *Strategic Trade Policy and the New International Economics* talks about the need for new thinking about trade policy, and suggests that the classical case for free trade is beginning to look increasingly unrealistic because it may be more in tune with the workings of the economy in the past than with the economy of today.[5]

To be sure, there is need for new thinking, which may well inspire a new pedagogy. There is a set of constructs that clearly disclose the rich country–poor country problem. They may serve as the core of the new thinking, hence the new pedagogy. Exhibits 13.1 through 13.4 represent the constructs in question.

Exhibit 13.1, the Human Development Paradigm, portrays a conceptual makeup of issues pertinent to developing a fundamental understanding of the human development problem. This is crucial to forging a new pedagogy on profit making, particularly one that emphasizes *profit satisficing*. The principle of human development is premised on the notion that people have a fundamental right to a range of life choices that lead to enhanced capability and empowerment. Human development as envisaged here has five core features from which life choices emanate— productivity and participation, equity and equality, sustainability and longevity, empowerment and self-determination, and governance and accountability.[6]

Productivity and participation call for an enabling of the productive capacity of people to enhance their ability to compete for jobs and command a living wage. Investment in people and in employment creation initiatives support development of human skills and capability, and promote participation in productive and financially rewarding work arrangements. Equity and equality prescribe elimination of barriers to economic, social, and political opportunities. As such, life-choice constraints are diminished, thereby producing greater equity in and more equal access to opportunities.

Exhibit 13.1
Human Development Paradigm

Productivity and Participation:	People must be enabled to increase their productivity and to participate fully in the process of income generation and paid employment.
Equity and Equality:	People must have equal access to opportunities. Barriers to economic, social, and political opportunities must be eliminated.
Sustainability and Longevity:	Access to opportunities must be inter-generational. Present & future generations must be assured that all forms of capital—physical, human, environmental—will be replenished.
Empowerment and Self-Determination:	Development must be by people, not only for them. They must participate fully in the decisions & processes that shape their lives.
Governance and Accountability:	Best practices, transparent administration, and public oversight must be employed to provide resource allocation, systems development, and program design to enhance people's capacities.

On the matter of sustainability and longevity, the key is to preserve the capacity to produce for future generations a level of well-being comparable to what is currently enjoyed. Replenishing the various forms of capital—physical, human, and environmental—assures their availability so that human life can be sustained for greater duration. Empowerment and self-determination focus on the enabling of people such that they participate freely in decision making that affects their lives. Development initiatives intended to expand their life choices must be determined by them, not simply for them. Finally, good governance is essential to expanding life choices and reducing life-choice constraints. People must have ready and free access to governing bodies, which in turn must be accountable to the people. Best practices, transparent administration, and public oversight must be employed to provide resource allocation, systems development, and program design to enhance people's capacities through the promotion of increased productivity, impartial access to opportunities, capital replenishment, and individual choice.[7]

Exhibit 13.2 offers important insight into what capital flows and international trade have not accomplished for poor countries through the eyes of what they have accomplished for rich countries. The multinational corporation symbolizes well the character of rich countries; the Third World represents the poor. An array of the multinational's characteristics, disposed to shareholder wealth maximization, provides important details about the organization that facilitate development of a new pedagogy.

Exhibit 13.2
The Rich Country–Poor Country Makeup

Who is the MNC?	Who is the THIRD WORLD?
1. Large corporation comprised of many subsidiaries characterized by progressive posture.	An economic grouping of countries, small, medium and large, character ized by backward/developing posture.
2. Financially wealthy with the ability to raise large sums of capital through the stock market and other financing opportunities.	Financially poor with little ability to raise significant funds relative to needs: natural resource exports, and foreign aid are the primary financing sources.
3. Strong negotiating powers in achieving locational advantages and other benefits that lower the cost of production, lower taxes, lower pollution standards, lower export-import tariffs, lower wages, flexible work hours, lower workplace standards.	Weak negotiating powers in controlling MNC, particularly when pursuing the attraction of direct foreign investment; flexible taxation policies, pollution standards, wage rates, import-export restrictions, etc., are used to persuade investors (MNCs) to locate there.
4. MNCs strive to maximize the value of stockholders' wealth and corporate profit.	Host nations strive to upgrade the quality of life of their citizenry.
5. Primary strength in raw material conversion.	Primary strength in raw material production (supply). (Some have an abundance of raw materials.)
6. Realizes considerable revenues from the production of consumer goods.	Realizes far lower revenues due to inability to engage in consumer goods production, especially big-ticket items, e.g., stoves, refrigerators, cars, televisions, etc.
7. Mobile: can relocate either in short run or long run to take advantage of new opportunities.	Immobile: impossible to relocate; must address objectives with given resources.

Exhibit 13.2 *(continued)*

8. Education rich: characterized by highly skilled workforce readily adaptable to technological changes and very capable of producing technology advances.	Education poor: characterized by poorly skilled workforce not easily adaptable to technological changes and largely incapable of producing advances in technology.
9. Represents the "Haves," the well-off, the progressive.	Represents the "Have-Nots," the needy, the poor.
10. Represents the "North" in terms of global geographic boundary.	Represents the "South" in terms of global geographic boundary.
11. Strong ability to initiate investment projects from the preliminary study to the economic and technological feasibility study to the engineering study.	Lacks the ability and capacity to initiate projects from the preliminary study to the economic and technological feasibility study to the engineering study.
12. Strong management ability.	Lacks strong management ability.
13. Access to and control of markets for movement of goods and services.	Little access to and control of markets for movement of goods and services.
14. Strong marketing skills.	Weak marketing skills.

And, an outline of the characteristics of the Third World, which is disposed to upgrading the quality of life and expanding life choices of its citizenry, further facilitates pedagogy development, but more profoundly provides a comparative context that facilitates critical thinking about the rich country–poor country makeup. Opportunities for direct foreign investment and trade among nations have given rise to multinational firms as they pursue *firm-specific* and *location-specific* advantages (these factors are discussed in Chapter 12). The *firm-specific* advantages are outlined in *Who is the MNC?* Financial wealth, strong negotiating powers, mobility, raw material conversion, highly skilled employees, and strong project conceptualization and implementation capability create a very formidable capacity to successfully compete in the global marketplace. Such capacity in ways facilitates *location-specific* advantages, making the multinational even more competitive.[8]

As noted, the character of the multinational well conveys the character of rich countries. Recall that Andre Gunder Frank argues that capital diffusion within and among Third World countries—that is, direct foreign investment occasioned by multinational enterprise—has led to the development of rich countries at the expense of poor countries. In any new pedagogy, it is important to understand that the multinational not only represents the power and prowess of the rich, but also by its very nature contributes greatly to the enabling of the rich country human development paradigm. Therefore, the requirement of a new pedagogy is to advance a new concept of enablement that has the potential of redressing the distressed poor country paradigm. The characteristics outlined in *Who is the Third World?* clearly suggest why the human development paradigm in poor countries is in distress. Backward development posture; financially poor, weak negotiating powers; raw materials supply; immobile, poorly skilled workforce; and minimal capability to conceptualize and implement investment initiatives create a rather limited capacity to generate significant revenues to support economic development. The proposed *profit satisficing* coupled with the capital diffusion powers of the multinational as envisaged in this discourse, particularly as prescribed in Chapter 12, can conceivably push poor countries in the direction of enablement enjoyed by rich countries. Once adequately spurred, the human development paradigm and wealth development generate a self-propelling momentum. This notion, therefore, is the platform for the new pedagogy.

No doubt the new pedagogy will require a new mind-set about shareholder wealth maximization. Exhibit 13.3 presents a framework of questions that are central to raising the consciousness about the capacity of shareholder wealth maximization, that is, what it does or does not promote, what it should or should not promote, and so on. Each question provides a basis for query and deliberation that is critically important to pedagogy development. A simple perusal of selected questions makes the point. Does or should shareholder wealth maximization seek to maximize the wealth of those most able; people who have the capacity to invest in corporations and thereby place themselves in a position to reap the

Exhibit 13.3
Shareholder Wealth Maximization
A Query and Deliberation Framework

Does/Should SWM ⟶ max. the wealth of the able, the rich, the fittest, etc.
Does/Should SWM ⟶ max. the efficient allocation of scarce resources
Does/Should SWM ⟶ max. employee income
Does/Should SWM ⟶ max. employee wealth
Does/Should SWM ⟶ max. economic (GDP) value
Does/Should SWM ⟶ max. social (society) value
Does/Should SWM ⟶ max. global economic value
Does/Should SWM ⟶ max. global social value
Does/Should SWM ⟶ refute Andre Gunder Frank's proposition

benefits of corporate growth? How did some obtain this capacity but not others? Does or should shareholder wealth maximization seek to maximize the efficient allocation of scarce resources—resources that belong to all humans? Why don't all humans share equitably in the utilization of scarce resources? Does or should shareholder wealth maximization seek to maximize employee income; compensation to those who do the heavy lifting, so to speak, in the production of goods and services? Why do some executives receive compensation that literally dwarfs that of rank-and-file workers? Does or should shareholder wealth maximization seek to maximize global economic value; produce a living wage in all countries? Why are there a few rich countries and a plethora of poor ones? Does or should shareholder wealth maximization seek to refute Andre Gunder Frank's proposition that capital diffusion has resulted in the development of underdevelopment? Why haven't capital flows from developed to underdeveloped countries resolved the rich country–poor country dilemma?

From a pedagogical perspective, these questions provide a platform from which to direct and encourage critical thinking, not only about the capacity of shareholder wealth maximization, but its values as well. In other words, what values are conveyed by the corporate goal of maximizing shareholder wealth? Are these values consistent with the social norm, should they be consistent with the social norm, and are they ethical? What values should shareholder wealth maximization project? Such questions assist in framing the pedagogy and facilitating the dialogue.

Redress of the rich country–poor country situation is well within the means and resources of available capacities. Policymakers, corporate managers, academicians, investors, and the general public have the capacity to change the course of events that produced the current dilemma. This discourse calls upon the multinational corporation to take the lead in this effort, but recognizes fully that the support of all stakeholders is requisite, particularly academicians. Under current pedagogy in the business school, academicians follow the conventional mode of thinking about shareholder wealth maximization and profit making. This is conveyed to future managers who will be charged with operating the multinational. It should be clear by now that redress of the rich country–poor country situation will be problematic under the current way of thinking about business enterprise.

To further raise consciousness about shareholder wealth maximization, Exhibit 13.4 engages the framework from two perspectives. First, it views current business school pedagogy as predicated upon thinking "inside the box," that is, analyzing issues through the conventional mode of pedagogical query and deliberation. Second, it calls for an expansion of the conventional mode to a broader dimension of introspection, extroversion, and critical analysis—thinking "outside the box" (this matter is given some attention in Chapter 12). Stipulation of shareholder wealth maximization

Exhibit 13.4
Thinking Outside the Box

T H E B O X	• B-SCHOOL EMPHASIZES SWM • MANAGERS ARE AGENTS OF SHAREHOLDERS • THE PRIMARY GOAL OF THE FIRM IS SWM • SHAREHOLDER INTEREST IS OF ABSOLUTE AND FOREMOST CONCERN

O U T S I D E T H E B O X	• SHAREHOLDER INTEREST IS PRIMARY 1 • STAKEHOLDER INTEREST (SOCIETY) IS PERHAPS PRIMARY 2 (I.E., MORE IMPORTANT THAN SECONDARY) • THIRD WORLD STAKEHOLDER HAS PRIMARY-LEVEL INTEREST IN FIRM GROWTH EQUATION • MANAGERS ARE VIEWED AS AGENTS OF STAKEHOLDERS • STAKEHOLDER HAPPINESS RESULTS IN LARGER PIE

---

as the goal of the firm in introductory finance textbooks and profit maximization in introductory economics textbooks[9] set the stage for developing critical thinking about the growth of the firm that resonates throughout business school pedagogy and beyond. Both the academician and the student (the future corporate manager) are products of convention. Academicians teach based upon a prescribed framework of concepts, theory, and practice; students, in turn, learn based upon what is conveyed and employed by academicians. Hence, pedagogy and learning takes place within a bounded environment governed by conventionally, as well as traditionally, accepted arts and sciences. This, for all practical purposes, is tantamount to thinking inside "the box." In the context of business school pedagogy, the primary mandate of the firm is profit making and maximizing shareholder wealth. Managers are seen as agents of shareholders duty bound by contractual obligation to act in the best interest of the shareholder (see Chapter 11 for this discussion). The shareholder's interest is of absolute and foremost concern; the stakeholder's interest is of secondary concern. The process of reasoning is governed by the mandate.

Clearly, the conventional mode of pedagogy has not assisted multinational enterprise well in remedying the condition of poor countries. But it can. The solutions to many great problems facing humankind have been achieved by thinking about the problem and the solution in a different way, leading to critical breakthroughs. A different way, of thinking is no less called for here. Viewing shareholder interest as a primary concern is crucial to maintaining a flow of capital into the corporation. But this concern need not be so elevated in stature that all other interests are simply secondary at best. The interest of the stakeholder, of which the shareholder is a component, deserves more than secondary consideration. This perspective has been previously articulated. It is important here to reiterate that solving the rich country–poor country dilemma necessarily requires a change in the thinking about business enterprise, and that the Third World stakeholder receive more than secondary priority in the firm growth equation. In this context, managers should be viewed as agents of stakeholders, and not simply duty bound to acting primarily and exclusively in the best interest of those who provide the investment capital.

Chapter 11 conveys this notion, and suggests *profit satisficing* as the means of achieving this objective. *Profit satisficing* is an enabler. It enables the firm in redressing the rich country–poor country dilemma, and it enables the human development paradigm in rescuing it from distress. Facilitating life-choice opportunities and fuller realization of life choices among Third World stakeholders in turn facilitates Third World economic development as it provides these economies fuller benefit of their participation. Despite opposing viewpoint, this is quite compatible with the best interests of the firm, particularly long-run interests. *Profit satisficing* is quite literally thinking "outside the box." It is outside the conventional or normal way of thinking about profit making, yet it is not counter to profit making but a complement to it. Thinking "outside the box" is necessary to developing an approach to solving the rich country–poor country dilemma.

The intent here is not to construct a new pedagogy but to offer grounds for its development. The firm currently pursues shareholder wealth maximization with profit maximization as a pillar. The proposal is to adapt the current goal of the firm to a broader construct—stakeholder wealth enhancement with *profit satisficing* as a pillar. The proposed pedagogy does not replace the existing pedagogy, but complements it. The profit maxim would not be impaired, shareholder interest would not be compromised, and the firm would suffer no injury. In fact, development of the whole business environment, as the proposed stakeholder framework suggests, rather than simply focusing on the elements essential to making a quick profit leads to erection of a more enduring and sustaining relationship with host environments. This clearly offers a win-win outcome. Profit making is more assured in the long run. The long-run return to shareholders is more stabilized. The human development paradigm, particularly for the "have-not" stakeholders, is enhanced. Economic development in host environments is facilitated. And, the multinational assumes a new role as change agent in ushering in a new mode of direct foreign investment in the Third World. All in all, the rich country–poor country dilemma takes center stage in global enterprise.

NOTES

1. Peter McLaren and Remin Farahmandpur, "Teaching Against Globalization and the New Imperialism: Toward a Revolutionary Pedagogy" *Journal of Teacher Education* 52, no. 2 (2001), 2.

2. Ibid., 1.

3. In chapter 10, it was noted that 40 percent of the population in sub-Saharan Africa live on less than $1 a day.

4. Donald R. Escarraz and Patrick B. O'Neill, "The Theory of the Firm and Finance Theory,"*Journal of Financial Education* (1997), 68.

5. Paul R. Krugman, ed., *Strategic Trade Policy and the New International Economics* (Cambridge, MA: The MIT Press, 1986).

6. Mahbub ul Haq has prepared original discourse on the human development paradigm, prescribing four components: equity, sustainability, productivity, and empowerment. See Mahbub ul Haq, *Reflections on Human Development* (Oxford: Oxford University Press, 1995), 16.

7. Mahbub ul Haq, ibid., 16–20.

8. Leon Grunberg, ibid; and Krugman and Obstfeld, ibid.

9. See David F. Scott, Jr., et al., *Basic Financial Management* (Upper Saddle River, NJ: Prentice Hall, Inc., 1999), 2–3; and N. Gregory Mankiw, *Principles of Microeconomics* (New York: The Dryden Press, 1998), 286.

CHAPTER 14

Epilogue

Solutions to problems of development are difficult to fashion and even harder to implement, particularly in light of forces at play that contradict and countermand rational approaches and efforts. The proposed change agent treatise is advanced in an environment characterized by many ills. Closing the discourse in epilogue form allows a conclusion of sorts without actually concluding. With the many open and outstanding issues impinging Third World inequality, a conclusion seems inappropriate. The following epilogue outlines several outstanding issues that may have a decidedly pejorative impact on the approach to Third World inequality resolution proposed herein, and cautions that persistence of the noted issues may render any approach impractical.

As this discourse draws to a close, a comment by Mahbub ul Haq seems appropriate:

I have found nothing more fascinating than the birth and evolution of new ideas. . . . The first stage is characterized by organized resistance. As new ideas begin to challenge the supremacy of the old, all the wrath and scorn is heaped upon the heads of those who have the audacity to think differently . . . The second stage can generally be described as widespread and uncritical acceptance of new ideas. At some point, there is a sudden realization that the time for a new idea has arrived and all those who had opposed it thus far hurry over to adopt it as their own. Their advocacy becomes even more passionate than those of the pioneers, and they take great pains to prove that they discovered the idea in the first place . . . It is the third stage which is generally the most rewarding—a critical evaluation of ideas and their practical implementation.[1]

This discourse is undertaken neither with eyes open and mind closed, nor with eyes closed and mind open. It is well understood and fully recognized that the task of redressing the predicament of poor countries is profoundly difficult and that any prescription for redress will very likely encounter rejection. But questions must be asked and solutions sought. Leonard Silk reminds us of the riddle Marx posed: "What is to take the place of capitalism once the historical conditions that gave rise to it no longer exist?" "That question shook the world," Silk asserts, "and is still shaking it."[2] Other questions are just as resounding. What is the fate of the world? Can the "haves" and "have nots" coexist? Will the meek inherit the earth? Can our intellectual abundance guide us to peace and tranquility for all?

Much has been articulated herein about the underlying purpose set in pursuit of a solution to Third World poverty, hence a redress of the rich country–poor country dilemma. Completion of this work, however, would be remiss without recognizing certain realities. Some have been previously articulated and simply restated here. Others not central to the primary focus of the discourse are noted as important in the larger scheme of things. All point to the inescapable realization that there is no simple way to bring resolve to the Third World poverty problem. It is exceedingly complex, it is profoundly misunderstood, and it is ultimately the world's foremost challenge, but it is not without remedy. Poverty is centrally a wealth issue. Creating greater wealth through the reallocation and utilization of resources in a manner conducive to facilitation of the human development paradigm is the key challenge. There are essentially three forces powerful enough to address the Third World wealth issue: foreign aid (principally a wealth redistribution tool), free enterprise (conventionally capitalism enabled by the free market mechanism and free trade), and good governance (essentially domestic politics of the people, by the people, and for the people). Foreign aid has one especially serious drawback. Its political objective often overshadows the strategic plan. Third World nations in particular are driven by a seemingly love-hate regard for G8 subsidy. They love the help but hate the price. This not withstanding, the poverty problem cannot be solved by wealth redistribution alone. New wealth must be created and lots of it. This calls for involvement of an entity that by objective specializes in new capital formation—the multinational corporation. Multinational enterprise in the Third World sets in place forces of capitalism through capital diffusion that foster investment incentive, development efficiency, and economic expansion. Implementation of the proposed *profit satisficing* through *stakeholder givebacks* can assist the multinational in very directly facilitating the human development paradigm. The combined forces of capital diffusion and *stakeholder givebacks* can mount a powerful assault on Third World poverty.

While the multinational corporation has enormous potential and delivers many benefits, it is no Sir Galahad. The proposition that the multinational can serve as change agent for Third World poverty is advanced in light of Andre Gunder Frank's assertion that capitalism has generated the development of underdevelopment. There is much wisdom in Frank's argument. We should not fail to keep in mind that the world "system" is a manifestation perhaps less by accident than by design. The "system" has grown out of a collective cornucopia of wants and expectations, and the initiative to realize them—the more limited the wants and expectations, the less initiative put forth; the more expansive they are, the more aggressive the effort for attainment. Over time, the more aggressive behavior manifests itself into a system structure and functional process that ultimately imposes itself on the collective form. The multinational corporation is a reflection of the more aggressive behavior. Hence, it has contributed to a systemic design that has facilitated the rich country–poor country makeup.

But any design can be changed. The world "system" can be made a better purveyor of equity and equality. Through capital diffusion and *stakeholder givebacks*, along with the support of foreign aid, the "system" can be retooled and restructured. Clearly though, the multinational corporation and G8 subsidy cannot stand alone in the struggle to abate Third World poverty; many hands are needed to lift the burden of disadvantagement. Despite the power of the multinational and the G8, a profoundly important and crucial responsibility must be assumed by the hand of governance. Governance, and indeed good governance, cannot be overlooked in facilitating and enabling Third World development. Sadly, governance in all too many Third World countries is in distress. At center stage are corruption and human rights violation followed closely by racism and ethical misdoing. While the origin of these matters may be internal, they also have external linkages, as outsiders conducting business with Third World countries and interacting through other means do so in ways that facilitate corruption, encourage human rights violation, perpetuate racial preference, and condone unethical practices.

Corruption—the abuse of the public trust or the use of political influence for personal gain at the public's cost—is widespread and deeply rooted in the Third World. It has compromised the whole of the institutional mapping in some cases and seriously constricted it in others. The constitution is little more than words on paper, the policy apparatus is bypassed, institutional capacity is impaired, political feasibility is violated, and government capacity is restricted. These conditions lead to undermined property rights, rule of law, investment incentives, development objectives, and the human development paradigm. Corruption is quite literally an assault on the political, social, and economic well-being of a nation. It creates systemic inefficiencies that severely restrict economic development and modernization. Key public officials and principal members of civil society from more than 60 developing countries ranked public sector corruption as the most severe impediment to development and growth.[3]

Standing shoulder to shoulder with corruption in the Third World is human rights violation. There is scarcely an aspect of human dignity that has not been compromised in the Third World. To address the problem, the United Nations set forth the Universal Declaration of Human Rights proclaiming freedom of speech and belief, and freedom from fear and want as the highest aspirations of common people. The articles of the declaration specifically address matters of slavery, torture, equal protection of the law, property ownership, trade unions, right to education, and a number of other important concerns.[4] Through the Universal Declaration of Human Rights, the United Nations has made an exhaustive attempt to recognize, stipulate, and protect the rights and freedoms of every aspect of human dignity. Despite this effort, the human rights violation problem persists.

Also, there is the matter of race relations and, specifically, racism. The rich country–poor country dilemma no doubt has been fueled by racial attitude, and as with corruption and human rights violation, racism hinders the development process. It stands as one of the world's greatest, if not the foremost, social ills, literally handcuffing society and destabilizing social interaction. Racial background and skin color are the primary targets of racism. While racial background is used as a measure of one's content and character, skin color is the more exploited feature of one's humanity. Skin color intolerance is quite literally the epitome of man's inhumanity to man. But there is a strong belief that we live in a color-blind society. In fact, many argue that skin color is insignificant in the socioeconomics and politics of, for example, G8–Third World relations. Does this view suggest that resource allocation, trade policy, capital diffusion, and other rich-country decisions involving Third World nations imply a color-blind society? In reality, does a color-blind society exist anywhere?[5]

Derald Wing Sue notes that after 30 years of work on the psychology of racism, he continues to be mystified by the failure of many to recognize the falsehoods of the color-blind society. Sue confides that the notion of a color-blind society can be employed only in the context of a level playing field where equal access and opportunity exist for all groups. Since this condition does not exist in society, Sue argues that the practice of color-blindness perpetuates and creates greater disparities in society.[6] In the Third World context, it will undermine accountability for human rights violation, income inequality, capital diffusion disparity, trade policy inequity, resource allocation patterns, and the like. If the policy apparatus assumes equal access and equal treatment as givens, then outcomes will be self-serving. That is, if social, economic, and/or political policies employed in the Third World ignore the realities of racism, the resulting outcomes will be skewed to the advantage of those in control of the policy apparatus.

Finally, there is the matter of ethics. Simply put—what is right, what is just, what is humane, what is passionate, what is tolerant? Discussions on ethics lead in many directions. Despite one's culture, race, color, sex, religion, language, nationality, social or economic position, political persuasion, or other status, there are matters of common interest among all humankind that set forth ethical behavior. It is suggested that ethical behavior of humankind emanates from common values that all societies desire: longevity and quality of life, respect and appreciation, and freedom and security. Rational people everywhere value life; they want a long, healthful, and prosperous existence. People everywhere value respect and appreciation; they want to be accepted as equals and treated with dignity. All people want freedom from fear and human bondage, and want to feel safe as they go about their daily lives.[7] The common values and their social pathos give rise to an ethics framework. Observing these values and operating within the framework should lead to ethical practices in social, economic, and political interaction and decision making. But nothing is certain, particularly when facing the power of tyranny, wealth, political influence, and the like. Ethics compromised are ethics minimized. The more complex the ethics framework, the greater the opportunity for co-option.

Perhaps ethics should simply concern matters of "right" and "wrong" and the capacity of humankind to display common sense. One doesn't need to grasp economic theory to understand income inequality. One doesn't need to be a brain surgeon to comprehend the inhumanity of human rights violation. If one has difficulty recognizing acts of inhumanity, then one has not been the victim of inhumanity. Switch sides. That is, imagine that because of the decisions and actions of others, you do not have food for mere sustenance, you do not have the freedom to publicly express your personal opinion, you do not feel secure and safe in your daily life or have the opportunity to expand your life choices, you do not feel equal to other human beings, and so on. How do you feel? How do you feel about those who victimize you? How do you feel about a society that permits victimization? No one appreciates being disenfranchised, persecuted, or oppressed. One doesn't have to be superintelligent to reach these conclusions. These are simply commonsense realities. Being your neighbor's keeper is right; persecuting your neighbor is wrong. Decisions and actions that support the survival of humankind are right; decisions and actions that support the survival of the fittest are wrong. Being ethical is doing the right thing.

So then, in a world where corruption, human rights violation, racism, and ethical misdoing abound, let it be clear that every word written herein is done with clear conscious and sound recognition that the multinational corporation in its own right stands apart as a purveyor of many "goods" and many "harms," and is responsible for much "propriety" as well as much "impropriety." Be it also clear that abating Third World poverty is absolutely and unequivocally a monumental task that requires the marshalling of resources, the development of strategy, and the implementation of plans on a scale one may find difficult to imagine. But our past accomplishments in tackling disease, discovering life-support fuels, and exploring outer space, among others, give us much cause for optimism. We know that we can accomplish the thought-to-be unimaginable, the presumed impossible. The enormous feat of resolving Third World poverty is so characterized. The deliberation herein argues that resolution of poverty conditions in the Third World, while presumed impossible, is obtainable. And the multinational, as this deliberation counsels, is best suited to lead the charge.

Having said all of this, closing with the words of Conrad N. Hilton seems fitting: "There is a natural law, a Divine law, that obliges you and me to relieve the suffering, the distressed and the destitute."[8] "If we show the willingness to stop along the broad hiway [sic] of economic prosperity [to help others] . . . we can have the right to expect that if we fall, we will be helped."[9]

NOTES

1. Mahbub ul Haq, Reflections on Human Development. Oxford: Oxford University press, 1995, 228–229.

2. Leonard Silk, *Economics in Plain English* (New York: Simon & Schuster, 1986), 34.

3. Cheryl W. Gray and Daniel Kaufmann, "Corruption and Development," *Finance & Development* 35, no. 1 (1998), 7. See also Robert Klitgaard, "Subverting Corruption," *Finance & Development* 37, no. 2 (2000), 2–5; and S.M. Ghazanfar and Karen S. May, "Third World Corruption: A Brief Survey of the Issues," *The Journal of Social, Political and Economic Studies* 25, no. 3 (2000), 351–68.

4. *Universal Declaration of Human Rights*, adopted and proclaimed by United Nations General Assembly resolution 217 A(III), 1948.

5. See Nancy Murray, "Somewhere Over the Rainbow: A Journey to the New South Africa," *Race & Class* 38, no. 3 (1997), 1–24; Alejandro de la Fuente, "The Resurgence of Racism in Cuba," *NACLA Report on the Americas* 34, no. 6 (2001), 29–34; (Anonymous), "The Darkening of South Africa," *The Economist* 335, no. 7915 (1995), 18–20; and Jonathan Rieder, "Our Complexion Complex," *The Washington Post* (2003), C04.

6. Dr. Derald Wing Sue is a professor of psychology and education at Columbia University's Teachers College. See Derald Wing Sue, "Dismantling the Myth of a Color-Blind Society," *Black Issues in Higher Education* 20, no. 19 (2003), back cover.

7. Denis Goulet, "On the Ethics of Development Planning," *Studies in Comparative International Development* 11, no. 1 (1976), 26–28.

8. Conrad N. Hilton, *Excerpt from the Last Will and Testament of Conrad N. Hilton*, Conrad N. Hilton Foundation, Los Angeles, CA.

9. Conrad N. Hilton, National Prayer Breakfast, Mayflower Hotel Ballroom, Washington, DC, 1956, Conrad N. Hilton College Library and Archives, Houston, TX.

Bibliography

Abadi, Jacob. 1993. "India's Economic Policy Since Nehru: The Failure of Democratic Socialism and the March Toward Free Trade." *Journal of Third World Studies*, 10(2): 12–35.

"Action on the Problem of Corrupt Practices." 1978. *The CTC Reporter*, 1(4), April.

Alchian, Armen. 1950. "Uncertainty, Evolution and Economic Theory." *Journal of Political Economy*, 21: 39–50.

Alchian, Armen A., and William R. Allen. 1969. *Exchange and Production, Theory in Use*. Belmont, CA: Wadsworth Publishing Company.

Ali, Sheikh R. 1989. "The Third World Debt Crisis and U.S. Policy." In *Third World at the Crossroads*, ed. Sheikh R. Ali. New York: Praeger, 193–204.

Amartya, Sen, ed. 1970. *Growth Economics*. Baltimore: Penguin Books.

Ammer, Christine, and Dean S. Ammer. 1977. *Dictionary of Business and Economics*. New York: The Free Press.

Anthony, R.H. 1960. "The Trouble with Profit Maximization." *Harvard Business Review*, 38: 126–134.

Appelbaum, Nancy P., Anne S. Macpherson, and Karin A. Rosemblatt, eds. 2003. *Race and Nation in Modern Latin America*. Chapel Hill: The University of North Carolina Press.

Arpan, J.S. 1972. *International Intra-corporate Pricing: Non-American Systems and Views*. New York: Praeger.

———. 1972. "International Intra-corporate Pricing: Non-American Systems and Views." *Journal of International Business Studies*, 7, Spring.

Asante, S.K.B. 2003. "A Partnership of Unequal Partners." *New African*, 419, June: 14–17.

Ashok, Kapoor. 1975. *Foreign Investments and the New Middle East*. Princeton, NJ: Darwin Press.

Ashok, Kapoor, and James E. Cotton. 1972. *Foreign Investments in Asia*. Princeton, NJ: Darwin Press.

Ayert, Richard, and James March. 1963. *A Behavior Theory of the Firm*. Englewood Cliffs, NJ: Prentice Hall.

BaNikongo, Nikongo, 1995. "The Splintered Caribbean in an Integrated World: Planning for the 21st Century." *Journal of Third World Studies*, 12(2), 106.

Barnet, Richard J., and Ronald E. Muller. 1974. *Global Reach*. New York: Simon and Schuster.

Barrera, Albino. 1997. Exchange-Value Determinization: Scholastic Just Price, Economic Theory, and Modern Catholic Social Thought. *History of Political Economy*, 29(1), Spring.

Berger, Peter L. 1974. *Pyramids of Sacrifice*. New York: Basic Books.

Bhide, A. 1994. Efficient Markets, Deficient Governance. *Harvard Business Review*, 72, November/December: 128–139.

Bigsten, Arne, and Andres, Danielsson. 1999. "Is Tanzania an Emerging Economy?" *Emerging Africa* (an OECD project). Paris, France: OECD, May.

Blake, D., and R. Walters. 1976. *The Politics of Global Economic Relations*. Englewood Cliffs, NJ: Prentice-Hall.

Bobo, Benjamin F. 1981. "Corporate and Third World Involvement: A Reciprocal Relationship." *Unpublished*. Riverside, CA: University of California.

———. 1982. "Multinational Corporations in the Economic Development of Black Africa." *Journal of African Studies*, 9(1), March: 15.

———. 1996. "Multinationals, the North and the New World Order: Objectives and Opportunities." *Proceedings of the International Management Development Association, Fifth World Business Congress*, July 17–21. Hamilton, Bermuda: International Management Development Association, 107–114.

———. 1999. "Multinationals and the Caribbean: A Post-Colonial Perspective." *Journal of the Third World Spectrum*, 6(1), Spring: 96–97.

———. 2000. "Whose Wealth to Maximize: The Third World as Stakeholder." *International Third World Journal and Review*, 11: 19–26.

———. 2001. *Locked In and Locked Out: The Impact of Urban Land Use Policy and Market Forces on African Americans*. Westport, CT: Praeger Publishers.

Bobo, Benjamin F., and Lawrence S. Tai. 1994. "Topicos Sobre Las Relaciones Norte-Sur y El Nuevo Order Mundial [Issues in North-South Relations and the New World Order]." *Revista de Contabilidad Y Auditoria*, 25, April: 95–118.

———. 1995. "Internationalizing Decision Making and the Global Interdependency Sensitivity Thesis." Unpublished working paper. Los Angeles, CA: Loyola Marymount University: 15–16.

———. 1995. "MNC–Third World Relations: A Comparative Study of Policymakers' Attitudes and Perceptions." *12th Annual Meeting: Association of Third World Studies Inc., ATWS Proceedings*. Williamsburg, VA: ATWS Publications, 45–53.

———. 1994. "Issues in North-South Relations and the New World Order." Paper presented at the *1st Annual Conference on Multinational Financial Issues*, June 2–4. Camden, NJ: Rutgers University.

———. 1996. "Multinationals in the Third World: Reciprocity, Conflict Resolution and Economic Policy Formulation." *Journal of the Third World Spectrum*, 3(1), Spring.

———. 1997. "Internationalization Decision Making and the Global Interdependency Sensitivity Thesis." *Journal of the Third World Spectrum*, 4(2): 23–41.

Brigham, Eugene. 1995. *Fundamentals of Financial Management*. New York: Dryden Press.

Browne, Robert S. 1996. "How Africa Can Prosper." In *Readings in International Political Economy*, ed. David N. Balaam and Michael Veseth. Upper Saddle River, NJ: Prentice-Hall, Inc.

Bulmer-Thomas, Victor. 1995. *The Economic History of Latin America Since Independence*. Cambridge, MA: Cambridge University Press.

Calleo, D., and B. Rowland. 1973. *America and the World Political Economy: Atlantic Dreams and National Realities*. Bloomington: Indiana University Press.

Campbell, Leland, and Charles S. Gulas. 1999. "Corporate Giving Behavior and Decision-Maker Social Consciousness." *Journal of Business Ethics*, 19(4), May.

Chaitram, Singh. 1989. *Multinationals, the State, and the Management of Economic Nationalism: The Case of Trinidad*. New York: Praeger.

Chang, S.J. 1997. "Whose Wealth to Maximize." *Journal of Financial Education*, 23, Fall: 1–13.

Clotfelter, Charles T., and Thomas Ehrlich. 1999. "Philanthropy and the Nonprofit Sector in a Changing America." *Wilson Quarterly*, 23(3), Summer: 125.

Clower, Robert. 1966. *Growth Without Development*. Evanston, IL: Northwestern University Press.

Coakley, George J., Philip M. Mobbs, Philip A. Szczesniak, David R. Wilburn, and Thomas R. Yager. 2001. "The Mineral Industries of Africa." *U.S. Geological Survey Minerals Yearbook*. Washington, DC: Bureau of Mines.

Coase, R.H. 1937. "The Nature of the Firm." *Economica*, November: 386–485.

Coffman, R.B. 1983. "Is Profit Maximization vs. Value Maximization Also Economics vs. Finance?" *Journal of Financial Education*, 12: 37–40.

Cohen, Benjamin J. 1973. *The Question of Imperialism: The Political Economy of Dominance and Dependence*. New York: Basic Books, Chapter 6.

Cornell, B., and A.C. Shapiro. 1987. "Corporate Stakeholders and Corporate Finance." *Financial Management*, 16: 5–14.

Cornwell, Richard. 2002. "A New Partnership for Africa's Development?" *African Security Review*, 11(1): 91–96.

Crespi, Irving. 1961. "Use of a Scaling Technique in Surveys." *Journal of Marketing*, 25(5), July: 69–72.

Crook, Clive. 2002. "Wealth of Nations—When Economic Development Just Isn't Enough." *National Journal*, 34(33–35): 2436.

Crookell, H. 1975. "Investing in Development—A Corporate View." *Columbia Journal of World Business*, Spring.

Curry, Robert L., Jr., and Donald Rothschild. 1974. "On Economic Bargaining between African Governments and Multinational Companies." *The Journal of Modern African Studies*, 12(1), February: 13–182.

Cyert, Richard, and James March. 1990. *A Behavioral Theory of the Firm*, 2nd ed. Cambridge, MA: Blackwell Business.

Dana, Leo Paul. 2002. *When Economies Change Paths*. Singapore: World Scientific Publishing Co. Pte. Ltd.

Daron, Acemoglu. 2003. "Root Causes: A Historical Approach to Assessing the Role of Institutions in Economic Development." *Finance and Development* (The International Monetary Fund), 40(2), June: 27.

De la Fuente, Alejandro. 2001. "The Resurgence of Racism in Cuba." *NACLA Report on the Americas*, 34(6), May/June: 29–34.

Declaration on the Establishment of a New International Economic Order. 1974. United Nation's 2,229th plenary meeting. New York: UN publications, 1 May.

Deepa, Ollapally. 1993. "The South Looks North: The Third World in the New World Order." *Current History*, 92(573): 175–179.

Demographic Yearbook 2000. 2002. New York: United Nations Department of Economic and Social Affairs, Issue 52.

Diebold, John. 1993. "Multinational Corporations: Why Be Scared of Them?" *Foreign Policy*, 12, Fall: 87.

Dymsza, W.A. 1972. *Multinational Business Strategy*. New York: McGraw Hill.

ECOSOC. 1976. Centre on Transnational Corporations, Document E/C. 10/17, July.

ECOSOC. Undated. "Corrupt Practices, Particularly Illegal Payments in International Commercial Transactions." Resolution 2/22 (63).

Eiteman, David K., and A.I. Stonehill. 1986. *Multi-national Business Finance*, 4th ed. Reading, MA: Addison-Wesley.

Elson, Diane. 1988. "Dominance and Dependency in the World Economy." In *Survival and Change in the Third World*, ed. Ben Crow, Mary Thorpe et al. New York: Oxford University Press.

Embree, Ainslie T., and Carol Gluck, eds. 1997. *Asia in Western and World History*. Armonk, NY: M. E. Sharpe, Inc.

Escarraz, Donald R., and Patrick B. O'Neill. 1997. "The Theory of the Firm and Finance Theory." *Journal of Financial Education*, Fall.

European Round Table of Industries. 1993. *Survey on Improvement of Conditions for Investment in the Developing World*. Brussels, Belgium: European Round Table of Industrialists.

Fayerweather, John. 1964. "LRP for International Operations." In *International Business Management Readings and Cases*, ed. John S. Ewing and Frank Meissner. Belmont, CA: Wadsworth Publishing Company.

———. 1972. "The Internationalization of Business." *Journal of the American Academy of Political and Social Science*, September: 403.

Financial Times. 1969. London, 12 September.

Findlay, M.C., III, and G.A. Whitmore. 1974. "Beyond Shareholder Wealth Maximization." *Financial Management*, 3, Winter.

FitzRoy, Felix, and Kornelius Kraft. 1986. "Profitability and Profit Sharing." *Journal of Industrial Economics*, 35, December: 113–130.

Frank, Andre Gunder. 1966. "The Development of Underdevelopment." *Monthly Review*, September.

Freeman, Gerene L. 1994. *What About My 40 Acers And A Mule?* New Haven, CT: Yale-New Haven Teachers Institute.

Friedman, Milton. 1953. *Essays in Positive Economics*. Chicago: University of Chicago Press.

Ghazanfar, S.M., and. Karen S. May. 2000. "Third World Corruption: A Brief Survey of the Issues." *The Journal of Social, Political and Economic Studies*, 25(3), Fall: 351–68.

Gilpin, Robert. 1975. *U.S. Power and the Multinational Corporation: The Political Economy of Foreign Direct Investment*. New York: Basic Books, Inc.

———. 1975a. "Three Models of the Future." In *International Organization*, ed. C. Fred Bergsten and Lawrence B. Krause, 29(1), Winter: 37–47.

Gitman, Lawrence J. 2003. *Principles of Managerial Finance*. New York: Addison-Wesley.

"Global Five Hundred: The World's Largest Corporations." 2003. *Fortune*, 148(2), July: 106–119.

Goulet, Denis. 1976. "On the Ethics of Development Planning." *Studies in Comparative International Development*, 11(1), Spring: 26–28.

Gray, Cheryl W., and David Kaufmann. 1998. "Corruption and Development." *Finance & Development*, 35(1), March: 7.

Greanias, George C. 1982. *The Foreign Corrupt Practices Act: Anatomy of a Statue*. Lexington, MA: Lexington Books.

Green, December, and Laura Luehrmann. 2003. *Comparative Politics of the Third World*. Boulder, CO: Lynne Rienner Publishers, Inc.

Greene, J., and M. Duerr. 1970. *Intercompany Transactions in the Multinational Firm*. New York: The Conference Board.

Grossman, S.J., and J.E. Stiglitz. 1977. "On Value Maximization and Alternative Objectives of the Firm." *Journal of Finance*, 32, 387–415.

Grunberg, Leon. 1996. "The IPE of Multinational Corporations." In David N. Balaam and Michael Veseth, *Introduction to International Political Economy*. Upper Saddle River, NJ: Prentice-Hall, Inc.

Guillaumont, Paprick, Sylviane Guillaumont-Jeanneney, and Aristomene Varoudakis. 1999. "Economic Policy Reform and Growth Prospects in Emerging African Economies," *Technical Papers*. Paris, France: OECD Development Center.

Gunder Frank, A. 1966. "The Development of Underdevelopment," *Monthly Review*, September.

———. 1996. "The Development of Underdevelopment." In *Readings in International Political Economy*, ed. David N. Balaam and Michael Veseth. Upper Saddle River, NJ: Prentice-Hall, Inc.

Gurley, John G. 1979. *Challengers to Capitalism*. New York: W.W. Norton & Company.

Hamilton, Nora, and Eun Mee Kim. 1993. "Economic and Political Liberalization in Mexico and South Korea." *Third World Quarterly*, 14(1), April: 109–136.

Harbison, Frederick, and Charles A. Myers. 1959. *Management in the Industrial World*. New York: McGraw-Hill Book Company.

Heenan, David A., and Warren J. Keegan. 1979. "The Rise of Third World Multinationals." *Harvard Business Review*, January/February.

Hilton, Conrad N. 1956. National Prayer Breakfast, 2 February, Mayflower Hotel Ballroom, Washington, DC. Conrad N. Hilton College Library and Archives, Houston, Texas.

———. 1984. *Excerpt from the Last Will and Testament of Conrad N. Hilton*, Los Angeles, CA: Conrad N. Hilton Foundation.

Hoisti, K. 1975. "Underdevelopment and the 'Gap' Theory of International Conflict." *American Political Science Review*, 69, 827–839.

Hughes, Helen. 1979. "Debt and Development: The Role of Foreign Capital in Economic Growth." *World Development*, 7(6), February: 105.

Hungry for Profit. 1994. New York: Richter Productions, Video.

"ILO: Draft on Trans-nationals Ready for Approval." 1977. *The CTC Reporter*, 1(2). UNCTAD: Code of Conduct on the Transfer of Technology, June.

International Chamber of Commerce. 1972. *Guidelines for International Investment*. Paris: ICC Publishing.

International Financial Statistics Yearbook. 1993. Washington, DC: International Monetary Fund.

Jacoby, N.H. 1972. "The Multinational Corporation." In *The Multinational Enterprise in Transition*, ed. A. Kapoor and Phillip D. Grub. Princeton, NJ: The Darwin Press.

Jacoby, Neil H. 1972. "The Multinational Corporation", In *The Multinational Enterprise in Transition*, ed. Ashok Kapoor and Phillip D. Grub Princeton NJ: Darwin Press.

Jalee, P. 1968. *The Pillage of the Third World*. New York: Monthly Review Press.

Jomo, K.S. 2001. "Globalization, Liberalization, Poverty and Income Inequality in Southeast Asia." *Technical Papers*. Paris, France: OECD Development Center, December.

Kapoor, Ashok. 1975. *Foreign Investments and the New Middle East*. Princeton, NJ: The Darwin Press.

Kapoor, Ashok, and J.E. Cotton. 1972. *Foreign Investments in Asia*. Princeton, NJ: The Darwin Press.

Kay, Cristobal. 1993. "For a Renewal of Development Studies: Latin American Theories and Neoliberalism in the Era of Structural Adjustment." *Third World Quarterly*, 14(4), November: 691–702.

Kim, Seongsu. 1998. "Does Profit Sharing Increase Firm's Profits?" *Journal of Labor Research*, 19(2), Spring: 351–352.

Kindleberger, Charles P., and Bruce Herrick. 1977. *Economic Development*. New York: McGraw-Hill Book Company.

King, Martin Luther, Jr. 1963. *Why We Can't Wait*. New York: Harper & Row.

———. 1965. "Remaining Awake Through A Great Revolution." *Commencement Address for Oberlin College*. Oberlin, OH.

———. 1968. "Remaining Awake Through A Great Revolution." *Congressional Record*, Washington, DC.

Klitgaard, Robert. 2000. "Subverting Corruption." *Finance & Development*, 37(2), June.

Kornai, Janos. 2000. "What the Change of System from Socialism to Capitalism Does and Does Not Mean." *Journal of Economic Perspectives*, 14(1), Winter.

Krugman, Paul R. 1992. "Is Free Trade Passé?" In *Current Issues in the International Economy*, ed. Linda S. Goldberg and Michael W. Klein. New York: HarperCollins College Publishers.

Krugman, Paul R., ed. 1986. *Strategic Trade Policy and the New International Economics*. Cambridge, MA: The MIT Press: 23–26.

Krugman, Paul R., and Maurice Obstfeld. 1994. *International Economics*. New York: HarperCollins College Publishers.

Kuhn, W.F. 1970. *The Evolution of Economic Thought*. Chicago: South-Western.

Kuznets, Simon S. 1955. "Toward a Theory of Economic Growth." In *National Policy for Economic Welfare at Home and Abroad*, ed. R. Lekachman. Garden City, NY: Doubleday: 36.

———. 1971. *Notes on Stage of Economic Growth as a System Determinant*. In *Comparison of Economic Systems*, ed. Alexander Eckstein. Berkeley: University of California Press.

Laird, Landon E., Jr. 1971. "Order Bias, the Ideal Rating, and the Semantic Differential." *Journal of Marketing Research*, 8, 375–378.

Lecraw, D. 1977. "Direct Investment by Firms from Less-Developed Countries." *Oxford Economic Papers*, 29(3), November.

Legrain, Philippe. 2002. "Africa's Challenge," *World Link*, 15(3), 3.

Leo, Paul Dana. 2002. *When Economies Change Paths*. Singapore: World Scientific Publishing Co. Pte. Ltd.

Lipsey, R.G., P.N. Courant, D.D. Purvis, and P.O. Steiner. 1994. *Economics*, 10th ed. New York: HarperCollins.

Madura, Jeff, and Theodore E. Veit. 1988. *Introduction to Financial Management*. New York: West Publishing Company.

Mahbub ul Haq. 1995. *Reflections on Human Development*. Oxford: Oxford University Press.

Mainuddin, Robin G. 1995. "The New World Order Transition in the Third World: Implications for the Nation-State." *Journal of Third World Studies*, 12(1), Spring: 51.

Mandle, Jay R. 1996. *Persistent Underdevelopment*. The Netherlands: Gordon and Breach Science Publishers SA.

Mankiw, Gregory N. 1998. *Principles of Microeconomics*. New York: The Dryden Press.

Manuel, Trevor A. 2003. "Africa and the Washington Consensus: Finding the Right Path." *Finance & Development* (The International Monetary Fund), 40(3), September: 19–20.

Martin, Wolk. 2002. *Rich Country, Changing Role*. MSNBC, 4 September.

Mason, Colin. 2000. *A Short History of Asia*. New York: St. Martin's Press.

Mason, Hal R. 1978. *Technology Transfers: A Comparison of American and Japanese Practices in Developing Countries*. Paper prepared for the Japan Society's Business Educational Program Workshop. CA: UCLA Graduate School of Management, 3 May–4 June.

Mbeki, Thabo. 2001. "New Partnerships for Africa's Development." *Presidents & Prime Ministers*, 10(6), November/December: 30–32.

———. 2003. "Mbeki: African Union Is the Mother, NEPAD Is Her Baby." *The New African*, 415, February: 44.

McConnell, Campbell R., and Stanley L. Brue. 1996. *Economics*. New York: McGraw-Hill, Inc.

McLaren, Peter, and Remin Farahmandpur. 2001. "Teaching Against Globalization and the New Imperialism: Toward a Revolutionary Pedagogy." *Journal of Teacher Education*, 52(2), March/April.

Meade, James E. 1961. *A Neoclassical Theory of Economic Growth*. Oxford: Oxford University Press: 10.

Meier, Gerald M. 1995. *Leading Issues in Economic Development*, New York: Oxford University Press: 453–457.

———. 1989. *Leading Issues in Economic Development*. New York: Oxford University Press.

Meier, Gerald M., ed. 1970. *Leading Issues in Economic Development*. New York: Oxford University Press.

Merriam, Allen H. 1988. "What Does 'Third World' Mean?" In *The Third World: States of Mind and Being*, ed. Jim Norwine and Alfonzo Gonzalez. Boston, MA: Unwin and Hyman.

Michaels, Marguerite. 1993. "Retreat from Africa." *Foreign Affairs*, 72(1): 103.

Mikesell, Raymond E. 1971. "Conflict in Foreign Investor–Host Country Relations: A Preliminary Analysis." In *Foreign Investment in the Petroleum and Mineral Industries: Case Studies in Investor–Host Country Relations*, ed. Raymond E. Mikesell. Baltimore, MD: The John Hopkins Press.

Mills, Greg, and Jonathan Oppenheimer. 2002. "Partners, Not Beggars." *Time Europe*, 160(2), 35.

Mitchell, Daniel J.B., David Lewin, and Edward E. Lawler, III. 1990. "Alternative Pay Systems, Firm Performance and Productivity." In *Paying for Productivity: A Look at the Evidence*, ed. Alan S. Blinder. Washington, DC: The Brookings Institute.

Moran, Theodore H. 1994. *Multinational Corporations and the Politics of Dependence: Copper in Chile*. Princeton, NJ: Princeton University Press.

Morley, Samuel A. 2001. "Distribution and Growth in Latin America in an Era of Structural Reform: The Impact of Globalization." *Technical Papers*. Paris, France: OECD Development Center, December.

Mullen, Jennifer. 1997. "Performance-Based Corporate Philanthropy: How Giving Smart Can Further Corporate Goals." *Public Relations Quarterly*, 42(2), Summer.

Muller, Ronald E., and David H. Moore. Undated. "Inter-American Relations and Latin American Investment by U.S. Multinational Corporations: Exploration of an Emerging New Harmony." Prepared for U.S. Department of State, 25–27, Appendix A, 66–75.

"Multinational Corporation and the Law of Uneven Development." 1972. In *Economics and World Order: From the 1970s to the 1990s*, ed. Jagdish Bhagwati. New York: The Macmillan Co.

Murray, Nancy. 1997. "Somewhere Over the Rainbow: A Journey to the New South Africa." *Race and Class*, 38(3), January–March: 1–24.

Nafziger, E. Wayne 1990. *The Economics of Developing Countries*, 2nd ed. Englewood Cliff, NJ: Prentice Hall, Inc.: 165, 379–380, 390–393, 403–406.

Nelson, R., and S.G. Winter. 1982. *An Evolutionary Theory of Economic Change*. Cambridge, MA: Belknap Press.

Nisser, Carl, and Don Wallace, Jr. 1978. "National Treatment for Multinational Enterprises: Will the OECD Governments Meet the Challenge?" *Columbia Journal of World Business*, Fall: 14.

Norwine, Jim, and Alfonso Gonzalez, eds. 1988. *The Third World: States of Mind and Being*. Boston, MA: Unwin and Hyman.

OECD. 1977. "Guidelines for Multinational Enterprises." *The CTC Reporter*, 1(2), June.

Okun, A.M. 1975. *Equality and Efficiency: The Big Tradeoff*. Washington, DC: The Brookings Institute.

Oliver, Coney T. 1972. "The Andean Foreign Investment Code: A New Phase in the Quest for Normative Order as to Direct Investment." *American Journal of International Law*, 66, October.

Ollapally, Deepa. 1993. "The South Looks North: The Third World in the New World Order." *Current History*, April: 175–179.

Organization of American States. 1978. *Transnational Enterprises*. AG Doc. 1003/78, 30 June.

Osvaldo, Sunkel. 1972. "Big Business and 'Dependencia': A Latin American View." *Foreign Affairs*, 50: 517–531.

Packenham, R. 1973. *Liberal America and the Third World: Political Development Ideas in Foreign Aid and Social Science*. Princeton, NJ: Princeton University Press.

Panayiotopoulos, Prodromos, and Gavin Capps, eds. 2001. *World Development*. London: Pluto Press.

Peter, L.B. 1974. *Pyramids of Sacrifice*. New York: Basic Books.

Poitras, G. 1994. "Shareholder Wealth Maximization, Business Ethics and Social Responsibility." *Journal of Business Ethics*, 13: 125–134.

"Poor vs. Rich: A New Global Conflict." 1975. *Time*, 2 December: 34–35.

Porter, M. 1987. "From Competitive Advantage to Corporate Strategy." *Harvard Business Review*, 65: 43–59.

Prahalad, C.K. 1994. "Corporate Governance or Corporate Value Added? Rethinking the Primacy of Shareholder Value." *Journal of Applied Corporate Finance*, 44: 40–50.

Primeaux, P., and J. Stieber. 1994. "Profit Maximization: The Ethical Mandate of Business." *Journal of Business Ethics*, 13: 287–294.

Report of the South Commission. 1990. *The Challenge to the South*. New York: Oxford University Press.

Richardson, Harry W. 1993. *Regional Growth Theory*. London: The Macmillan Co.

Ricupero, Rubens. 1999. *Foreign Direct Investment in Africa: Performance and Potential*. Geneva: United Nations, June.

Rieder, John. 2003. "Our Complexion Complex." *The Washington Post*, 23 July: C.04.

Root, Franklin R. 1968. "Attitudes of American Executives Toward Foreign Government and Investment Opportunities." *Economic and Business Bulletin*, 20(2), January: 15–23.

Root, Hilton L. 1996. *Small Countries, Big Lessons: Governance and the Rise of East Asia*. New York: Oxford University Press, Chapter 10.

Rostow, W.W. 1959. "The Stages of Economic Growth." *Economic History Review*, August: 36–40.

———. 1990. *The Stages of Economic Growth*. New York: Cambridge University Press.

Rostow, W.W. et al. 1963. *The Economics of Take-Off into Sustained Growth*. New York: St. Martin's Press.

Sahlgren, Klaus A. 1977. "A View from the United Nations." *California Management Review*, 20(1): 84–85.

Sandeep, Bhargava. 1994. "Profit Sharing and the Financial Performance of Companies: Evidence from U.K. Panel Data." *Economic Journal*, 104, September: 1044–1056.

Sanjaya, Lall. 1979. "Transfer Pricing and Developing Countries: Some Problems of Investigation." *World Development*, 7: 59.

Schumpeter, Joseph A. 1961. *The Theory of Economic Development*. Cambridge, MA: Harvard University Press.

Scott, David F., Jr., John D. Martin, William Petty, and Arthur J. Keown. 1999. *Basic Financial Management*. Upper Saddle River, NJ: Prentice Hall, Inc.

Sheikh, R. Ali. 1989. "The Third World Debt Crisis and U.S. Policy." In *Third World at the Crossroads*, ed. Sheikh R. Ali. New York: Praeger.

Shoup, Carl S. 1974. "Taxation of Multinational Corporations." In *The Impact of Multinational Corporations on Development and on International Relations. Technical Papers: Taxation*. United Nations, Department of Economic and Social Affairs, STE/SA/II.

Silk, Leonard. 1986. *Economics in Plain English*. New York: Simon & Schuster.

Simon, Herbert A. 1947. *Administrative Behavior*. New York: Free Press.

———. 1958. *Organizations*. New York: Wiley.

Singer, Hans W., and Javed A. Ansari. 1975. "Poor vs. Rich: A New Global Conflict." *Time*, 22 December: 34–35.

———. 1988. *Rich and Poor Countries: Consequences of International Disorder*, 4th ed. Boston: Unwin and Hyman.

Sparkman, John. 1976. "Declaration of OECD Member Governments on International Investment and Multinational Enterprises." *Economic Interdependence*, 21 June: 89.

———. 1977. "Economic Interdependence and the International Corporation." *California Management Review*, 20(1), Fall: 88.

Spero, J. 1977. *The Politics of International Economic Relations*. New York: St. Martin's.

Statistical Abstract of the United States. 1993. Washington, DC: Bureau of Statistics.

———. 2002. Washington, DC: Bureau of Statistics.

———. 2003. Washington, DC: Bureau of Statistics.

Steade, Richard D. 1978. "Multinational Corporations and the Changing World Economic Order." *California Management Review*, 21(2): 6.

Stewart, B. 1985. "The Fragile Foundations of the Neoclassical Approach to Development." *Journal of Development Studies*, 21(2): 282–292.

———. 1993. "Continental Bank Roundtable on Global Competition in the 90s." *Journal of Applied Corporate Finance*, 6: 51–55.

Stone, Roger D., and Eve Hamilton. 1991. *Global Economics and the Environment: Toward Sustainable Rural Development in the Third World*. New York: Council on Foreign Relations Press.

Survey on Improvements of Conditions for Investment in the Developing World. 1993. Brussels, Belgium: European Round Table of Industrialists.

"The Darkening of South Africa." 1995. *The Economist*, 335 (7915): 18–20.

Thomas, Clive Y. 1975. "Industrialization and the Transformation of Africa: An Alternative Strategy to MNC Expansion." In *Multinational Firms in Africa*, ed. Carl Widstrand. Uppsala: Scandinavian Institute of African Studies.

Tomlinson, B.R. 2003. "What Was the Third World?" *Journal of Contemporary History*, 38(2): 307–321.

Tugwell, Franklin. 1995. *The Politics of Oil in Venezuela*. Stanford: Stanford University Press.

Tull, Donald S., and Gerald S. Albaum. 1973. *Survey Research: A Decisional Approach*. New York: Intext Educational Publishers, 120–123.

UNCTAD. 1978. *Dominant Positions of Market Power of Transnational Corporations: Use of the Transfer Pricing Mechanism*. New York: United Nations Publications.

———. 1978. *Handbook on the Acquisition of Technology by Developing Countries*. E. 78.II.D.15. New York: United Nations Publications.

Universal Declaration of Human Rights. 1948. Adopted and proclaimed by United Nations General Assembly Resolution 217 A (III), 10 December.

Van de Walle, Nicholas. 1999. "Aids Crisis of Legitimacy: Current Proposals and Future Prospects." *African Affairs*, 98: 346.

Vernon, Raymond. 1971. *Sovereignty at Bay.* New York: Basic Books.

Veseth, Michael. 1996. *Readings in International Political Economy.* Upper Saddle River, NJ: Prentice Hall, Inc.

Wagona Makoba, J. 2002. "Nongovernmental Organizations (NGOs) and Third World Development: An Alternative Approach to Development." *Journal of Third World Studies*, 19(1), Spring: 53–55.

Walleri, Dan R. 1978. "The Political Economy Literature on North-South Relations." *International Studies Quarterly*, 22(4): 587–590.

Ward, Runnalls B., and L. D'Anjou, eds. 1971. *The Widening Gap: Development in the 1970s.* New York: Columbia University Press.

Weintraub, Sidney. 1979. "The New International Economic Order: The Beneficiaries." *World Development*, 7(3): 251.

Widyono, Benny. 1978. "Transnational Corporations and Export-Oriented Primary Commodities." *Cepal Review*: 138.

Wield, David, and E. Rhodes, eds. 1988. "Divisions of Labour or Labour Divided?" In *Survival and Change in the Third World*, ed. Ben Crow, Mary Thorpe et al. New York: Oxford University Press.

Wing Sue, Derald. 2003. "Dismantling the Myth of a Color-Blind Society." *Black Issues in Higher Education*, 20(19), November.

World Bank Annual Report 1976. 1976. Washington, DC: World Bank.

World Development Factbook. 2003. Washington, DC: Central Intelligence Agency.

World Economic Factbook 1993. 1993. London: Euromonitor.

World Development Indicators. 2003. Washington, DC: World Bank.

World Development Report 1993. 1993. New York: Oxford University Press.

World Development Report 1994. 1994. New York: Oxford University Press.

World Development Report 1995. 1995. Washington, DC: World Bank.

World Development Report 2003: Sustainable Development in a Dynamic World. 2002. Washington, DC: World Bank, 240–241.

Index

1980 survey, xv, 64–73, 105, 123
1994 survey, xv, 64–73, 75–83, 86–87, 92, 95, 102–103, 105, 123

able factor, 184, 190, 192
accept–reject criteria, 179, 182
Acemoglu, Daron, 145, 150, 219
Africa, xv–xvi, 8, 9, 11, 12, 14–23, 25–33, 35–39, 43, 45–46, 49, 53, 55, 98, 101, 139–149
African predicament, xvi, 139–149
African Union, 147
agency relationship, 162, 182–183
aggregate production function, 189, 193
Alchian and Allen, 192
Alchian and Friedman, 157
Amartya, Sen, 128, 144, 217
American firms, 8, 60
Anglo–Saxon world, 155
appropriate technology, 29, 72–73, 86–87, 101
April 1955, 49
Argentina, 11, 16, 18–19, 21, 46, 54
argument, 1–5, 12–14, 48, 56, 59, 122, 140, 142, 154–158, 179, 184, 197, 211
Asia, xv, 12, 14–15, 17, 19–20, 23, 46, 49, 53, 55, 98, 101, 134–135, 143–144, 148
Asian NICs, 134–135
assimilation of technology, 29, 101

Balling, 155
Bandung, Indonesia, 49
BaNikongo, 130–131, 137, 218
bargaining framework, xv, 111, 118–119, 122, 124
bargaining models, 119, 125
Barnet and Muller, 163
behavioral theory of the firm, 154, 165, 219
Berger, Peter, 26, 48
Bobo and Tai, 93, 102, 105, 106, 111, 131
Bourgeoisie, 170
Brazil, 11, 16, 18–20, 44, 52, 54
British firms, 8, 159
Browne, Robert S., 140–143, 149–150, 219
B-School pedagogy, 197–208
Buffer stock, 100
Business practices, x, xiv, 70–72, 84–85, 104
Business school, xiv, xvi, 107, 197–199, 205–206

capital creation, 28
capital diffusion, xiv, 1, 3, 5, 19, 203–205, 210–213
capital flows, 15, 19–20, 70–71, 84–85, 197, 200, 202, 205
capital formation, 28, 59, 210
capital-intensive, 4, 27, 49, 59–60, 134

capitalism, 1, 164, 167, 170–172, 182,
    194, 198–199, 210–211
capitalist model, 172
capitalist system, 51
capstone, 124
Caribbean, xvi, 17, 46, 49, 129–137, 139,
    148, 166, 218
Caribbean development strategy, 131
Caribbean economic integration, 132,
    134, 137
Chang, S. J., 154–155, 163–165, 167,
    219
change agent, xiv, xvi, 3, 7, 82, 84, 95,
    105, 135, 149, 153, 155, 167, 169, 172,
    182, 188, 193, 207, 209, 211
Chernick, 133
Chile, 11, 16–17, 19–22, 27, 224
China, 8, 11, 16–19, 22–23, 46, 140
Coase, 155, 165, 219
code of conduct, 37, 41, 52, 56, 221
code of ethics, 56
collective self–reliance, 143
Colombia, 11, 16, 18–22, 46
commodity agreements, 44, 56, 91, 100
commodity price stabilization, 100
comparative advantage, xi, xiv, 2–5,
    30, 58, 99, 127, 129–137, 140–142,
    149–150, 172, 186, 188
comparative attitude profiles, 66
compensatory financing, 100
competitive advantage, 2, 30, 166,
    175, 225
concession agreements, 121
concessionary system, 121
conflict, x, xv, 36–37, 44, 48, 56, 59–61,
    75–76, 78, 81–83, 92, 111–112, 114,
    121–122, 125, 127–128, 137, 177, 180,
    183–184, 193
contractual agreements, 31
core, 1–3, 5, 28, 145, 200
corporate good, 154, 189–190
corporate objective, 159, 164, 180, 182,
    185–186, 191–193
corporation-to-government model,
    148–149
corruption, 17, 92, 211–212, 214,
    220–222
cost-benefit analysis, 114

counterargument, 13–14
countervailing argument, 2
countervailing power, 114
covert activities, 89–90
created comparative advantage, 134,
    142
critical mass, 141–143
cultural factors, x, 65, 88
cumulative and circular causation, 116
Curry-Robert, 119, 120, 127
Curry-Rothchild model, 119, 120
Cyert and March, 154

debt financing, 31, 55
debt relief, 44, 52, 54, 92, 147
degree of specificity, 34
dependencia, 104–105, 115–117, 119,
    125–126
dependency theory, 50–51
development of underdevelopment, 1,
    5, 23, 27, 38, 49, 140, 150, 166, 197,
    205, 211, 220, 221
direct foreign investment, ix, xiv, 1, 8,
    15, 17–20, 23, 26, 30, 44, 47, 53,
    58–59, 65–70, 72, 74, 76, 78–81,
    86–93, 97, 149, 203
disharmony, 92, 95–96, 107, 118, 122
distribution effects, 2, 3
domestic policy formulation, x, 89–90
Dutch firms, 8
dynamic models, 119

East Asian Miracle, 19, 24
Eastern bloc, 49
East–West axis, 49
Economic Community of West African
    States (ECOWAS), 143
economic complementarity, 142
economic diffusion, 2
economic irrationalism, 141
economic nationalism, 50–51, 127, 219
economic parity, 52, 55
economic rent appropriation, 30, 39
economies of scale, 2, 39, 130,
    132, 135
efficiency with equity, 158
efficient allocation of resources, 159,
    173, 185, 199, 205

Eiteman and Stonehill, 155, 165, 220
empowerment and self-determination, 200–201
endowment, 133, 135–137, 171
Engels, Friedrich, 170–171
engine of growth, 141
enhancement of firm value, 159–160
entrepreneur, 3, 36, 69, 72, 83–84, 86, 170, 187–188
equity and equality, 54, 200, 201, 211
ethics, xi, xv, 28, 36, 56, 162, 166–167, 189–193, 213, 215, 219, 221, 225
European Union, 140, 141
expatriate managers, 112, 177
exploitation, 2–3, 5, 14, 26, 48, 104, 107, 120, 123, 133, 156–157, 159, 164, 166, 188
export-led development philosophy, 144
export substitution strategy, 143
expropriation, 68, 79
external factor supply, 134

factor endowment, 133, 135–137
factors of production, 2, 3, 126, 186–188
fair-sharing, 114, 159, 164, 191
Fayerweather, John, 112, 125, 165, 220
fear of nationalization, 106
feudalism, 170
firm's primary goal, xvi, 107, 109, 162, 170, 206
firm-specific competitive advantages, 175–176, 203
first world, 23, 49, 158, 162, 166
FitzRoy and Kraft, 159, 166, 220
five core features, 201
fixed factors, 102
Foreign Corrupt Practices Act of 1977, 56, 62, 221
foreign exchange, 3, 70–71, 84, 90
Fortune 500, xxi, 65, 77
free market oriented, 82
free rider, 161, 191
free trade, 61, 127, 140–141, 150, 200, 210, 217, 222
Friedman, Milton, 138, 156, 166

G8, 1, 3, 4, 10, 12, 23, 141–142, 147–149, 153, 171, 210–212
GDP, 15, 17, 204
Generalized System of Tariff Preferences (GSP), 99
Gilpin, Robert, 1, 5, 61, 102, 104–105, 111, 115–119, 122, 124, 126–127, 165, 220
Gilpin's models, 1, 104–105, 112, 115, 118–119, 122, 124, 126, 221
Girvan, 133
GIST, xi, xiv, 111–127, 139, 169–195, 197
give-and-take, 13, 14, 50–51, 89
Global Interdependency Sensitivity Thesis, xiv, 111, 121, 193, 218
GNP per capita, 19–20, 24, 26, 45–47
good ethics, 189, 191, 192
good governance, 2, 3, 143–147, 201, 210–211
good government capacity, 145, 146
good institutions, 145, 146
good policy apparatus, 145, 146
good political feasibility, 145, 164, 211
good rules, 145, 146
governance and accountability, 200, 201, 212
government codes, x, 70–72, 84–85
government-to-corporation model, 148
government-to-government model, 148
great development failure, 140, 143
greater good, 154, 189, 190
greed, 198, 199
greedy, 198, 199
gross domestic product (GDP), 15, 17, 204
gross margin, 33
gross national product, ix, 9–12, 16, 20–21, 23, 24
GSP, 99
guiding principles, 144
Gunder Frank, Andre, 1, 5, 23, 27, 49, 140–142, 150, 154–155, 158, 197, 203–205, 211

Haq, Mahbub ul, 208, 209, 214, 223
happy medium, 64

Harbison and Myers, 112, 221
have-nots, xix, 49–50, 107, 136, 184,
    203, 210
haves, xix, 49–50, 107, 136, 184,
    203, 210
highest and best use, 136, 158–159,
    164, 173, 195, 198
Hilton, Conrad N., 214–215, 221
historical stage of social development,
    170
host country management team,
    176, 177
hub and spokes trap, 132
human development paradigm, xi,
    200–201, 204, 207–208, 210–212
human rights violation, 17, 211–214
Hymer, Stephen, 116

ill feeling, 44, 64, 114
illegitimate practices, 68, 79
International Monetary Fund (IMF),
    57, 58, 100, 150, 222, 223
impatience and reciprocal demand
    intensity, 119, 122
implantation, 113
import substitution, x, 87, 131, 133,
    135, 143
inappropriate technology, 72–73,
    86–87
income disparity, 20
income distribution, 20, 60
income gap, 15, 20, 162
income inequality, xiii, 20, 24,
    213, 222
indebted countries, 139
India, 8, 9, 11, 16–19, 22, 29, 44, 46, 61,
    140, 217
indigenous capital, 59
inequality and dependency, 117, 149
initiator of change, 103
institutional arrangements, 30, 39
institutional mapping, 144–146, 211
integrating force, 135
intergenerational blueprint, xix
international currency, 142
international donor community, 148
international trading system, 99,
    100, 102

internationalism, 50, 51
intra-continental system of linkages,
    142
intra-firm pricing, 32
investment bundle, 113
issue of inequality, 47, 50

Jamaica, 18, 19, 46, 132
joint ventures, x, 30, 65, 67–68, 71–72,
    78–80, 82, 83, 85, 89, 103, 113

Kindleberger and Herrick, 39, 192,
    195, 222
King, Martin Luther Jr., xx, xxi, 222
know-how, xx, 4, 27–28, 30, 96, 101,
    112, 135, 172, 175, 187–188
knowledge-intensive, 4, 134
Krugman, Paul R., 141, 150, 195,
    200, 208
Kuznets, Simon, 6, 101

labor endowment, 136
labor-intensive, 4, 27, 49, 59, 99,
    133, 134
lack of uniformity, 35, 36
ladder and queue, 130, 134–135
ladder of comparative advantage, xi,
    3, 4, 5, 134, 135, 172, 186, 188
Latin America, xv, 12, 14, 15, 17, 19, 20,
    23, 24, 35, 41, 46, 49, 52–53, 55, 61,
    68, 79, 91, 93, 98, 101, 125, 126, 148,
    217, 219, 222, 224
law of increasing firm size, 116
law of uneven development, 116,
    127, 224
laws of development, 116
LDC, x, xi, 64, 67–74, 78–91, 100, 103,
    105, 123
leading sectors, 4, 160, 166
learning curve, 120, 122
less-developed countries (LDCs), 64,
    67–74, 78–91, 100, 103, 105, 123
Lewis, 131
liberalism, 50–51, 61, 222
life-choice constraints, xiii, xiv, 7, 43,
    200, 207
location-specific advantages, 175–176,
    203

mail survey, 64
majority ownership, 69–70, 80–81
Manifesto of the Communist Party,
    170
market efficiency, 2, 3
Marshall Plan for Africa, 147–148
Marx and Engels, 170–171
Marx, Karl, 170, 171
Marxian Principles, 164
Marxist, 5, 51, 116, 149
Mason, R. Hal, 29 39–40
Mbcki, Thabo, 143–144, 150, 226
Meier, 6, 61, 96, 99, 126–127, 134, 137,
    195, 223
mercantilist, 104–105, 115,
    117–119, 125
method of ownership, x, 65, 68–70,
    80–81
metropolis, 1, 26, 48
Mexico, 11, 16, 18–19, 21, 52, 54,
    61, 221
Middle East, 12, 15, 17, 53, 55, 74, 93,
    98, 101, 217, 222
Mikesell model, 120
Mikesell, Raymond, 120
mini-states, 141
minority ownership, 69, 70, 81
Mitchell et al., 159, 166, 224
MNC–host country, xv, 70, 73, 75, 80,
    82, 90, 92, 104, 106, 111, 112, 114–116,
    118–125
MNC–host government power sharing
    arrangement, 106
model of shareholder wealth maxi-
    mization, xvi, 173
model of third world stakeholder
    inclusion, 193
models of international economic
    interdependence, 121
Moran, Theodore, 120, 127, 224
Moran's model, 120, 127, 224

NAFTA, 140, 141
Nafziger, E. Wayne, 99–100, 102, 166,
    195, 224
nationalization, 36, 96, 106, 114, 122,
    123, 160
nation-state, 7, 48, 149, 223

natural order of social development,
    170
natural resources, 2, 13–14, 19, 44,
    47–49, 52, 55, 61, 81, 92, 97, 101–102,
    104, 107, 133, 135, 140, 141, 186
Nelson, Richard, 156, 166, 224
neoclassical assumption, 59
neocolonialist exploitation, 26, 48
NEPAD, 147–148, 150, 226
net present value, xxi, 171, 178, 182
New International Economic Order,
    28, 38, 41, 54, 90, 93, 220, 227
New Partnership for Africa's
    Development (NEPAD), 147
new pedagogy, xvi, 198–200, 202–204,
    207
new world order, 105–109, 129–130,
    138, 165, 166, 218, 220, 223, 224
NGOs, 147–148, 150, 227
Nkrumah, Kwame, 26, 48
nonaligned, 45–47, 49, 61
nongovernmental organizations
    (NGOs), 147, 150, 227
non-maximizing, 156
Northern Hemisphere, 44, 50
North South, xv, 43–61, 92, 98, 101,
    165, 218, 227
North–South axis, 49
North–South concept, 47, 49

OECD, 24, 37, 41, 56, 98, 99, 218, 221,
    222, 224, 226
OECD code of conduct, 37
Oil Crisis, 54
on-the-job training, 187, 188, 189, 193
one-person-one-vote rule, 146
Organization for Economic
    Cooperation and Development
    (OECD), 37, 56
Organization of African Unity, 147
outside the box, xi, 184, 189, 193,
    205–207

Pareto optimality, 124
path to stakeholder inclusion, 193
pedagogy, xiv, xvi, 107, 171, 197–208,
    223
pent-up demand, 190, 192

periphery, 1–3, 5
perspective, xiv, xix–xxi, 5, 25, 75,
    81, 84, 89, 102, 105, 115, 122,
    129–137, 155, 158, 162, 166–167, 177,
    182, 199, 205, 207
Pharaon, Ghaith R., 9
policymakers, 39, 59, 63–73, 77–92,
    102, 205, 218
port of despair, 140, 143–144,
    147–148
Porter, Michael, 156, 166, 225
postcolonial opportunities, 130
poverty, xiii, xiv, xix–xxi, 2, 12, 17, 24,
    44, 61, 96, 116, 140, 147, 164,
    179–184, 197, 210–211, 214, 222
poverty abatement, xx, xxi, 96
predecessors of multinational
    corporations, 7
predestination, xix
predicament, xvi, 12, 130, 139–151, 210
preferential tariffs, 44, 52, 57, 91, 92,
    97, 100
Preferential Trade Area of Eastern and
    Southern Africa (PTA), 143
prescription for good governance, 145
price stabilization, 56–57, 91, 100
price makers, 141
price takers, 141
Primeaux and Stieber, 158–159, 166,
    225
principal-agent problem, 162
principal-agent relationship, 162, 163
principle of comparative advantage,
    xiv, 3, 141
producer cartels, 56, 100
product cycle model, 99
productivity and participation,
    200–201
profit-maxim rule, 159, 185
profit maximization, xiv, xxi, 107,
    130, 136, 153, 156–159, 162–163,
    165–166, 171, 184, 199, 206–207, 217,
    219, 225
profit motive, xxi, 107, 153, 171, 188,
    199
profit satisficing, xi, xiv, xxi, 95,
    108–109, 130, 136, 137, 153, 155–167,
    169–195, 197–200, 204, 207, 210

profit satisficing–stakeholder equity
    enhancement, 193

racism, xx, 211–214, 219
ready, willing, and able, xi, 180,
    189–191
reciprocity, 27, 65, 67, 73, 75, 77–79, 92,
    128, 137, 218
redistribution doctrine, xv, 52
redistribution of wealth, 3, 52,
    96, 158
resource-intensive, 4, 134–135
restrictive power of the G8, 141
return on investment, 106, 108, 122,
    136
Ricardian comparative advantage, 130,
    133
Ricardo, David, 3, 133
rich country–poor country, xi, xiv, xvi,
    2, 5, 12, 14, 25, 95, 111, 139, 170, 184,
    185, 189, 192, 197, 199–200, 202–203,
    205, 207, 210–212
Root, Hilton, L., 144, 150, 225
Rostow, 4, 6, 160, 166, 167, 225
Rothchild, Donald, 119
rule of law, 114, 146–147, 211

Schumpeter, Joseph A., 188, 195, 225
Second World, 49
seed capital, 28
self-determination, 49, 200–201
semantic differential technique, 65
September 11, 2001, 63, 179
shareholder–stakeholder paradigm,
    179
shareholder–stakeholder wealth
    maximization, xi
shareholder wealth maximization, xi,
    xvi, 107, 136, 153–158, 162–166,
    169–193, 197–207, 220, 225
Silk, Leonard, 210, 214, 226
Singh, Chaitram, 119, 127, 219
Smith, Adam, 141, 154, 163
social distress, 19
social norms, 88
socialism, 50, 51, 61, 167, 170–172,
    217, 222
socialist model, 172

sole ownership, 69, 70, 79, 81
Southern Hemisphere, 43, 50
sovereignty-at-bay, 104, 105, 115–117
sovereignty over natural resources, 44,
    52, 55, 92, 97, 101
Spearman rank correlation coefficient,
    66, 68, 70, 72, 73
stage theory, xiv, 4, 5
stage theory of economic growth,
    xiv, 5
stakeholder, xi, xiv, xvi, xxi, 153–166,
    169, 172–173, 175, 177–194, 198–199,
    205–207, 210–211, 218, 219
stakeholder givebacks, xi, xiv, 159–163,
    185–189, 193, 210, 211
stakeholder premise, 155, 156
staple scale, 65, 66
static bargaining model, 119
stock ownership loans, 71, 85
sustainability and longevity, 200, 201
sustainable change, xx
SWM, 154–156, 158–159, 163, 169–195,
    204, 206
SWM-driven corporate governance,
    155

tariff barriers, 57, 99
taxation, xv, 28, 35, 41, 56, 83, 160, 202,
    225
technology transfer, x, xv, 2, 20, 28–32,
    38–40, 44, 57, 72, 80, 86–88, 91,
    96–97, 101, 103, 113, 120, 131, 160,
    223
technology transplant, 29
the box, 184, 205, 206
the customer is always right, 162
the whole is greater than the sum of
    the parts, 106
theory of a just price, 163
thinking outside the box, xi, 206
Third World debt servicing, 98
Third World multinational, 8, 23, 221

Third World stakeholder, xvi, 156, 159,
    163, 172–173, 175, 180–182, 190, 193,
    206–207
Third World stakeholder inclusion,
    173, 175, 193
Thomas, Clive, 123, 128, 226
trade liberalization, 57, 91
transfer pricing, 34–35, 38, 40–41, 72,
    96, 121, 225, 226
transfer pricing decisions, 35
tripartite agreements, 133
Tugwell, Franklin, 121, 127, 226

U.N. General Assembly, 37, 214, 227
UNCTAD, 24, 39–41, 100, 221, 226
underdevelopment, 1, 2, 5, 17, 23,
    27–28, 38, 49–50, 61, 116, 137, 140,
    142, 150, 166, 197, 205, 211, 220, 221,
    223
United Nations, 24, 37, 41, 100, 212,
    214, 220, 225–227
Universal Declaration of Human
    Rights, 212, 214, 227
user-friendly, xiv, 169–195, 197–207

Venezuela, 11, 16, 18–21, 55,
    127, 226

wealth redistribution doctrine, xv
weighted average rating, x, xi, 66–73,
    78–91, 103
Who is the MNC?, 202, 204
Who is the Third World?, 202, 204
whose wealth to maximize, 153–167,
    218, 219
win-win scenario, xi, 193, 194
Wing Sue, Derald, 212, 215
Winter, Sidney, 156, 166, 224
Wonnacott, 132
World Bank, 139, 143, 148, 227
World Health Organization, 96
wretchedness of being, xx

About the Author

BENJAMIN F. BOBO is Professor of Finance of Loyola Marymount University, Los Angeles. His research focuses on life-choice constraints of the economically disadvantaged in the United States and around the world. He is the author of many articles and books, including *Locked in and Locked Out: The Impact of Urban Land Use Policy and Market Forces on African Americans* (Praeger, 2001).

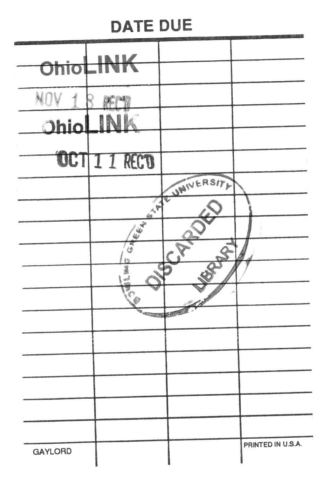